D1478832

Catholic Activism in South-West France, 1540–1570

Catholic Activism in South-West France, 1540–1570

KEVIN GOULD

ASHGATE

© Kevin Gould, 2006

All rights reserved. No part of this publication may be reproduced, stored in a retrieval system, or transmitted in any form or by any means, electronic, mechanical, photocopied, recorded or otherwise without the prior permission of the publisher.

Kevin Gould has asserted his moral right under the Copyright, Designs and Patents Act, 1988, to be identified as the author of this work.

Published by
Ashgate Publishing Limited
Gower House
Croft Road
Aldershot
Hants GU11 3HR
England

Ashgate Publishing Company
Suite 420
101 Cherry Street
Burlington, VT 05401–4405
USA

Ashgate website: http://www.ashgate.com

British Library Cataloguing-in-Publication Data
Gould, Kevin
    Catholic activism in south-west France, 1540–1570. – (St
Andrews studies in Reformation history)
    1. Catholic Church – France, Southwest – History – 16th
century 2. Catholics – France, Southwest – History – 16th
century 3. France, Southwest – Church history – 16th century
    4. France, Southwest – History – 16th century
    I. Title
    282.4'47'09031

Library of Congress Cataloging-in-Publication Data
Gould, Kevin, 1964–
    Catholic activism in south-west France, 1540–1570 / Kevin Gould.
        p. cm. – (St. Andrews studies in Reformation history)
    Includes bibliographical references and index.
    ISBN 0-7546-5226-2 (alk. paper)
    1. Counter-Reformation – France. 2. Catholic Church – France –
History – 16th century. 3. France – Church history – 16th century. I.
Title. II. Series.

    BX1529.G68 2006
    274.4'706–dc22

                                                                2005034905
ISBN 10: 0 7546 5226 2
Printed on acid-free paper
Typeset in Sabon by Saxon Graphics Ltd, Derby
Printed and bound in Great Britain by MPG Books Ltd, Bodmin, Cornwall

Contents

Acknowledgements   *vi*

List of Abbreviations   *viii*

1. Themes and Sources   1
2. The Birth of Catholic Activism at Bordeaux   18
3. The Bordeaux Syndicate   34
4. The Nobility of the Bordelais   50
5. Catholic Consolidation at Bordeaux   67
6. Coalition and Consensus at Agen   83
7. The Defence of Agen   97
8. Confrontation and Insurrection at Toulouse   110
9. Militant Ascendancy at Toulouse   124
10. Rebellion and Wider Catholic Activism: Béarn and Navarre   143
11. Conclusion   159

Select bibliography   167

Index   183

Acknowledgements

This project has been enriched by the kindness and support of numerous people. I am greatly indebted to Penny Roberts, my PhD supervisor and mentor, under whose expert direction much of this book was completed. It was Penny who first encouraged me to explore more deeply the convoluted machinations that were the French Wars of Religion, and whose suggestion that I immerse myself in Monluc's *Commentaires* served to shape much of my subsequent research. I am also grateful to Andrew Pettegree, who commissioned the book, and whose guidance on matters of organization and argument has greatly influenced the final text, and to Mark Greengrass, the external examiner of my doctoral thesis, for his advice concerning the minutiae of confessional rivalries in the south-west. Other academics have shared their knowledge freely: Michael Jones advised on the activities of confraternities in northern France; Pierre-Jean Souriac helped identify manuscript sources relating to the crusade of 1568 within the archives at Toulouse; Steve Hindle discussed local affinities and 'loops of association' in the English setting; and the staff and students of the History Departments at the Universities of Warwick and St Andrews offered critical comment on various papers. I would additionally like to thank Joe Bergin, Alan James, Bruce Gordon, and Humfrey Butters for their encouragement and friendship over recent years – it has meant a great deal.

I extend my appreciation to the Arts and Humanities Research Board for providing the funds that made my research trips to France possible, and to the archivists and librarians of the French archives at Agen, Bordeaux, Toulouse, and Paris, who were welcoming and helpful at all times. I would like to express my gratitude to Ashgate Publishing for their diligence, and to acknowledge the St Andrews Studies in Reformation History board for their consideration and care over the past year.

Monographs are seldom written in isolation, and I am grateful to the following friends and colleagues for their words of encouragement: David Morris; Angela McShane-Jones; Tim Reinke-Williams; Michael Cahill; James Nott; Mark Bryant; Graeme Murdoch; Ann and Andy Barnes; Graham Sadler; Jim Shields; Pete Jacobs; Andy Rawlings; Matthew Hargraves; Bridget Heal; and Rona Johnston Gordon. Thanks are especially due to Graham Harwood for creating the detailed map of south-west France, and for the endless cathartic discussions about nothing in particular. It is only fitting that I also acknowledge the soundtrack to this experience: Nine Inch Nails, A Perfect Circle, Amplifier and many others. And to Nigel Krohn, wherever you are now, take care – you will be sorely missed.

Finally, I would like to express my love and gratitude to my family. My parents, Helena and Christopher Gould, and my grandparents, Agnes and Ted Gould, and Joan and Joe Connell, continue to be a tremendous influence on my life. My brothers, Ian, Adrian, and Patrick, and their families, have been a great support over the years, while the courage of the various Gould, Connell, and Craig clan members has been a constant source of inspiration. And to Carran Craig, who has had to endure so much in the researching and writing of this project, yet has been loving and supportive throughout – thank you so much. This book is dedicated to you.

Kevin Gould
April 2005

Abbreviations

ADG	Archives départementales de la Gironde
ADHG	Archives départementales de la Haute-Garonne
ADLG	Archives départementales de Lot-et-Garonne
AHG	*Archives historiques du département de la Gironde*
AHR	*American Historical Review*
AMB	Archives municipales de Bordeaux
AMT	Archives municipales de Toulouse
ARG	*Archiv für Reformationsgeschichte*
BMB	Bibliothèque municipale de Bordeaux
BN	Bibliothèque nationale de Paris
BSHPF	*Bulletin de la société de l'histoire du protestantisme français*
EHR	*English Historical Review*
FH	*French History*
FHS	*French Historical Studies*
HGL	*Histoire générale de Languedoc*
HJ	*Historical Journal*
JEH	*Journal of Ecclesiastical History*
JMH	*Journal of Modern History*
P&P	*Past and Present*
SCJ	*Sixteenth Century Journal*

CHAPTER ONE

Themes and Sources

Favorable Bordeaux, le nom de favourable
Se perdit en suivant l'exemple abominable.[1]

Perceptions of Catholic conduct during the French Wars of Religion (1562–98) have traditionally been shaped by two episodes: the bloodlust of the Saint Bartholomew's massacres of 1572 and the militancy of the Catholic League during the 1580s and 1590s. Protestant contemporaries observed Catholic behaviour during these periods as provocative, ferocious and brutal, a characterization that gained greater licence as subsequent historians determined to interpret the conflict as a struggle for legitimacy by a persecuted minority in the face of uncompromising Catholic aggression.[2] The pre-eminence of studies of League belligerence in the historiography of Catholic endeavours has done little to lessen this partiality, with the result that Catholic *faits et mentalités* during the first decades of the wars have been largely overlooked. Scholars have only recently begun to redress these imbalances. A.N. Galpern, Philip Benedict and Robert Sauzet were among the first to reappraise earlier Catholic pursuits, adopting a more sensitive approach that balanced traditional accounts with fresh archival research, and which set Catholic conduct within its regional milieu rather than as a facet of conventional narratives such as court faction, noble intrigues and international conspiracies.[3]

---

[1] Théodore Agrippa d'Aubigné, *Les tragiques* (2 vols, ed. F. Lestringant, Paris, 1995), p. 260.

[2] See, for example, Théodore de Bèze, *Histoire ecclésiastique des églises réformées au royaume de France* (3 vols, eds W. Baum and E. Cunitz, Nieuwkoop, 1974); Condé, *Mémoires de Condé, ou recueil pour servir à l'histoire de France, contenant ce qui s'est passé du plus mémorable dans le Royaume* (6 vols, London, Paris, 1743). Other Protestant polemic against Catholic aggression can be found in Théodore de Bèze, *Correspondance de Théodore de Bèze* (26 vols, ed. H. Aubert, Geneva, 1960–2002); Michel de Castelnau, *Les mémoires de Messire Michel de Castelnau, seigneur de Mauvissiere et de Concressaut, ausquelles sont traictées les choses plus remarquables qu'il a veues et negotiées en France, Angleterre, et Escosse, soubs les rois François II et Charles IX, tant en temps de paix qu'en temps de guerre* (Paris, 1671); Théodore Agrippa d'Aubigné, *Histoire universelle* (10 vols, ed. A. de Ruble, Paris, 1886–1909); Brantôme, *Oeuvres complètes de Pierre de Bourdeille, seigneur de Brantôme* (2 vols, ed. L. Lalanne, Paris, 1864–82).

[3] A.N. Galpern, *The Religions of the People in Sixteenth-Century Champagne* (Cambridge, MA, 1976); Philip Benedict, *Rouen during the Wars of Religion* (Cambridge, 1981); Robert Sauzet, *Contre-réforme et réforme catholique en Bas-Languedoc* (Louvain, 1981). Janine Garrisson-Estèbe also provided a useful account of Catholic responses to the domination of political and social institutions of the 'United Provinces of the Midi' in her *Protestants du midi 1559–1598* (Toulouse, 1980).

Denis Crouzet's two-volume opus, *Les guerriers de Dieu*, published in 1990, was a significant milestone in this approach. Crouzet argued that Catholic activism was certainly not the preserve of the elites of France but had been embraced by many among the urban and rural communities from the mid-sixteenth century, the early confessional clashes heightened by a pervading sense of millenarian *angoisse* and growing penitential fervour.[4]

The affinity for localized studies during the 1990s did much to develop this perspective. Barbara Diefendorf's and Ann Ramsey's work on Paris, for example, showed how Catholics sought to unify the community against an increasingly potent reform movement by reinforcing traditional concepts of orthodoxy: confirming doctrine, re-emphasizing ritual and collective piety, employing polemic.[5] David Nicholls's examination of confessional relations at Tours found that it was the usurpation of local institutions by leading Catholic magistrates rather than Catholic military prowess that was the key to countering Protestant hegemony – a policy Penny Roberts has revealed was also employed by militant Catholics at Troyes.[6] Wolfgang Kaiser's work on the port of Marseille assessed the growth of militant Catholicism in an urban setting devoid of the influence of a sovereign court and lacking the strong participation of royal officials, while Marc Venard detailed how the presence of numerous well-established confraternities and a Jesuit school facilitated greater authoritative control for Avignon's Catholic leadership.[7] Such revisionist

[4] Denis Crouzet, *Les guerriers de Dieu* (2 vols, Seyssel, 1990).

[5] Barbara B. Diefendorf, *Beneath the Cross. Catholics and Huguenots in Sixteenth-Century Paris* (Oxford, 1991); Ann W. Ramsey, *Liturgy, Politics, and Salvation: The Catholic League in Paris and the Nature of Catholic Reform 1540–1630* (Rochester, NY, 1999).

[6] David Nicholls, 'Protestants, Catholics and magistrates in Tours, 1562–1572: The making of a Catholic city during the religious wars', *FH*, 8, 1 (1994), pp. 14–33; Penny Roberts, *A City in Conflict. Troyes during the French Wars of religion* (Manchester, 1996). Interestingly, Mark W. Konnert has revealed that it was the determination of the civic corporation at nearby Châlons-sur-Marne to tolerate rather than exploit religious differences that ensured the town would escape serious sectarian violence during the 1560s – this despite Champagne being the epicentre of Guise power in the region. See Mark W. Konnert, *Civic Agendas and Religious Passion. Châlons-sur-Marne during the French Wars of Religion, 1560–1594* (Kirksville, MS, 1997); Mark W. Konnert, 'Provincial governors and their regimes during the French Wars of Religion: the duc de Guise and the city council of Châlons-sur-Marne', *SCJ*, 25 (1994), pp. 823–40.

[7] Wolfgang Kaiser, *Marseille au temps des troubles. Morphologie sociale et luttes de factions 1559–1595* (Paris, 1992); Marc Venard, *Réforme Protestante, réforme catholique, dans la province d'Avignon au XVIe siècle* (Paris, 1993); Marc Venard, 'Catholicism and resistance to the Reformation in France, 1555–1585', in Philip Benedict, Guido Marnef, Henk van Nierop and Marc Venard (eds), *Reformation, Revolt, and Civil War in France and the Netherlands 1555–1585* (Amsterdam, 1999), pp. 133–48.

methodology underscored Stuart Carroll's assessment of militancy within Normandy and Mack P. Holt's evaluation of Catholic ascendancy within the staunchly orthodox province of Burgundy, while Olivier Christin's examination of the Catholic riposte to Protestant iconoclasm provided valuable new insights into confessional contention within the communities of France.[8] Catholic endeavour in the volatile south-western provinces of Guyenne and Western Languedoc is served by several apposite studies. Jonathan Powis's work on contestation at Bordeaux scrutinized the political wrangling between Catholics and moderates within the town's *parlement* and civic administration, while the articles of Joan Davies and Mark Greengrass offered a detailed analysis of confessional strife at Toulouse during the first religious war.[9] Both René Souriac's analysis of government and local bureaucracy at Comminges and Michel Cassan's assessment of confraternal activism at Limoges proffered comprehensive studies of Catholic organizational and administrative skills, while Philip Conner's analysis of Protestant government at Montauban revealed Catholic reaction to the loss of political power within an important urban centre.[10]

One theme evident in these latter studies is the ferocity and violence of sectarian relations in the south-west. James Wood's review of the impact of war in the 1560s on the communities of France demonstrated this

---

[8] Stuart Carroll, *Noble Power during the French Wars of Religion. The Guise Affinity and the Catholic Cause in Normandy* (Cambridge, 1998); Stuart Carroll, 'The Guise affinity and popular protest during the Wars of Religion', *FH*, 9 (1995), pp. 125–51; Mack P. Holt, 'Burgundians into Frenchmen: Catholic identity in sixteenth-century Burgundy', in Michael Wolfe (ed.), *Changing Identities in Early Modern France* (Durham, NC, 1997), pp. 345–70; Mack P. Holt, 'Wine, community and Reformation in sixteenth-century Burgundy', *P&P*, 138 (1993), pp. 59–93; Olivier Christin, *Une révolution symbolique. L'iconoclasme huguenot et la reconstruction catholique* (Paris, 1991), esp. Part Two: 'La riposte', pp. 177–285.

[9] Jonathan Powis, 'The Magistrates of the Parlement of Bordeaux c. 1500–1563' (unpublished PhD thesis, Oxford University, 1975); Jonathan Powis, 'Order, religion, and the magistrates of a provincial parlement in sixteenth-century France', *ARG*, 71 (1980), pp. 180–97; Joan Davies, 'Persecution and Protestantism: Toulouse, 1562–1575', *HJ*, 22 (1979), pp. 31–51; Joan Davies, 'Languedoc and its Governor, Henri de Montmorency-Damville, 1563–1589' (unpublished PhD thesis, University of London, 1974); Mark Greengrass, 'The anatomy of a religious riot in Toulouse in May 1562', *JEH*, 34 (1983), pp. 367–91; 'The *Sainte Union* in the provinces: the case of Toulouse', *SCJ*, 14, 4 (1983), pp. 469–96; Mark Greengrass, *War, Politics and Religion in Languedoc in the government of Henri de Montmorency-Damville, 1574–1610* (PhD thesis, University of Oxford, 1979).

[10] René Souriac, *Décentralisation administrative dans l'ancienne France. Autonomie commingeoise et pouvoir d'état, 1540–1630* (2 vols, Toulouse, 1992); Michel Cassan, *Le temps des guerres de religion. Le cas du Limousin (vers 1530–vers 1630)* (Paris, 1996); Philip Conner, *Huguenot Heartland. Montauban and Southern French Calvinism during the Wars of Religion* (Aldershot, 2002).

phenomenon succinctly. Wood showed that of the seventeen dioceses of France worst affected by financial ruin, twelve (71 per cent) were located in or on the borders of Guyenne and Western Languedoc, with Guyenne witnessing especially high levels of abuse against Catholic priests and canons throughout the decade.[11] Crouzet concurred, calling the region 'a laboratory of violent experiences',[12] a view supported by contemporary Catholic testimony: a report from the Toulouse *parlement* to the crown in January 1562 asserted that 'by violence and insidious means, the reformers are conspiring to be dominant in this kingdom',[13] while the governor of Narbonne, Raymond de Pavie, *sieur* de Fourquevaux, informed the French ambassador in Spain six months later that 'the seditious of Guyenne are the worst of all'.[14] Indeed, the scale of military activity across the region during the 1560s caused Florimond de Raemond, a *conseiller* of the Bordeaux *parlement*, to remark that Guyenne had now become 'a shop of soldiers and the breeding ground of armies'.[15] Several factors exacerbated these tensions: the large reform population in the south-west (almost 10 per cent of the region by 1561); the high percentage of urban centres of the region that featured substantial Protestant communities, and that subsequently fell under Protestant control over the 1560s; and the large number of landholding nobles that converted to 'la nouvelle religion' across the countryside, thereby ranging their armed retinues against those of local Catholic elites. Indeed, Crouzet has concluded that it was the scale and intensity of the Protestant expansion that resulted in such explosive sectarian tensions across the region during the 1560s.[16]

With confessional affairs so strained, Catholics of the south-west became energized from an early stage, and began to form associations to better defend their communities. Confederation and coalition soon became the standard medium for security for Catholics, with the result that Guyenne and Western Languedoc would witness Catholic 'leaguing' on a scale rarely

---

[11] J. B. Wood, 'The impact of the Wars of Religion: A view of France in 1581", *SCJ*, 15 (1984), pp. 148–53.

[12] Crouzet, *Les guerriers de Dieu*, I, p. 524. Crouzet devoted more attention to the south-west than any other region in his *Les guerriers de Dieu*, even titling one section: 'Pourquoi le sud-ouest?'

[13] *Parlement* of Toulouse to Charles IX (7 January 1562). A. de Ruble, *Jeanne d'Albret et la guerre civile* (Paris, 1897), p. 101.

[14] Fourquevaux to Saint-Sulpice, ambassador of Charles IX in Spain (17 June 1562), Edmond Cabié, *Guerres de religion dans le sud-ouest de la France et principalement dans le Quercy, d'après les papiers des seigneurs de Saint-Sulpice de 1561 à 1590. Documents transcrits, classés et annotés* (Paris, 1906), pp. 5–6.

[15] Paul Courteault, *Histoire de Gascogne et de Béarn* (Paris, 1938), p. 210.

[16] Crouzet, *Les guerriers de Dieu*, I, p. 524.

seen elsewhere in France at this time. Yet, while a number of these militant bodies are identified within historical commentaries, the specifics of their evolution and the mechanics of their organization and activity have rarely been assessed in any detail: of the few dedicated surveys, Joseph Lecler's short paper proved effective, while the narrative essays of James Westfall Thompson, A. Dupré and Charles Dartigue offered only limited fare.[17] Why such a paucity in the historiography? The long-standing, and largely unchallenged, assumption that the Leaguers were the pre-eminent Catholic activists of the wars is partly to blame, as it identified all earlier episodes of militancy as little more than precursors to the *Sainte Union*. Lecler typified this approach, examining the associations of the 1560s as antecedents to a later construction rather than as independent entities in themselves, even framing his discourse under the title: 'Aux origines de la Ligue'. Another contributory factor was the reluctance of historians to see pre-League Catholic bodies as anything other than disparate, localized entities, whose parochial nature tended to render them inconsequential in provincial affairs.[18]

This book will refute the assumptions that have bolstered such historiographies, and will present in their place an alternative history of Catholic militancy in south-west France. At Bordeaux, Toulouse, Agen and Cadillac, for example, elite-led foundations and multifarious collectives offered formal vehicles for Catholic dissent. At their core were authority and community figures alike: high and low nobles, court officials, local clergy and *confrères*, and an energized citizenry. The vitality of popular sentiment often drew upon the experience of confronting reform evangelism at local levels, and in some cases served to prepare the ground for the emerging associations. Significantly, in most instances individual Catholic militant bodies united in solidarity with neighbouring and regional allies across the south-west to form potent entities – they were certainly not the 'limited, ephemeral, unconnected' *ligues* as described by Lecler. For John Bossy, the failure to explore such complex forces in greater detail has precluded valuable insights being made into Catholic *mentalités* during the early years of sectarian conflict, a time, he asserted, of seismic shifts in Catholic perspectives and posture.[19] This has resulted

---

[17] Joseph Lecler, 'Aux origines de la Ligue: Premiers projets et premiers essais (1561–1570)', *Études*, 227 (1936), pp. 188–208; James Westfall Thompson, *The Wars of Religion in France, 1559–1576* (New York, 1958), esp. Chapter IX: pp. 206–31; A. Dupré, 'Projet de ligue catholique à Bordeaux en 1562 et 1563', *Revue catholique de Bordeaux*, 12 (1891), pp. 372–78; Charles Dartigue, 'Une cabale politico-religieuse à Bordeaux en juillet 1562: le syndicat contre le parlement', *BSHPF*, 98 (1951), pp. 141–52.

[18] Again, Lecler is culpable, portraying the associations of the 1560s as 'limited, ephemeral, without connections': Lecler, 'Aux origines de la Ligue', p. 189.

[19] John Bossy, 'Leagues and associations in sixteenth-century French Catholicism', *Studies in Church History*, 23 (1986), pp. 171–89.

in wider controversies being marginalized in deference to the obsession with League studies. The existence of widespread militancy in the south-west during the 1550s and 1560s, for instance, challenges the historio-graphical axiom that places the Council of Trent at the centre of the sixteenth-century movement of Catholic renewal in France. The nascence of so many associations suggests that Catholicism did not wait upon Trent, not in Guyenne and Western Languedoc at least, but instead deter-mined individuals sought to defend orthodoxy long before the Tridentine decrees ever reached the royal court, insistent that heresy should not prevail within their community. This posits a new schema for the profile of Catholic activism, positioning the militant bodies of the mid-decades of the century at the vanguard of Catholic renewal, and the associations of the 1560s as arbiters of the Catholic counter-offensive, rather than the post-1584 Leaguers as assumed in existing historiographies.

This study will reflect on these controversies and will provide a detailed analysis of Catholic militancy across the south-west of France during the pre-League period. It will examine three distinct loci: Bordeaux and the Bordelais; Agen and the Agenais; and Toulouse and its environs. This delineation is a natural one. Not only were these regions hotbeds of Catholic activism from the early 1540s, but the three towns were the only sizeable urban centres of the south-west to resist fully the inexorable gains made by the reform movement over the period. Chapters Two to Five will examine key elements of activism at Bordeaux and the Bordelais: the defence of Catholic traditions and practices within the community and the emergence of confraternal activism during the 1540s and 1550s; the creation of a syndicate of militant officials within the sovereign court during the early 1560s; the formation of elite associations to secure Bordeaux's hinterland after 1563; and the usurpation and domi-nation of government offices by Catholic activists after 1567. Chapters Six and Seven will assess events at Agen and across the Agenais: the formation of a coalition 'government' of Catholic notables to maintain authority over local institutions; its subsequent union with proactive elite associations intent on leading a Catholic counter-offensive within the region; and the coalescing of local Catholic bodies into an entity capable of defending the town from a concerted Protestant onslaught after 1567. Chapters Eight and Nine will focus on Toulouse and its environs: pre-war communal and confraternal activism across the town; the Protestant coup of May 1562 and the Catholic response; the creation of an oath-bound elite league and subsequent coalition council to confront Protestant gains within the locality; and the reinvigoration of Catholic missionary zeal through the calling of a crusade. Chapter Ten will explore the involve-ment of militants of the south-west in the Catholic rebellions in the neigh-bouring territories of Béarn and Navarre, and the interconnectedness of

Catholic forces in the decade-long attempt to oust the monarch of these lands, Jeanne d'Albret, from power.

Why the south-west? The rising Protestant population, the aggressive posture of evangelicals, the infiltration of council chambers by reformed officials and the violent sectarian confrontations have been noted above, but there were several extraneous circumstances that also heightened tensions across the south-west. The support offered to militants at Bordeaux and Toulouse by external Catholic powers such as Spain and the papacy was one such factor. As frontier provinces, Guyenne and Languedoc had long resisted military, political and economic pressure from exterior powers. During the 1550s and 1560s, however, resident Catholics actively sought alliances with neighbouring co-religionists to bolster their standing, trading intelligence for funds and military provisions. The resulting influx of papal gold and Spanish troops complicated matters, with Protestants asserting repeatedly that Catholic captains were colluding with the enemies of France and taking bribes to 'sell' the kingdom to the highest bidder. Another extenuating factor that intensified the instability of the south-west was the lack of effective governorship and grandee influence. Robert Harding and Sharon Kettering have identified the provincial governor as a leading determinant of the strength of regional political government in sixteenth-century France.[20] It was through the office of governor that patronage networks, local alliances and bonds of fidelity usually permeated, especially at times of weak central authority, as occurred during the religious wars. Yet during the 1550s and early 1560s, neither Guyenne nor Languedoc saw their incumbent for any length of time. The governor of Guyenne, Antoine de Bourbon, king of Navarre, was absent from his seat of office for long periods, preferring to administrate by communiqué from the royal court, while Languedoc's governor, Anne de Montmorency, the Constable of France, rarely visited his province either.[21]

Surprisingly, this power vacuum was not filled by leading grandee families of France, with the result that royal officials and local elites of the south-west profited from this rupture in the traditional hierarchy of provincial authority and managed their affairs with a licence not

---

[20] Robert R. Harding, *Anatomy of a Power Elite, The Provincial Governors of Early Modern France* (New Haven, 1978), pp. 21–107; Sharon Kettering, 'Clientage during the French Wars of Religion', *SCJ*, 20 (1989), pp. 221–39; Sharon Kettering, 'Patronage and kinship in Early Modern France', *FHS*, 16 (1989), pp. 408–35.

[21] The two heirs to these seats of power fared little better during the 1560s. At the death of Navarre in November 1562, his office remained vacant as his son, Henri de Bourbon, was too young to assume the title and so remained disenfranchised until late in 1569. The successor to the Constable in Languedoc, Henri de Montmorency-Damville, fared only slightly better, spending a short time in his *gouvernement* in 1564 before leaving to head the royal army as marshal of France after 1565.

normally tolerated under the auspices of a dominant governor. The dearth of Guise influence here is especially unexpected, given that the machinations of this powerful Catholic family are seen as integral to most studies of the French Wars of Religion, and that Catholicism in the region badly needed a potent patron during much of the 1560s.[22] There are three possible reasons for Guise absence from the south-west. Firstly, the great distance from the region to the north-eastern centres of Guise patrimony may have been too constraining. Communication between the crown and the region had proved troublesome enough, so it was unlikely that the Guise's evolving influence would have fared any better. Secondly, as Stuart Carroll has outlined, the main factor determining political strategy for the Guise at this time was their feud with the Admiral, Coligny, and so involvement in sectarian confrontations in the south-west would have been peripheral to court rivalries.[23] This is confirmed by Harding and Benedict, who have argued that, despite their bluster, it is doubtful that the Guise intended to undertake a concerted campaign to extirpate Protestantism from France during the early 1560s.[24] That the family was adopting a circumspect approach at this time is evident from two contemporary sources: the minutes of the Assembly of Fontainebleau, in August 1560, at which the provincial governors and local officials were cautioned that large-scale repression of the reform movement would be more of a threat to public order than a cure; and a royal directive of early 1561 that warned the militant duke d'Etampes, governor of Brittany, that 'as long as Protestants, in praising God make no scandal for others and assemble in small numbers and peaceably, they should not be prevented from so doing … In the times we are in, we must conduct all things cautiously with reason, great calmness, and moderation, precipitating nothing'.[25] Certainly, such reticence may well have been a realization of

---

[22] The Guise had risen to prominence following their part in the military successes of the 1550s, with the duke, François, playing a leading role in the Italian campaigns against Spanish forces, while his brother, Charles, cardinal of Lorraine, became a successful and highly prominent diplomat. The defining moment for Guise ascendancy came with the defeat and capture of the Constable of France, Anne de Montmorency, by Spanish troops at Saint-Quentin in August 1557. Until this point, the Montmorencies had edged the rivalry between the two houses. Now, with François promoted to *lieutenant-général* of France in the Constable's absence, and with the cardinal of Lorraine appointed to oversee domestic and foreign policy, the brothers were the new dominant force at court. See Carroll, *Noble Power*; Jean-Marie Constant, *Les Guise* (Paris, 1984); Henri Forneron, *Les ducs de Guise et leur époque: Étude historique sur le seizième siècle* (2 vols, Paris, 1893).

[23] Carroll, *Noble Power*; Carroll, 'The Guise affinity', pp. 125–51.

[24] Harding, *Anatomy of a Power Elite*, pp. 49–51; Philip Benedict, 'The Saint Bartholomew's Massacres in the Provinces', *HJ*, 21 (1978), p. 214.

[25] Charles IX to Étampes (March 1561), quoted in Harding, *Anatomy of a Power Elite*, p. 51.

the difficulty any pogrom would encounter: one moderate voice at Bordeaux warned in 1560 that 'at this moment royal ministers may be unwilling to proceed with a policy aimed at the total annihilation of Huguenot supporters',[26] while Jean de Monluc, bishop of Valence, writing in 1562, noted that 'the number of sectarians of the new religion is so great and they are so firm and constant in their belief that those who would oppose them would have to kill them all, otherwise those that survived would resuscitate their movement'.[27]

A third factor that may explain Guise absence is that their client network rarely penetrated into the south-west. This was, after all, the heartland of Bourbon patrimony, and while the region did feature three high-ranking former clients of the Guise – Christophe de Roffignac, *président* of the *parlement* at Bordeaux; George, Cardinal d'Armagnac, *lieutenant du roi* at Toulouse; and Blaise de Monluc, *lieutenant-général* (later *lieutenant du roi*) in Guyenne – their affiliation had occurred earlier in their careers during service in the north of France. On their return to the south-west, all three had little contact with their former patrons. Events surrounding Monluc's association capture this succinctly. The Gascon captain had served in the royal army under the Guise in Italy during the 1550s, gaining promotion to the post of *colonel-général des gens de pied* in May 1558, and fighting alongside the duke in the victory over the Spanish army at Thionville later that year.[28] But relations had become strained as a result of the backlash that greeted Monluc's promotion. Essentially the office had become a focal point of renewed hostility between the Guise and Montmorency families at court: François, *duc* de Guise, now *lieutenant-général* of France, had removed the incumbent *colonel-général*, François de Châtillon, *seigneur* d'Andelot, the nephew of the Constable, to spite his adversary. Monluc had become a pawn in the manoeuvrings of the Guise; the office a poison chalice. Courteault stated that Monluc was sufficiently insignificant in court circles to prevent civil war breaking out at his appointment, but would serve as the perfect scapegoat should the French military offensives of 1558 ultimately fail.[29] Monluc was equivocal about the d'Andelot affair in his *Commentaires*, claiming that it was regrettable that the Constable had

---

[26] Powis, 'Order, religion, and magistrates', p. 183.

[27] Myriam Yardeni, *La conscience nationale en France pendant les guerres de religion (1559–98)* (Paris, 1971), p. 89.

[28] Monluc's career had seemingly reached a new height – from archer in the Gascon regiments of Francis I to *colonel-général* of Henry II's royal army. For further details of his military service under the Guise at Picardy in 1558, see Jules Andrieu, *Histoire de l'Agenais* (2 vols, Agen, 1893), I, p. 211.

[29] Paul Courteault, *Blaise de Monluc, Historien* (Geneva, 1970), p. 349.

been offended, and that he had only accepted the role after being urged to do so by the king and the cardinal of Lorraine.[30] There may be a glint of truth in this as, when Montmorency was returned to power and re-instated as Constable in November 1558, Monluc immediately resigned his commission and allowed d'Andelot to resume his office so as to avoid any recriminations. In fact, Monluc seems to have been keen to extricate himself completely from this situation, as he requested permission to leave the royal army and join the king of Navarre's military expedition against rebel forces in Béarn and lower Navarre.[31]

Yet Monluc's affiliation to the Guise would still cause problems. When Henry II died in July 1559, François de Guise seized power at court, isolating Catherine de Medici, the king's widow, Montmorency and Antoine de Bourbon, the first prince of the blood, who most expected would assume the role of regent for the boy king, Francis II. This put Monluc in an awkward position, for he was now settled at Navarre's court at Pau. To choose one party and sever ties with the other would have been political suicide at such a fluid time, so Monluc became a pragmatist, serving Navarre in the south-west, but staying in contact with the duke of Guise through his brother, Jean, bishop of Valence.[32] The situation became more complicated in May 1560, though, when Monluc's intervention in the trial of two Calvinist ministers at Agen, Jean Voisin and Jacques Fontaine, resulted in complaints from local reformers to Navarre. Monluc received a reprimand from Pau for presiding over the case without official jurisdiction, but, when further sanctions were mooted, the duke of Guise intervened to spare Monluc further censure.[33] While Guise mediation may suggest that ties were still strong between the two parties, Paul Courteault believed that the duke's motive was to secure a spy in the south-west to watch over Navarre. Monluc had the perfect credentials for the task, and this may account for his recall to the royal court in August 1560, and the flurry of correspondence with the cardinal of Lorraine later the same year.[34]

---

[30] Blaise de Monluc, *Blaise de Monluc, Commentaires 1521–1576* (eds Paul Courteault and J. Giono, Paris, 1964), p. 424.

[31] When his release was granted in January 1559 by the *conseil privé*, Monluc withdrew with haste to the security of his homeland of Guyenne, leaving the Guise and Montmorency families to resume their power struggle without him. See A.W. Evans, *Blaise de Monluc* (London, 1909), p. 19.

[32] For rivalry between Navarre and the Guise in the late 1550s, see Sutherland's chapter: 'Antoine de Bourbon, King of Navarre and the French crisis of authority, 1559–1562', Nicola M. Sutherland, *Princes, Politics and Religion 1547–1589* (London, 1984), pp. 55–72.

[33] Paul Courteault, *Un Cadet de Gascogne au XVIe siècle. Blaise de Monluc* (Paris, 1909), pp. 148–9.

[34] Courteault, *Blaise de Monluc. Historien,* p. 390.

It would be a short-lived reconciliation, though, as the death of Francis II in December 1560 released Monluc from his obligations. This time, Catherine de Medici wasted no time securing the reins of power, promoting Montmorency and sending for Navarre so as to counter the Guise element within the royal council. With the Guise ostracized from court, Monluc was able to return to Guyenne, to remain there as *lieutenant-général* after December 1561.

Their relationship after this point is unclear. Communications between the two were rare during the 1560s, and the Guise seemed too preoccupied with affairs in the north and north-east to intervene in Catholic intrigues in Guyenne or Languedoc. Mark Greengrass did find a tentative connection between the parties in his examination of the indentures of a client of the Guise, Guy de Daillon, *comte* de Lude, with transcripts, dated August 1563, revealing that Lude promised to serve the Guise family faithfully, but also to recognize Monluc as '*lieutenant-général* and head of the enterprise in Guyenne'.[35] This is supported by archival evidence that revealed Lude to be an active supporter of Catholic activists at Bordeaux (he would be identified by moderates within the court as one of those Catholic nobles accused of attempting to usurp power in September 1563[36]) but little additional material survives to confirm or reject the supposition that Lude was a conduit between the Guise and Monluc at this time. What should be remembered, however, is that, in February 1563, François de Guise, Monluc's patron during the 1550s, died at Orléans, and so it was his son, Henri de Guise, who now headed the family. Perhaps the lack of Guise involvement in Catholic affairs of the south-west is explained by the fact that Henri did not enjoy the same bond with the militants there as had his father. A brief examination of the diminishing relationship between another leading Catholic activist of the south-west, George, Cardinal d'Armagnac, and the Guise tends to confirm this supposition. Armagnac had acted as diplomatic envoy on many of François de Guise's foreign campaigns during the early 1550s, and had also served on several diplomatic missions for the duke's brother, the cardinal of Lorraine, during the same period. Indeed, it was on one such campaign in Italy that Armagnac met and became friends with Monluc – the beginning of a long-standing friendship that would prove pivotal to the extensive relations between Catholics of Guyenne and those

---

[35] Mark Greengrass, 'Functions and limitations of political clientage in France before Richelieu', in Neithard Bulst, Robert Descimon and Alain Guerreau (eds), *L'état ou le roi. Les fondations de la modernité monarchique en France (XIVe-XVIIe siècles)* (Paris, 1996), p. 89.

[36] D'Escars to Catherine de Medici (6 September 1563), BN nouv. acq. français, 20 598, fo. 197.

at Toulouse.[37] Yet Armagnac also began to distance himself from the turmoil of court politics after 1560, owing no doubt to the complicated position he now found himself in – this one-time Guise client now held several important provincial offices directly responsible to the governor, Montmorency, yet as Inquisitor General for the south-west he still had contacts with the cardinal of Lorraine, who oversaw the implementation of inquisitorial episodes in France. It seems, then, that the Guise–Montmorency rivalry was effectively isolating the Catholic militants of the south-west from grandee affiliation, as it placed the key protagonists in a compromising situation.

Such was the contention that wracked political and religious affairs in the south-west of France during the 1550s and 1560s. Before the study turns to examine Catholic activism at Bordeaux, Agen and Toulouse during this period, it is worth reviewing the various sources used in researching this book. While the centralized holdings of the *Bibliothèque Nationale* in Paris proved essential for royal correspondence, troop muster and appeal judgements to the king and *conseil privé*, the bulk of the manuscript sources used here were drawn from the departmental and municipal archives of the south-west. The richest vein of material relating to Catholic militancy at Bordeaux was found in the numerous *registres du parlement* and *arrêts du parlement*, with the *fonds ancien* containing important if disparate information on ecclesiastical affairs, town council deliberations, military affairs, town guard provisioning, punitive taxation and the fining of Protestant communities. The *Archives historiques du département de la Gironde* and Ducourneau's *La Guienne historique et monumentale* were also useful here, as both reproduced transcriptions of manuscripts, some of which have since been lost or irrevocably damaged.[38] The researcher is ably supported by a wealth of antiquarian *histoires et chroniques* of

---

[37] Armagnac to Henry II (30 April 1555), Philippe Tamizey de Larroque, 'Lettres inédites du Cardinal d'Armagnac', *Collection Méridionale*, V (Paris, Bordeaux, 1874), pp. 66–8. See also letter from pope Pius IV to Monluc reporting that cardinal Armagnac had informed Rome of the brave deeds achieved by Monluc in Guyenne in defence of the Catholic faith (April 1562), [Condé], *Mémoires de Condé*, III, pp. 317–18. In fact, Armagnac also attempted to boost Monluc's profile with the Montmorency circle at court, writing a letter of recommendation to the Constable praising the Gascon captain's endeavours in March 1555. See Cardinal Armagnac to Constable Montmorency (March 1555), *Revue d'Aquitaine*, V (Auch, 1861), pp. 559–60.

[38] *AHG* (58 vols, Bordeaux, 1858–1932); Alex Ducourneau, *La Guienne historique et monumentale*, II (2 vols, Bordeaux, 1844).

Bordeaux, reminding us that the art of local history was once alive and well.[39]

Similar resources were to be found at Toulouse. Again, the various *registres du parlement* and *arrêts du parlement* provided the staple of manuscript references, with Privat's 15-volume *Histoire de Languedoc* (1872–90) proving indispensable, as it contains numerous transcriptions of sixteenth-century *preuves*.[40] Devic and Vaissète's *Histoire générale de Languedoc* also holds a number of pertinent transcriptions of manuscript documentation, though this life-work of two Dominican monks requires careful reading as it often overstates Catholic sensibilities and is prone to denigrate any and all Calvinist thought and actions.[41] Arnaud's *Histoire des Protestants du Vivarais et du Velay, pays de Languedoc* and Gachon's *Histoire de Languedoc* offer a Protestant counter-perspective to this work, while the *Revue d'Aquitaine* presents a fairly neutral view of the region's sectarian conflict.[42] As at Bordeaux, a number of valuable local studies of Toulouse and its *parlement* are available to the researcher.[43] Archival collections at Agen are more limited, as much of the town's administrative dealings fell under the jurisdiction of the Bordeaux *parlement*. Manuscript resources relating to affairs across the Agenais

[39] See especially Dom Devienne, *Histoire de Bordeaux* (Bordeaux, 1771); Ernest Gaullieur, *Histoire de la réformation à Bordeaux et dans le ressort du parlement de Guyenne*, I (2 vols, Bordeaux, 1884); Robert Boutrouche (ed.), *Bordeaux de 1453 à 1715* (Bordeaux, 1966); Camille Julian, *L'histoire de Bordeaux depuis les origines jusqu'à 1895* (Bordeaux, 1895); Abbé Patrice-John O'Reilly, *Histoire complète de Bordeaux* (6 vols, Bordeaux, 1863). For works relating to the Bordeaux *parlement*, see Jean de Métivier, *Chronique du parlement de Bordeaux* (2 vols, Bordeaux, 1886); C.B.F. Boscheron-Desportes, *Histoire du parlement de Bordeaux depuis sa création jusqu'à sa suppression (1451–1790)* (2 vols, Bordeaux, 1877); A. Communay, *Le parlement de Bordeaux, notes biographiques sur ses principaux officiers* (Bordeaux, 1898); F. Hauchecorne, 'Le parlement de Bordeaux pendant la première guerre civile (décembre 1560–mars 1563)', *Annales du Midi*, 62 (1950), pp. 329–40; Philippe Tamizey de Larroque, 'Jean Lange, conseiller au parlement de Bordeaux', *Revue Catholique de Bordeaux*, 1883 (Bordeaux), pp. 685–97.

[40] *Histoire de Languedoc* (15 vols, ed. Privat, Toulouse, 1872–90).

[41] Devic and Vaissète, *Histoire générale de Languedoc* (2 vols, Toulouse, 1872–92).

[42] Arnaud, *Histoire des Protestants du Vivarais et du Velay, pays de Languedoc* (Toulouse, 1888); Gachon, *Histoire de Languedoc* (Toulouse, 1921); *Revue d'Aquitaine* (16 vols, Auch, 1857–68).

[43] For local histories of Toulouse, see Germain de Lafaille, *Annales de la ville de Toulouse* (2 vols, Toulouse, 1687; 1701); Robert A. Schneider, *Public Life in Toulouse 1463–1789. From Municipal Republic to Cosmopolitan City* (Ithaca, 1989); Jacques Gaches, *Mémoires sur les guerres de religion à Castres et dans le Languedoc (1555–1610)* (Geneva, 1970); Henri Ramet, *Histoire de Toulouse* (Toulouse, 1935). For works relating to the Toulouse *parlement*, see Raymond A. Mentzer, 'Calvinist propaganda and the Parlement of Toulouse', *ARG*, 68 (1977), pp. 268–83; Jean-Baptiste Dubédat, *Histoire du parlement de Toulouse* (2 vols, Paris, 1885); André Viala, *Le parlement de Toulouse et l'administration royale laïque, 1420–1525 environ* (Albi, 1953).

were thus dispersed across the region's centres, though the collection of *fonds ancien* maintained within Agen's municipal archives proved especially informative. Antiquarian local histories of the Agenais were similarly useful, as they contained a wealth of sixteenth-century correspondence and documentation that had been subsequently transcribed and published.[44]

Access to material relating to Béarn and Navarre was difficult. The Navarrais archives were ruined by fire in 1716, with much of its manuscript collection destroyed.[45] Fortunately, a number of documents relating to the religious wars had been transcribed by Pierre de Salefranque in the late seventeenth century, intended as appendices to his life work: *Histoire de l'hérésie de Béarn et Navarre*. The work remained unpublished, though, until 1910, when it was unearthed by Abbé Dubarat and published in four parts in the *Bulletin de la société des sciences, lettres et arts de Pau*.[46] Such material proved highly contentious, causing Dubarat to offer an extensive account of the veracity of Salefranque's work within his editorial preface.[47] In fact, it was only in 1934, when a second expert in the history of Béarn, Charles Dartigue-Peyrou, confirmed their reliability, that the *preuves* were finally accepted by the historical community.[48] Scholars are compelled to explore the numerous antiquarian local histories for additional detail on these southern border regions, though the sectarian bias within these texts is more prominent than their counterparts at Bordeaux or Toulouse. Protestant apologies, for example, are to be found in Olhagaray's *Histoire de Foix, Béarn et*

---

[44] For the Agenais, see *Revue de l'Agenais* (1871 on); Andrieu, *Histoire de l'Agenais*; Abbé Joseph Barrère, *Histoire religieuse et monumentale du diocèse d'Agen, depuis les temps les plus reculés jusqu'à nos jours* (2 vols, Agen, 1855–56); Georges Tholin, 'La ville d'Agen pendant les guerres de religion du XVIe siècle', *Revue de l'Agenais et des anciennes provinces du sud-ouest* XIV–XVI (Agen, 1887–89).

[45] A similar fate befell the *Registres de la jurade* at Bordeaux for the period 1560–80. It is thought that these documents were either burned in the numerous fires that plagued the town's archives over the centuries or destroyed by officials keen to eradicate certain events from history.

[46] Pierre de Salefranque, 'Histoire de l'hérésie de Béarn. Manuscrit de Pierre de Salefranque, conseiller du roi, secrétaire du parlement de Navarre', in *Bulletin de la société des sciences, lettres et arts de Pau*, IIe Série, XLIII–XLVI (ed. Abbé Dubarat, Pau, 1920–23). Nancy Roelker believed that Salefranque, a minor official from an important *robin* family in Béarn, may have written his history in preparation for the revocation of the edict of Nantes in 1685. See Nancy Roelker, *Queen of Navarre, Jeanne d'Albret 1528–1572* (Cambridge, MA, 1968), p. 128.

[47] Abbé Dubarat, 'Histoire de l'hérésie de Béarn. Manuscrit de Pierre de Salefranque, conseiller du roi, secrétaire et Darde-sacs du parlement de Navarre', *Bulletin de la société des sciences, lettres et arts de Pau*, IIe Série, XLIII (Pau, 1920).

[48] Charles Dartigue-Peyrou, *La vicomté de Béarn sous le règne d'Henri II d'Albret (1517–1555)* (Paris, 1934), pp. 455–75.

Navarre, Dartigue's *Jeanne d'Albret et le Béarn*, Communay's *Les Huguenots dans le Béarn et la Navarre*, and Bordenave's *Histoire de Béarn et Navarre*,[49] while Catholic narratives are contained in the works of Dubarat, Labenazie's *Histoire de la ville d'Agen and pays d'Agenois*, and Lestrade's 'Les Huguenots en Comminges'.[50] For more impartial analysis of the region's confessional history there are a number of apposite texts, with the recent studies by Bryson, Greengrass and Roelker the more even-handed.[51]

Finally, a note on the *Commentaires* of Blaise de Monluc, used extensively throughout this study to provide important insights into the activities of and dichotomies facing Catholic commanders of the southwest. Of course, extreme caution needs to be exercised when reading these memorial accounts of the civil wars, but Monluc's work, once dismissed as blatant Catholic propaganda, has undergone something of a revision in recent years. Paul Courteault, Monluc's biographer, for example, claimed that the *Commentaires* 'merit their place on the top rung of narrative histories of France during the sixteenth century. Monluc is nearly always well informed, his accounts are exact, his detail is accurate, his judgements are moderate and circumspect'.[52] Similarly, Pierre Michel sees no reason to dismiss Monluc as an unreliable source: 'The objectivity of Monluc is remarkable ... Generally, historians and Protestant commentators confirm his version of

---

[49] Pierre Olhagaray, *Histoire des comptes de Foix, Bearn, et Navarre, diligemment recueillie tant des precedens historiens, que des archives desdites maisons* (Paris, 1629); C. Dartigue, *Jeanne d'Albret et le Béarn* (Mont-de-Marsan, 1934); A. Communay, 'Les Huguenots dans le Béarn et la Navarre. Documents inédits', *Archives historiques de la Gascogne*, 6 (Paris, Auch, 1885); Nicolas de Bordenave, *Histoire de Béarn et Navarre* (ed. P. Raymond, Paris, 1873).

[50] Abbé Dubarat, *Le Protestantisme en Béarn et au pays basque* (Pau, 1895); Abbé Dubarat, *Documents et bibliographie sur la réforme en Béarn et au pays basque* (Pau, 1905); Labenazie, *Histoire de la ville d'Agen et pays d'Agenois*, I (Montauban, 1888); Abbé Jean Lestrade, *Les Huguenots en Comminges. Documents inédits*, I (Paris, Auch, 1900); 'Les Huguenots en Comminges. Documents inédits, II', *Archives Historiques de la Gascogne*, 14 (Paris, Auch, 1910), pp. 1–160.

[51] David Bryson, *Queen Jeanne and the Promised Land* (Brill, 1999); Mark Greengrass, 'The Calvinist experiment in Béarn', in A. Pettegree, A. Duke and G. Lewis (eds), *Calvinism in Europe, 1540–1620* (Cambridge, 1994), pp. 119–42; Roelker, *Queen of Navarre*. See also Courteault, *Histoire de Gascogne et de Béarn*; G. Bourgeon, *La Réforme à Nérac. Les origines (1530–1560)* (Toulouse, 1880); J. de Jaurgain, 'Les capitaines châtelains de Mauléon. Appendice', *Revue de Béarn, Navarre et Lannes*, III (1885), pp. 13–81; 'Les capitaines châtelains de Mauléon', *Revue de Béarn, Navarre et Lannes*, II (1884), pp. 241–341; P. Mirasson, *Histoire du Béarn* (Paris, 1770); Raymond Ritter, 'Jeanne d'Albret et les troubles de la religion en Béarn, Bigorre, Soule et Navarre, 1560–1572', *Revue de Béarn*, 3–6 (1928–33); Alphonse de Ruble, *Jeanne d'Albret et la guerre civile* (Paris, 1897).

[52] Courteault, *Blaise de Monluc, Historien*, pp. 618–19.

events.'[53] Certainly, neither of the two great Protestant histories of the religious wars, the *Histoire ecclésiastique* and the *Mémoires de Condé*, disputes the detail of Monluc's writings, even if they revile his sentiment and activities.[54] Two printed editions of the *Commentaires* will be used in this study: the nineteenth-century five-volume set edited by the baron Alphonse de Ruble; and Paul Courteault's more recent edition, featuring extensive notes and variants.[55] Monluc only began writing his *Commentaires* after his retirement in 1570 and, although he had finished them by 1572, they were amended and added to over the following years. It seems evident that many of these revisions were borrowed from the memoirs of Guillaume and Martin du Bellay, in an attempt by Monluc to augment his more vague recollections of early events. The result, then, saw his commentary on his life's deeds revised and extended with a vindication of his proud reputation in the face of recent allegations of corruption and malpractice.[56] Ruble and Courteault, however, drew from three distinct versions of the *Commentaires* for their editions: the extant original manuscript; the 1592 text, published by Florimond de Raemond; and a later incomplete edition held by Monluc's nephew, Jean de Monluc de Balagny, which featured Jean's additional notes in the margins. Ruble used Balagny's manuscript as the basis for his edition, drawing on the other two sources to fill the gaps as required; although much of the content and orthography of the original is retained, Ruble corrected many of Florimond's alterations and restored proper names throughout. Courteault, on the other hand, preferred to use the original manuscript as his basis, with Florimond's and Balagny's texts cited where necessary. Where the different editions offer supplementary original information, Courteault supplies multiple versions, something Ruble does not, highlighting text from alternate editions by the use of italics, parentheses and footnotes. He corrects the pre-1564 calendar, by which New Year began at Easter, to the modern equivalent, an amendment that Ruble also ignored. In fact, Courteault is extremely critical of Ruble's editorial method, describing it as '*un amalgame perpétuel, impossible à contrôler*'.[57] For Courteault, Ruble interchanged the different texts too often and too readily, with the result that a less than authentic complete

---

[53] Pierre Michel, *Blaise de Monluc* (Paris, 1971), pp. 128–9.

[54] [Bèze], *Hist. eccl.*; [Condé] *Mémoires de Condé*.

[55] Blaise de Monluc, *Commentaires et lettres de Blaise de Monluc, maréchal de France* (5 vols, ed. A. de Ruble, Paris, 1864–72); [Monluc], *Commentaires 1521–1576*.

[56] For the influence of Guillaume and Martin du Bellay on the text, and Monluc's desire for vindication through his *Commentaires*, see Robert J. Knecht, 'The sword and the pen: Blaise de Monluc and his *Commentaires*', *Renaissance Studies*, 9 (1995), pp. 104–18.

[57] [Monluc], *Commentaires 1521–1576*, p. xxx.

work is created from less than complete materials. For all references within this study, therefore, Courteault's more complete edition of 1964 will be used. Ruble's edition, though, will be cited for all references to Monluc's correspondence, as it contains two additional volumes of transcribed letters sent and received by Monluc during his career, something Courteault was unable to complete.

CHAPTER TWO

The Birth of Catholic Activism at Bordeaux

The province of Guyenne proved fertile ground for the fledgling reformed church in France. Situated in the south-western corner of the country, its great distance from the centre of court power, and isolation from the major patronage networks of Catholic grandees in the north-east, screened the activities of visiting ministers from prying eyes. Calvin was well aware of this potential, dispatching a higher proportion of ministers from Geneva to the south-west than to any other region: of the eighty-eight ministers arriving in France from Geneva between 1555 and 1562, twenty-eight – nearly one-third – headed to Guyenne, Bergerac and Western Languedoc.[1] The policy paid dividends as numerous landed families offered succour to itinerant preachers, while local communities clamoured to hear their evangelical message. By 1562, it was estimated that 10 per cent of Guyenne's population had converted to 'la nouvelle religion'.[2]

Yet, despite these gains, many reformers found it difficult to gain access to government offices within Guyenne throughout the 1550s, settling instead for positions within the universities of the south-west, the traditional centres of Humanist learning in the region. This would change after 1560 as the crown, weakened by minority, was forced to pursue conciliatory policies in order to placate Protestant nobles and ease confessional tensions across the provinces. Governmental offices were now opened to representatives of both faiths, and reformers penetrated the corridors of local power in large numbers. The confessional make-up of local institutions altered further as incumbents converted from Catholicism, while established Catholic foundations such as monasteries, convents and even the lesser clergy reported dwindling membership.[3] Rising Protestant representation within the councils and bureaucracies added to the pressure on the crown to make further concessions to the

---

[1] Sixteen ministers were appointed to Guyenne, nine to Western Languedoc and three to Bergerac. See Robert M. Kingdon, *Geneva and the Coming of the Wars of Religion 1555–1563* (Geneva, 1956), p. 55. For the distribution of ministers in the south-west, see also Mack P. Holt, *The French Wars of Religion, 1562–1629* (Cambridge, 1995), p. 38; Janine Garrisson-Estèbe, *Les Protestants au XVIe siècle* (Paris, 1988), p. 207.

[2] BN, Dupuy, 588, fo. 106.

[3] Courteault, *Histoire de Gascogne et de Béarn*, p. 209.

reform movement, with the edict of Saint-Germain (January 1562) seen as evidence that the royal court was prepared to compromise and accommodate Protestantism officially within the kingdom.

For Catholics, however, the new officials were little more than heretics and criminals, violators of the body politic. Catholic magistrates in the south-west expressed especial betrayal at this turn of events, claiming the crown was turning a blind eye to continuing outrages in its urgency to conciliate. There is little doubt that the number of attacks on Catholic clergy, churches and citizens was rising during this time. The Spanish Ambassador to the French court, Thomas Perrenot, *sieur* de Chantonnay, estimated that over four hundred Catholic churches were desecrated by Protestants during the first years of the 1560s,[4] while James B. Wood's recent study of violence against priests, canons and friars during the first decades of the religious wars showed that the highest incidences were found in Guyenne and lower Languedoc.[5]

At Bordeaux, magistrates of the *parlement* expressed concern at these events, forecasting that confessional rivalry within its legal chambers would paralyse local administration, with hostilities spilling over into communal violence as supporters of each faith rallied to defend their rights and privileges.[6] Analysis of the emerging Protestant infrastructure in the south-west also reveals that such fears were not unwarranted. In order to consolidate their gains, the reformed church had convened a synod at Clairac, on 19 November 1560, under the auspices of Calvin's chief minister, Boisnormand, to integrate the disparate churches of the region into a single entity.[7] The assembly determined that Guyenne would be divided into seven constituencies: Condommois, les Landes, Béarn, Agenais de la Garonne, Agenais vers Sainte-Foy, Bordelais et Bazadais and Quercy et Rouergue. Each constituency was to be governed through its colloquy but answerable only to the synod. The two largest colloquies established were at Agen, containing twenty-one churches, and at Condom, with fourteen, though all were charged with responsibility for affairs of their own churches irrespective of size.

These revisions established both a province-wide bureaucracy and an effective military infrastructure, with individual churches ordered to acquire military cadres capable of defending the local community. Each church was to recruit a professional captain and to finance any necessary troop provision by diverting money away from local taxes into a war chest, with additional sums put aside to fund the levying of mercenary

---

4 Ruble, *Jeanne d'Albret*, p. 139.
5 Wood, 'The impact of the Wars of Religion', p. 148.
6 Powis, 'Order, religion and magistrates', p. 181.
7 ADLG, E Sup. Agen, GG 201, fo. 1.

companies should they be required. The synod, however, made it clear these would not be autonomous commands. Orders were to be issued by the colloquy to the church leadership, and the captains were to follow these to the letter. No doubt aware that such innovations might alarm Catholic authorities, the synod urged all captains to make their military activities as unobtrusive as possible, with all muster rolls and manoeuvres to be undertaken in secrecy, or at night.[8] There was little difficulty in recruiting suitable commanders as the south-west had recently been inundated with military veterans, unemployed following the disbanding of the royal army at the peace with Spain of 1559.[9] The reformers were not averse to offering added incentives to attract these veterans, either, with the Catholic general, Blaise de Monluc, noting that certain ministers were tempting recruits 'not only with riches, but with the keys to heaven too'.[10]

Protestant military potential thus evolved at pace over this period. A second synod, held at Sainte-Foy, near Agen, in November 1561, devised the *assemblée politique*, a regional committee whose remit it was to oversee the organization, training and deployment of troops serving the local churches. This essentially formalized the military structure of the reform church in Guyenne, uniting Protestant communities across the province. The *assemblée politique* was charged with coordinating military affairs through the colloquies, with colonels appointed to govern each locality, and two *protecteurs*, stationed at Bordeaux and Toulouse, commanding the combined forces of the south-west.[11] As a model for organizing defence and uniting disparate centres of population across Guyenne, this pyramidal hierarchy would prove to be a great success. So much so, in fact, that it was quickly adopted by regional synods across France, and ultimately by the

---

[8] For further reading on the Synod at Clairac, see Bourgeon, *La réforme à Nérac*, pp. 83–4; Lucien Romier, *La conjuration d'Amboise* (Paris, 1923), pp. 222–5; Tholin, 'La ville d'Agen', XIV, p. 439; Lecler, 'Aux origines de la ligue', p. 190. For a broad picture of provincial synods across France during 1559/60, see Garrisson-Estèbe, *Les Protestants au XVIe siècle*, p. 193.

[9] The Venetian ambassador, Barbaro, noted that most of the Protestant infantry deployed during the first war was 'composée de vieux soldats, pour la plupart gascons'. [Monluc], *Commentaires 1521–1576*, p. 1207, note 10.

[10] [Monluc], *Commentaires 1521–1576*, p. 510. Ironically, Monluc would also receive such an offer from a captain of the Reformed church at Nérac in January 1562, promising money and the use of four thousand foot soldiers should he convert. This elicited a most vitriolic response: 'what diabolic churches are these that make captains?' [Monluc], *Commentaires 1521–1576*, p. 478.

[11] See Lucien Romier, 'A dissident nobility under the cloak of religion', in J.H.M. Salmon (ed.), *The French Wars of Religion. How Important were Religious Factors?* (Boston, MA, 1967), p. 28.

national synod as the blueprint for its military reforms after April 1562.[12]

Catholic reaction to such innovation was swift. Florimond de Raemond, a Catholic *conseiller* at Bordeaux, ridiculed the colloquies as little more than 'a gathering of ministers, advocates, merchants, solicitors, tailors, coppersmiths and gardeners'.[13] Senior magistrates, however, were less frivolous, accusing the reformers of wanting to 'introduce their religion at sword point, to bring down the monarchy, and to reduce Guyenne to cantons'.[14] Théodore de Bèze, Calvin's representative in the south-west, rejected these charges, arguing that the Clairac and Sainte-Foy initiatives were nothing more than a means to allow Protestants to contribute more effectively to royal military potential.[15] Monluc, though, was in no doubt that the synod's reorganization of its military structure was at the root of much of the region's troubles.[16] Certainly, the threat to Catholic security posed by these innovations was now very real, with authorities across the region inundated with complaints of iconoclasm, armed assemblies and abuses of the clergy.[17] But if Protestant aggrandizement in Guyenne seemed to be moving at pace, one major obstacle remained in its path: the fortified citadel and Catholic bastion of Bordeaux.

As the capital of the province of Guyenne, and the largest urban centre of the region by far – its population had swelled from 25 000 in 1515 to around 50 000 in 1559[18] – the stronghold of Bordeaux was undoubtedly a chief objective of Protestant expansionism. The town's wealth was founded on the export of wine across Europe, the principal of many benefits derived from its status as the premier trading port on the Atlantic, while its formidable defensive architecture reflected a chequered history, one in which French, English and Gascon troops had fought incessantly for dominion over the town. Encircled by an imposing curtain wall, Bordeaux was

---

[12] See especially the reorganization of the synod at Nîmes, in R.J. Knecht, *The French Civil Wars, 1562–1598* (London, 2000), pp. 74–5. For wider reformed military structures, see Kingdon, *Geneva and the Coming of the Wars of Religion*, pp. 106–9.

[13] Florimond de Raemond, *Histoire de la naissance, progrez et decadence de l'hérésie de ce siècle* (2 vols, Rouen, 1610), I, p. 994.

[14] Arlette Jouanna, Jacqueline Boucher, Dominique Biloghi and Guy le Thiec (eds), *Histoire et dictionnaire des guerres de religion* (Paris, 1998), p. 68.

[15] [Bèze], *Hist. eccl.*, I, p. 888.

[16] [Monluc], *Commentaires et lettres*, IV, p. 118. See [Monluc], *Commentaires 1521–1576*, pp. 472; 507.

[17] See, for example, AMB, ms 766, fos. 374–427 for April 1560; fos. 428–554 for May 1560; fos. 555–632 for June 1560; fos. 633–707 for July 1560; Bordeaux *parlement* to king (23 August 1560), BN, ms français, 15 873.

[18] For Bordeaux's growing population in the sixteenth century, see Anne-Marie Cocula, *Étienne de la Boétie* (Bordeaux, 1995), pp. 72–3.

fortified by seven stout gateways, two opening to the countryside and five facing the river Garonne. A decorated central gateway, the *porte de Cailhau*, provided a ceremonial entrance into the town from the port, while its battlements posed a daunting obstacle to any amphibious assault. Its location at the mouth of the river allowed the town fathers to control all waterway traffic along this important southern artery. In times of strife, chains could be thrown across the Garonne from its landing stage to prevent galleys from continuing downriver.[19] Incorporated into the curtain defences were two robust fortresses: the château Trompette, commanding the north-eastern approaches to Bordeaux; and the château Hâ, guarding the land to the west. Garrisoned within each were royal soldiers and the town guard, each commanded by professional captains.[20]

As in other large French towns, the administrative infrastructure of Bordeaux comprised a maelstrom of complex, competing entities. Civil government was the prerogative of the town council, the *jurade*. An *arrêt du parlement* of 1527 specified that the civic corporation should consist of a mayor and twelve serving officers, or *jurats*. In 1534 this number was halved, so that each of the six *quartiers* of Bordeaux – Saint-Éloi, Saint-Pierre, Saint-Michel, Saint-Rémy, Sainte-Eulalie and Saint-Mexent – was represented by a single *jurat*.[21] Following the revolt of the Gabelle in 1548, when numerous civic officials were implicated in the insurrection that saw the Catholic *lieutenant du roi*, Tristan de Moneins, dragged from his home and murdered on the streets of Bordeaux, the *jurade* was temporarily suspended. In its stead, twenty-four *prud'hommes* were elected from among the loyal bourgeoisie to serve under the mayor. When, in 1550, the king exonerated the six *jurats*, reinstating the ancient rights of the city corporation, the incumbent *prud'hommes* were kept on, forming a new body, the *Trente*. The office of mayor, previously named 'in perpetuity' by the king, was now made an elective post, restricted to a single two-year term.[22] By *lettres patentes* of 1559 and 1560, the *jurats* were then granted jurisdiction over the town's policing, with responsibility to appoint both the captain and lieutenant of the guard.[23]

---

[19] Chevalier describes the *porte de Cailhau* at Bordeaux as 'un véritable arc de triomphe': Bernard Chevalier, *Les bonnes villes de France du XIVe au XVIe siècle* (Paris, 1982), p. 125.

[20] Some useful general histories of Bordeaux can be found in Boutrouche, *Bordeaux de 1453 à 1715*; Ducourneau, *La Guienne historique*; Devienne, *Histoire de Bordeaux*; Julian, *L'histoire de Bordeaux*; O'Reilly, *Histoire complète de Bordeaux*; Gabriel de Lurbe, *Chronique Bordeloise* (Bordeaux, 1594); Jean Darnal, *Chronique Bordeloise. Supplement* (Bordeaux, 1619).

[21] AMB, Carton II, 17, *Cérémonies* (24 July 1527). See Ducourneau, *La Guienne historique*, II, p. 204.

[22] Boutrouche, *Bordeaux de 1453 à 1715*, pp. 541–5.

[23] AMB, Carton II, 14, *Guet de Garde* (1559/1560).

Bordeaux also featured the seat of *parlement* for Guyenne, a staunchly Catholic sovereign court that would prove a continual thorn in Protestant aspirations to secure the town and its hinterland. The origins of the *parlement* at Bordeaux date back to the late fifteenth century when a single courtroom, the *grand'chambre*, was established within the *palais de l'ombrière* to dispense royal justice. Over the following decades it expanded dramatically. Under Louis XII, a *chambre des enquêtes* was created, followed by a *chambre criminelle* in 1519, and two new chambers, a *chambre des requêtes* and a second *cour criminelle*, or *tournelle*, in 1546 and 1547, respectively.[24] Each chamber played a specific role in the judicial administration of the province. The *grand'chambre* provided the major appeal court for Guyenne, dealing largely with high-profile local and crown issues, while the *chambre des enquêtes* served as its annex, hearing lesser civil cases. The *chambre des requêtes* incorporated petitioning into the daily life of the *parlement*, allowing litigants to plead their case and offer a defence rather than to simply be judged. It also served to relieve the *chambre des enquêtes* of many of its petty cases, while the *cour criminelle* vetted appeals to decide whether they were worthy of proceeding before the *grand'chambre*.[25] With the expansion of legal chambers, the number of officials appointed to serve the *parlement* increased too. Originally, the court was served by two *présidents* and eighteen *conseillers*, of which nine served as *clercs*. In 1519, royal *lettres* created a new office, that of *premier président*, and added eight further offices of *conseiller*. Four more were created in 1537, five in 1543, while 1547 saw fifteen *conseillers* and two *présidents* added to serve in the new chambers.[26] Thus, when an up-and-coming *conseiller*, Etienne de la Boëtie, entered the *parlement* in 1553, he reported a professional corpus numbering one *premier président*, seven *présidents*, sixty-two *conseillers*, sixty-two *avocats*, eighty-five *procureurs*, eleven *huissiers*, eight *secrétaires*, two *greffiers* and two *receveurs aux amendes*.[27]

If the *parlement* would come to epitomize the defence of orthodoxy within the institutional framework of Guyenne throughout this period, lesser bodies such as the *présidiaux* and *cours des aides* would prove more susceptible to infiltration by Protestant officials and would champion the reform cause across the region. Guyenne boasted nine *présidiaux*, judicial

---

[24] Gaston Zeller, *Les institutions de la France au XVIe siècle* (Paris, 1948), pp. 153–4. The *parlement* suffered a similar fate to the *jurade* following the Gabelle riots of 1548, being suspended by royal order until the amnesty of 1 January 1550.

[25] Zeller, *Les institutions de la France*, pp. 177–81.

[26] Boutrouche, *Bordeaux de 1453 à 1715*, pp. 289–90; Boscheron-Desportes, *Histoire du parlement de Bordeaux*, p. 99.

[27] Cocula, *Étienne de la Boëtie*, pp. 72–3.

courts aimed at bridging the gap between the *parlement* and the lesser *seigneurial* and *sénéchaussée* courts.[28] The *présidiaux* were the cause of intense friction for the *parlement*, especially as the edict of Fontainebleau (1552) granted them 'last resort' jurisdiction over many criminal cases, a prerogative previously held by the court at Bordeaux. This became increasingly contentious during the initial stages of the religious wars, with cases involving Protestants regularly dismissed by *présidial* officers sympathetic to the new religion, even though Catholic magistrates had decided to the contrary.[29] The new *cour des aides* at Périgueux, an autonomous fiscal body formed by the crown in 1554, ostensibly to fund the royal war chest through the sale of offices, further complicated matters, not least because officials here were paid significantly higher wages than *parlementaires* – 500 *livres* per year as opposed to 375 *livres*.[30] This caused great resentment at Bordeaux, especially as many new offices were being sold to converts of the new religion. Indeed, at the first opportunity the magistrates moved to annex the *cour des aides*, absorbing it into a newly-established *chambre des requêtes et des aides* within the *parlement* in October 1557.[31] Wider representation also suffered as a result of the *parlement*'s determination to ostracize Protestant officials, with neither the *états de Guyenne* nor the *assemblées particulières* (the *états de l'Agenais, de Quercy, de Rouergue* and *de Périgord*) being convoked on a regular basis for fear of providing a platform for reform propaganda.[32] Jurisdictional squabbles and confessional tensions thus wracked the governance of Bordeaux throughout the 1550s and early 1560s, and it seems apposite that the first formal Catholic riposte to Protestant incursions would emanate from within the administrative corpus itself.

---

[28] Zeller, *Les institutions de la France*, pp. 175–7. Each *présidial* was officiated by a *président*, seven *conseillers*, a *procureur* and an *avocat du roi*.

[29] Powis has shown that many of these discrepancies centred on the *lieutenant-criminel* of the *présidial* at Bordeaux, whose leniency in cases of 'scandal and illegal assembly' forced the *parlement* to review and revise many decisions: Powis, *The Magistrates of the Parlement of Bordeaux*, pp. 77–8.

[30] Boscheron-Desportes, *Histoire du parlement de Bordeaux*, p. 104; Géralde Nakam, *Montaigne et son temps. Les événements et les essais* (Paris, 1982), p. 55.

[31] This was a serious blow to the consulate of Périgueux, who had paid the crown 50 000 *écus* in 1554 to guard against this very outcome. In November 1561, the *cour des aides* was fully integrated into the corpus of the *parlement*. See Powis, *The Magistrates of the Parlement of Bordeaux*, pp. 66–8; Zachary Sayre Schiffman, 'An intellectual in politics: Montaigne in Bordeaux', in Michael Wolfe (ed.), *Changing Identities in Early Modern France* (Durham, NC, 1997), p. 309; Boscheron-Desportes, *Histoire du parlement de Bordeaux*, pp. 107–11.

[32] Zeller, *Les institutions de la France*, pp. 57–70.

Throughout the 1540s and 1550s, spontaneous clashes between Catholic and evangelical groups on the streets of Bordeaux became a feature of everyday life. Prominent on the Catholic side were two groups in particular: the associates of the confraternity of Saint-Yves, the representative corporation of the *avocats* and *procureurs* of the *parlement* of Bordeaux; and the players of the *basoche*, the affiliated actors and musicians of the confraternity, whose performances brought colour and melody to the town's various religious processions and feast day celebrations. As the confrontations grew in size and violence, it would be the *confrères* and *basochiens* who spearheaded Catholic militant reactions. In this, they received the support of prominent Catholic *parlementaires*, who defended their actions within the court, and who came to play an ever increasing role in the administrative functions of the confraternity.

The cult of Saint-Yves had been a medieval phenomenon. Its patron, Yves Hélory, was born on 7 October 1253, at Kermartin, near Tréguier in northern France. The son of a local nobleman, Yves had been expected to pursue a military career, but instead entered the university at Orleans to embark upon a vocation in the legal profession. On qualifying as a *juge et avocat*, Yves quickly gained renown for his tireless defence of the poor, needy and abused of the region. At his death in 1303 locals immortalized his achievements in inscription on his tomb: 'Comforter of the afflicted, advocate to widows, tutor to orphans, defender of the innocent, patron of advocates'.[33] Over the following years, numerous miracles were reported at this site, prompting a papal inquest. On 19 May 1347, Yves was pronounced a saint by pope Clement VI at Avignon, and soon became *patron des avocats* within the courts of the land.[34]

While he was revered in various regions throughout the fourteenth and fifteenth centuries, it was the early decades of the sixteenth century that witnessed the widescale veneration of Saint-Yves across France. In the various *parlements*, confraternities dedicated to the protection of the needy were established by the *avocats* and *procureurs* as a mark of respect to their patron. The first appeared at Paris in 1517, celebrating its feast day on 19 May, the date of Yves' canonization, while the earliest reference to such a confraternity at Bordeaux is to be found in the *registres du*

---

[33] See Christian Chavanon, *Béatification professionnelle de Saint Yves* (Bordeaux, 1936), pp. 7–10.

[34] The best general histories of the cult of Saint-Yves in France are Jean François Fournel, *Histoire des avocats au parlement de Paris depuis Saint Louis jusq'au 15 octobre 1790* (2 vols, Paris, 1813); S. Ropartz, *Histoire de Saint Yves, patron des gens de justice* (Saint-Brieux, 1856); Louis Arthur de la Borderie, *Monuments originaux de l'histoire de Saint Yves* (Saint-Brieux, 1887).

parlement for May 1529.[35] An examination of the *registres* for subsequent years shows that this feast day ritual was observed each May without fail throughout the century. The entry for 19 May 1536 reveals that the ceremony was never restricted solely to the *avocats* and *procureurs*, but that significant numbers of magistrates were in attendance too: 'After dinner, having held vespers in the manner accustomed of the Confraternity of Saint-Yves, the presidents, councillors and advocates and procurers of the court gathered in the *salle de l'audience*, as was the custom, to elect and confirm syndics to serve the confraternity for the coming year.'[36]

The integral role of the attending *parlementaires* in the administrative affairs of the confraternity is best seen in an entry for May 1559, which reports that, once the mass in veneration of Saint-Yves had been completed, an election was held to appoint four *commissaires* to represent the confraternity before the court for the coming year.[37] Here, the *avocats* and *procureurs* nominated eight contenders, four from each corporation, with the gathered magistrates selecting their preferred candidates. Supervising this procedure were the four outgoing *commissaires*, whose terms of office would terminate at the swearing-in of the new electees before the altar of the palace chapel. To conclude proceedings, two *conseillers* were taken to examine the confraternity's accounts, a practice that suggests the *parlement's* financial division took a keen interest in the expenditure of the brotherhood. It is pertinent to note that many of the magistrates who regularly attended the Saint-Yves ceremonial, such as *présidents* Roffignac, Fauguerolles, Beraud and Lachassaigne, and *conseillers* Malvin, Baulon and de Nort, would prove to be among the more active Catholic zealots of the 1560s.[38]

Also present at these occasions was Jean de Lange, perhaps best known to historians of the religious wars for his distinguished performance at the *états-généraux* at Orleans in 1560, where he delivered a vibrant harangue against church abuses.[39] Lange had entered professional life at Bordeaux in July 1547, as an *avocat de la chambre de plaïde* in the *parlement*,

---

[35] BMB, ms 1497, III, fo. 89. Unfortunately, the articles of the Confraternity of Saint-Yves at Bordeaux are no longer extant. However, a complete set of articles, drawn up in 1527, is extant for the Confraternity of Saint-Yves at Rieux. See Le Palenc, 'La confrérie des avocats de Rieux au seizième siècle', *Bulletin de la société archéologique du midi de la France*, 25–8 (1899–1901), pp. 313–14.

[36] BMB, ms 1497, III, fo. 101.

[37] AMB, ms 765, fos 867–9.

[38] For Catholic magistrates attending the confraternity's ceremonial and participating in the administrative proceedings, see, for example, BMB, ms 369, II, fo. 155; AMB, ms 766, fo. 505; AMB, ms 767, fo. 443.

[39] See 'La harangue du peuple et tiers estats de toute la France au Roy tres-chrestien Charles neufiéme, tenant ses estats generaulx en sa ville d'Orleans le premier jour de janvier 1560, faicte par maistre Jean de Lange de Luxe, conseiller et advocat de la Royne au

subsequently serving two concurrent terms on the *jurade* between 1554 and 1556.[40] In 1556, he also secured appointment to the office of treasurer of the Confraternity of Saint-Yves, holding this position for several years.[41] As a rule passed in 1555 stipulated that all candidates wishing to hold administrative office must have served a minimum ten-year membership of the brotherhood before applying, it is evident that Lange was a regular affiliate of the confraternity.[42] He would therefore have been immersed in the penitential ethos of this increasingly militant brand of Catholicism, and well acquainted with its day-to-day confrontations with evangelicals across Bordeaux. Lange would also have been aware of the front-line protagonists in these altercations: the *clercs de la basoche*. The *basoche* were young, trainee *avocats* and *procureurs* of the court, who combined legal apprenticeship with the performance of music, acting and pageantry.[43] Only two such troupes were permitted to stage plays, ballads and processional songs on the streets of Bordeaux during the sixteenth century: the *basoche* and the *écoliers* of the *collège de Guyenne*. The two were almost exact contemporaries: the *collège de Guyenne* was founded in 1533, by members of the *jurade* keen to replace the town's defunct *collège de grammaire*, while the first mention of the *basoche* performing in Bordeaux appears in the *registres du parlement* for 1534.[44] But where both groups were permitted to rehearse and present standard performances across the town as part of their education and training, only the *basoche* were licensed to perform for the festivities surrounding the Saint-Yves ceremonial, as their players were affiliates of the confraternity too, albeit apprentices intent on serving in the court and obtaining full fellowship of the brotherhood one day.[45]

---

parlement de Bordeaux' (Orleans, August 1560), BMB, H 8613; BMB, ms 712, 8, II, fo. 208. Both Boscheron-Desportes and Tamizey de Larroque lauded Lange as 'a brilliant orator' who carried many a Catholic debate during the 1560s. See Boscheron-Desportes, *Histoire du parlement de Bordeaux*, I, p. 159; Tamizey de Larroque, 'Jean Lange, conseiller', p. 687.

[40] 'Serment prêté par Jean de Lange, l'un des Trente; il jure d'être obéissant aux mandements de MM. les Jurats, de bien les conseiller, sans égard pour personne, et de garder le secret' (15 September 1554), 'Inventaire sommaire des registres de la jurade, 1520–1783', I, *Archives Municipales de Bordeaux* (Bordeaux, 1896), fo. 22. See also Tamizey de Larroque, 'Jean Lange, conseiller', p. 687.

[41] ADG, 1B 165, *Arrêt du parlement* (2 March 1556), fo. 20.

[42] For the ten-year rule, see AMB, ms 763, fos 577–9; BMB, ms 1497, III, fo. 183.

[43] The origins of the *basoche* in France date back to 1303, when Philippe le Bel authorized the institution of a community of *clercs du parlement de Paris*. See Howard Graham Harvey, *The Theatre of the Basoche. The Contributions of the Law Societies to French Medieval Comedy* (Cambridge, MA, 1941), p. 17.

[44] AMB, ms 759, fo. 869. For the formation of the *collège du Guyenne* at Bordeaux, see Chevalier, *Les bonnes villes de France*, p. 231; Zeller, *Les institutions de la France*, p. 211.

[45] See Harvey, *The Theatre of the Basoche*, p. 14; Gaullieur, *Histoire de la réformation à Bordeaux*, I, pp. 251–5.

In their earlier years, the staple of *basoche* and *écolier* performances were traditional biblical tales and devotional songs. By the 1540s, however, each group had begun to favour the more controversial morality plays and farces so popular across France.[46] At first, this new material, which ridiculed church abuses and even mocked individual *jurats* and *parlementaires*, was well received by audiences. But, as the reform movement gained momentum in and around Bordeaux, its provocative content began to incite vocal outbursts from attending partisans. The sectarian nature of the plays was exacerbated as the two groups diverged along confessional lines. The *basoche*, as members of the confraternity, proffered the Catholic voice in Bordeaux, deriding reform ideology and innovation, and defending traditional church structures. By performing at the confraternity's feast-day celebrations the *basoche* were able to reach a wide audience across the town, especially as the festivities often lasted for eight days or more.[47] Thus their performances became a focal point for Catholic sentiment in Bordeaux, a forum at which Catholic identity within the town could be defined. The Protestant cause was championed by the *écoliers* of the *collège de Guyenne*, an institution once respected across France as a prominent seat of Humanist learning, but now renowned as an engine of reform evangelism in the south-west. By 1551, many *écoliers* could be seen openly espousing the Calvinist faith in Bordeaux, even attacking local ceremonies and chanting psalms to interrupt processions and masses.[48]

With public performances now a popular vehicle for the dissemination of sectarian propaganda, the authorities in Bordeaux were forced to deal with rising numbers of confrontations between the two troupes. By 1545, members of the *jurade* were regularly intervening to restore order, causing the *parlement* to rule that henceforth the content of every play was to be vetted before performance.[49] The court appointed a committee to validate each month's material, with representatives from both groups charged with presenting their proposed repertoires before the *grand'chambre* well in advance. In the Catholic case this duty fell to the incumbent artistic director of the company, an elected official notionally titled *roi de la basoche*. The office of *roi* had been honorific at best, although the holder

---

[46] For a detailed study of the various forms of *farce*, *moralité* and *sottie* performed by the *basoche* in France during the sixteenth century, see Harvey, *The Theatre of the Basoche*.

[47] 'La fête des basoches durant 8 jours avant la fête de St Yves. Le roi de la basoche se promenoit par les rues suivis par tous les élèves; deux à deux, l'epée au côté': BMB, ms 828, 5, fo. 53.

[48] For examples of urban violence committed by the youth during religious ceremonies, see Chevalier, *Les bonnes villes de France*, pp. 287–308.

[49] BMB, ms 367, fo. 81. For wider moves to censor the content of *basochien* performances across France at this time, see Harvey, *The Theatre of the Basoche*, p. 34.

did receive a *redevance annuelle* of 15 *sols* from the confraternity. The *parlement's* dictate altered this, however, so that when Jehan Pachabelier was confirmed as the new *roi*, in May 1545, he became the first *basochien* fully accountable to the court for the activities of his fellow players.[50]

This development had important ramifications for Catholic consensus at Bordeaux. Firstly, it legitimized the status of the *basoche* within the town; despite their affiliation to the confraternity the *basoche* had never been awarded formal recognition by the authorities. It also raised the profile of the *roi de la basoche* within the hierarchy of Bordeaux society. Thus from 1545 onwards the *roi* became an intrinsic part of formal cere-monial within the town, heading processions and welcoming visiting dignitaries on arrival. His status was raised further in May 1549, when Henry II formally integrated the office of *roi* into the administrative struc-tures of the Bordeaux *parlement*, effectively granting Catholics five distinct representative voices within the court: the four elected *commis-saires* of the Confraternity of Saint-Yves, and the newly-appointed *roi de la basoche*.[51] The zenith for the *basoche*, though, came in December 1559, with the royal visit of Elizabeth of Spain to Bordeaux. As the queen's entourage processed through the *porte de Cailhau* into the town, the elite guard that received her and led the parade through the streets was composed of the full corpus of the Confraternity of Saint-Yves, marching 'in arms and in good order under the emblem of the basoche', with the *roi*, Jehan Larquier, mounted on a white charger, in full armour, leading the cavalcade.[52]

As the reform movement continued to gain ground at Bordeaux – it is estimated that over seven thousand, around 14 per cent, of the town's fifty thousand inhabitants were sympathetic to *la nouvelle religion* by 1561[53] – the rivalry between the *basoche* and *écoliers* intensified. Their plays, literature and songs now became saturated with polemic, with both managing to circumvent the issue of censorship by performing in secret and not writing down the content of the plays.[54] This war of propaganda

---

[50] Ernest Gaullieur, *Histoire du collège de Guyenne* (Paris, 1874), p. 257.

[51] BMB, ms 367, fo. 96; AMB, ms 766, fo. 149. The *registres du parlement* confirm that *côtisations* were paid in full to the *procureur-général* of the court by the *basochiens*, ADG, 1B 211, *Arrêt du parlement* (16 February 1560), fo. 56; and by the *avocats* and *procureurs* of the confraternity of Saint-Yves, ADG, 1B 165, *Arrêt du parlement* (2 March 1556), fo. 20; ADG, 1B 212, *Arrêt du parlement* (18 March 1560), fo. 266.

[52] AMB, ms 766, fos. 89–94 and 104; BMB, ms 369, II, fos 179–88. See also ADG, 1B 207, *Arrêt du parlement* (29 November 1559), fos 40, 182.

[53] For Bordeaux estimates, see Nakam, *Montaigne et son temps*, p. 47; Boutrouche, *Bordeaux de 1453 à 1715*, p. 243.

[54] Harvey states that this may have led to fewer prosecutions, but it leaves the historian with fewer records to examine: Harvey, *The Theatre of the Basoche*, p. 223.

captured in microcosm the growing social tension between Catholics and Protestants across Guyenne. Inevitably, the initial weapons of the players – parody and satire – gave way to stones, swords and guns. At one *basochien* performance at Libourne, in May 1555, royal troops were needed to quell the riot that ensued after attending Protestants attacked the players with clubs, claiming that the material being acted was offensive to the reformed church.[55] As a result of this mêlée, the *roi*, and leading members of the Confraternity of Saint-Yves, were summoned by the *grand'chambre* at Bordeaux to explain Catholic involvement in the disturbances.[56] Matters escalated dramatically in 1556, with the institution of military-style structures within the *collège de Guyenne*. The *écoliers* had divided themselves into four divisions (*Gascogne*, *France*, *Navarre* and *Provence*), each headed by a captain and sub-lieutenant to oversee discipline. Each cell would be responsible for coordinating specific militant activity in Bordeaux, and be able to deploy separately or in conjunction with other units.[57] Gaullieur highlights the close resemblance between these measures and the innovations of the synods of Clairac and Sainte-Foy after 1560, and suggests that the schemes employed by the *écoliers* at this early date may well have been precursors to the military initiatives adopted by these reformed synods four years later.[58]

This escalation forced the *parlement* into stronger action. In April 1556, it issued an *arrêt* banning 'any pieces relating to religion, the Christian faith, the veneration of the saints, and the institutions of the church' from the plays and comedies of both the *basoche* and *écoliers*, censoring a large body of traditional content in the process.[59] The following year, the court went further still, proscribing any material that defamed the *jurats* and *parlementaires* themselves. Howard Harvey has shown that caricatures of royal and provincial magistrates had been rare during the early decades of the sixteenth century, with farces tending to reflect notorious criminal trials, as in the oft-performed 'La condamnacion des banquetz', or would parody the *basoche* and lesser officials themselves, as in 'La farce de Mestre Trubert et d'Artrongnart' and 'Plaidoyé de la Simple et de la Rusée'.[60] During the high period of evangel-

---

[55] ADG, 1B 158, *Arrêt du parlement* (14 May 1555), fos 93–7.

[56] ADG, 1B 161, *Arrêt du parlement* (September 1555), fo. 30.

[57] Gaullieur, *Histoire du collège de Guyenne*, pp. 257–60. It is interesting to note that the students of the University of Paris in the early thirteenth century were similarly divided into four nations: France, Picardy, Normandy and England. See David Nicholas, *The Evolution of the Medieval World* (London, 1992), p. 349.

[58] Gaullieur, *Histoire du collège de Guyenne*, p. 257.

[59] *AHG*, 3, p. 466.

[60] Harvey, *The Theatre of the Basoche*, pp. 72–103.

ism in the 1550s, however, Catholic sentiment turned on those magistrates and clergy suspected of sympathizing with the reform church, with
anti-magisterial and anti-clerical performances increasing dramatically
across France.[61] By 1559 both groups had taken to patrolling the streets
of Bordeaux in gangs, actively seeking out their rivals, with armed skirmishes the norm. On one occasion, in May 1560, a band of *écoliers* was
intercepted by the town guard before it could disrupt Catholic services at
Saint-André. In the ensuing fight, though, the guard found itself so
heavily outnumbered that only assistance from the soldiers at the nearby
Château Hâ allowed escape without too many casualties.[62] The
parlement ordered an immediate inquest into this outrage, requisitioning
all similar cases of accusations of armed bands of *écoliers* roaming the
region so as to track down the ringleaders.[63] On 16 May, the court took
the decisive step of banning the *écoliers* from assembling outside the walls
of their *collège*, warning that further transgressions would be severely
punished.[64]

The *collège de Guyenne*, though, had a powerful patron in Antoine de
Bourbon, king of Navarre, and governor of the province. Although
absent from the region, Navarre had been informed of this punishment,
and had dispatched letters to Bordeaux vilifying the magistrates for
showing favour to the *basoche*, forcing the court to rescind its punitive
arrêt.[65] This divided the *parlement* completely. Catholic *conseillers* and
confrères opposed vehemently such interference, urging that further
measures, not concessions, should be taken against the *collège*. The
moderate party within the court, however, led by the *premier président*,
Jacques-Benoît de Lagebâton, affirmed the governor's right to intervene
and urged conciliation between all parties. A compromise of sorts was
reached, with Catholic magistrates agreeing to re-examine the decision to
censure the *écoliers* so long as all accusations of illicit assemblies in
Bordeaux were investigated fully by the court.[66] Thus, in January 1561,
the *parlement* dispatched a number of its *conseillers* in pairs, and accompanied by soldiers from the Château Hâ for protection, to survey the
town and to arrest those caught attending any illegal gatherings. In fact,

[61] See for example the morality play 'Mars et Justice' (c. 1553), a prime example of a
diatribe against the latitude being granted to Calvinist ministers, and the anti-clerical farces
of the late 1550s: 'Les pauvres deables'; 'Le meunyer de qui le diable emporte l'ame'; 'Le
porteur de Patience'; 'Frère Guillebert'; 'Du pardonneur, du Triaculeur'; 'De la Tavernière':
Harvey, *The Theatre of the Basoche*, pp. 51, 173.
[62] AMB, ms 766, fos 433–42.
[63] ADG, 1B 214, *Arrêt du parlement* (3 May 1560), fo. 23.
[64] AMB, ms 766, fos 452–8.
[65] BMB, ms 367, fo. 213.
[66] AMB, ms 766, fos 461–6.

within two months, six *conseillers* were being employed on a full-time basis to search suspect houses and remove any weapons found to threaten the security of the *maison de ville*.[67] Yet difficulties remained. One Catholic merchant, whose name is missing from the *registres*, complained to Charles de Couci, *sieur* de Burie, the *lieutenant du roi* in Guyenne, that he had sent six communiqués to the *parlement* relating details of over thirty illegal armed assemblies within the town in recent months, but had heard nothing in return.[68] Similarly, Protestants who had lodged counter-complaints against Catholics suspected of contravening various clauses within recent royal edicts asserted that little had been done to satisfy their claims.[69]

Matters intensified in February 1561, when the incumbent *roi de la basoche*, Charles Amussat, marched a large force of armed *basochiens* to the gates of the *collège*, intent on gaining entry and attacking the *écoliers*. Fortunately, the *parlement* had been informed of this, and deployed a number of soldiers in the vicinity to forestall full-scale fighting.[70] The beleaguered magistrates were now compelled to act. On 15 February they issued an *arrêt* censuring the activities of both parties. The *écoliers* were ordered to disband their divisional structures, while the *basoche* were prevented from electing a *roi* for the immediate future.[71] Five days later, the *grand'chambre* issued a more detailed ordinance forcing both *écoliers* and *basochiens* to disarm and relinquish all weapons to the court.[72] Denied recourse to armed pursuits, the *écoliers* continued to vex the Catholics of Bordeaux by gathering on street corners and within the corridors of the *parlement* building itself to chant the psalms of Clément Marot. While apparently a more peaceable activity, this was no less illegal, as an *arrêt* of 26 March 1561 had banned the singing of psalms anywhere within the walls of Bordeaux on pain of death.[73] Catholics living near the *collège*, however, reported that these illegal assemblies were continuing unabated, with over five hundred people gathering to chant on some occasions.[74] An investigation launched by the *parlement* found numerous *écoliers* guilty of contravening the *arrêt* and charged

---

[67]   AMB, ms 767, fo. 300.

[68]   AMB, ms 767, fo. 400.

[69]   In one instance, numerous Catholic magistrates and notables of Bordeaux were accused of failing to surrender their arms, and of continuing their surreptitious patrols of the streets at night, in direct contravention of a recent *arrêt* calling for the disarming of the town's inhabitants. AMB, ms 767, fo. 339.

[70]   Gaullieur, *Histoire du collège de Guyenne*, p. 260.

[71]   BMB, ms 369, II, fo. 269.

[72]   ADG, 1B 226, *Arrêt du parlement* (20 February 1561), fo. 274.

[73]   ADG, 1B 227, *Arrêt du parlement* (26 March 1561), fo. 363.

[74]   BMB, ms 369, II, fo. 273.

them accordingly, although the judgement was not delivered until later in the year.[75] There were many who argued, though, and with some justification, that the deputation sent to examine the Catholic claims constituted a *fait accompli*, in that each of the four deputies assigned – Roffignac, Béraud, Baulon, and Monein – was known to be zealous in his adherence to orthodoxy. It would be interesting to know the response, if any, of those militant Catholics based within the *parlement* building to this provocation. The court was, after all, home to both the confraternity and the *basoche*, and would soon be the seat of the nascent syndicate too. The *registres*, though, are silent on this matter.

This survey of confraternal and *basochien* activism within Bordeaux has shown that Catholics did not wait for the outbreak of formal hostilities in 1562 to challenge the emerging Protestant movement, but that informal resistance and more organized counter-offensives were employed from the first confessional disputes, becoming more aggressive and calculating as the enmity between the faiths intensified. But informal militancy was about to give way to formal and ordered Catholic policy at Bordeaux, as the belligerence of the *confrères* and *basochiens*, and the coalescing of relations between these activists and their peers within the *parlement*, led to the formation of a syndicate of Catholic *avocats* and *procureurs* within the sovereign court, a militant corpus that would have a major impact on Catholic policy and play an integral role in shaping the form and timescale of Catholic resurgence at Bordeaux throughout the 1560s.

---

[75] ADG, 1B 236, *Arrêt du parlement* (29 November 1561), fo. 98.

CHAPTER THREE

The Bordeaux Syndicate

The birth of a syndicate of officials within the *parlement* at Bordeaux in November 1561 would prove to be an important milestone in the evolution of Catholic militancy in the south-west. No longer was the defence of orthodoxy the concern solely of impulsive communal activists such as the *confrères*, *basochiens* and clergy, but now urban patricians would come to the fore, seeking to gain control of government institutions so as to shape legislation and effect an anti-Protestant, pro-Catholic agenda. That is not to say that the officials of Bordeaux had been sedentary to this point. Concerted efforts had been made by key individuals to steer policy in favour of their cause throughout 1560 and 1561, most prominently in the matters of town defences and the size and deployment of the guard. Here the already flourishing symbiosis between certain Catholic magistrates and existing militant bodies is evident, with sizeable elements of the Confraternity of Saint-Yves and armed *basochiens* proffered to the civic corporation to supplement the guard on numerous occasions. This, of course, would prove too contentious a proposal to be accepted by Protestant communities and moderate magistrates alike, but it served to reveal that a synergy between patricians and militants existed even before the outbreak of hostilities in 1562.

Debate over the use of Catholic militia in urban and regional defence had, in fact, been going on throughout 1560 and 1561. A greater policing role for 'bon Catholicques' of Bordeaux had first been mooted within the *parlement* between May and September 1560, with the arrival of royal *lettres missives* sanctioning the deployment of a number of armed *avocats et procureurs* to augment the guard.[1] Encouraged by the crown's latitude in this matter, leading Catholics, including François de Peyrusse, *comte* d'Escars, *lieutenant* to the absent governor of the province, Antoine de Bourbon, urged the *parlement* to go one step further and assign Catholic-only units to patrol the town walls and gates.[2] The *lieutenant du roi* for

---

[1] AMB, ms 766, fo. 810.

[2] AMB, ms 766, fos 787–92. D'Escars would prove an important figure in Catholic hegemony within the south-west, holding numerous high offices: *lieutenant-général du Limousin* (22 September 1561); *seneschal de Toulouse* (25 May 1562); *gouverneur de Bordeaux* (4 May 1563); *gouverneur de la château Hâ* at Bordeaux (4 May 1563); *cappitaine de compagnie de cinquante hommes* (12 February 1565); *lieutenant des châtellenies de Rancon, Champagnac, et du Périgord* (7 February 1568). See Cassan, *Le temps des guerres de religion*, pp. 198–9.

Guyenne, Burie, on the other hand, expressed concern at the deployment of such overtly sectarian supplementary forces, claiming that they threatened the efficacy of patrols. He was especially troubled by plans to have Catholic officials assist in the monitoring of individuals entering the town gates and in the surveillance of hotels and taverns for 'troublemakers',[3] asserting that such roles should not be assumed by ad hoc bodies as they had long been the remit of the *jurade*.[4]

The *lieutenant du roi's* diffidence regarding attempts to bolster the defences of Bordeaux annoyed Catholics. In November 1560, Jean de Lange reported Burie to the crown for incompetence and misadministration, and for failing to defend the province adequately.[5] Attached to this complaint was a *mémoire*, signed by numerous Catholics of the *parlement*, which listed those magistrates suspected of having converted to the Protestant faith. This allegation was to polarize the *parlement*. Dubois, a moderate *conseiller*, retorted that the court had always striven to perform its duties with impartiality and rebuked Lange, a mere *avocat*, for speaking above his station. In response, Thomas de Ram, a solid Catholic, and the *lieutenant-général* of the *sénéchaussée* of Guyenne, disputed Dubois's assertions, arguing that the recent release of a number of Protestant prisoners arrested for assaulting Catholics was an injustice that stemmed directly from the policy of appeasement preferred by moderates and Protestant sympathizers.[6] The invective intensified as further allegations from Lange forced Burie to appeal to Catherine de Medici to clear his name, contrasting his lengthy, loyal service to the crown with the subterfuge being practised by certain Catholic officers at Bordeaux, and suggesting that Lange be detained for spreading 'falsehoods'.[7]

This charge would have proved immensely damaging for Lange had the *avocat* not been sheltered by sympathetic voices within the upper echelons of the *parlement*. Foremost among these was the *président*, Christophe de Roffignac. Roffignac's Catholic credentials were impeccable: a client of the cardinal of Lorraine during his time in Paris in the 1540s and 1550s, he became a keen supporter of grass roots Catholicism at Bordeaux after his appointment as *président* in December 1555, regularly presiding over festive and administrative ceremonial for the Confraternity of Saint-Yves – duties that first brought him into close

---

[3] AMB, ms 766, fols 787–92.

[4] Burie to Francis II (14 September 1560): BN, ms français, 15 873, fo. 8.

[5] O'Reilly, *Histoire complète de Bordeaux*, II, p. 204.

[6] O'Reilly, *Histoire complète de Bordeaux*, II, p. 204.

[7] Burie to Catherine de Medici (19 January 1561), *AHG*, 10, p. 38; Burie to Catherine de Medici (20 January 1561), *AHG*, 10, pp. 35–6.

contact with Lange, then the fellowship's treasurer.[8] Camille Julian described Roffignac as 'one of the most intelligent Catholic militants of Bordeaux',[9] while Tamizey de Larroque outlined the significance of the relationship between these two Catholic zealots: 'if the fiery *président* de Roffignac was at this time the head of the Bordeaux league, Lange was its secretary'.[10] Yet Lange would prove far more than a subordinate to Roffignac; theirs would be a partnership, reciprocal in nature, with Lange initiating Catholic exploits across Bordeaux while Roffignac acted as his guardian. In this, the *président* was ably supported by a number of loyal *conseillers*, the most prominent being Charles de Malvin and François de Baulon, each tireless defenders of orthodoxy within the court.[11] To have such high-ranking patrons would prove immensely important for Lange as he was, as Dubois had commented, merely an *avocat*, and so, in political terms, vulnerable to attack from moderate and Protestant magistrates alike.

Tensions between militants and moderates heightened once more in late 1561 over what to do about the increasing levels of violence within Bordeaux. With Burie still hamstrung by insufficient resources, the *parlement* decided to take the lead in organizing security for the town. But when orders were dispatched to the captains of Bordeaux's two fortresses, the châteaux Trompette and Hâ, requisitioning forty soldiers from each to augment the town guard, their respective captains, Vaillac and Noailles, refused to comply, claiming they possessed inadequate numbers to meet this demand while maintaining the integrity of their own defences.[12] The *parlement* had little option than to revisit its policy of arming 'bons Catholicques' from within the court, with Roffignac ordering all able-bodied officials to report to the *maison de ville* for deployment (the old and more infirm were granted exemption so long as they provided a trustworthy representative to take their place).[13] Again, Burie objected to this use of Catholic militia, and only gave his consent to the plan when it was agreed that recruits would be placed under the authority of a *jurat* and accountable to the *capitaine du guet* for their conduct.[14]

---

[8] See Powis, *The Magistrates of the Parlement of Bordeaux*, p. 107.

[9] Julian, *Histoire de Bordeaux*, esp. Chapter 12.

[10] Tamizey de Larroque, 'Jean Lange, conseiller', p. 687.

[11] Malvin frequently represented Catholic plaintiffs before the court, on occasion giving evidence in person to support their defence. See, for example, AMB, ms 767, fos 179–86. Baulon's most celebrated act would come later in the decade: securing the return of the Jesuits to Bordeaux in 1568.

[12] BMB, ms 369, II, fos 304–25.

[13] AMB, ms 768, fos 229–31.

[14] AMB, ms 767, fos 886–91; BMB, ms 369, II, fo. 331.

Throughout this period, relations between Burie and the militants were not helped by the rising number of complaints from Catholic victims of Protestant violence across the Bordelais, many aggrieved at the inability of the *lieutenant du roi* to secure the hinterland. With limited resources at his disposal, Burie had informed the *grand'chambre* in the spring of 1561 that, as the defence of Bordeaux was his priority, the policing of the Bordelais would have to be undertaken by the local nobility.[15] While neither Catholic nor Protestant communities expected this ad hoc expedient to be effective, the initial results seemed promising. For a time, order was maintained in many localities by noble retinues, aided by visits from deputations of Bordeaux *conseillers* to calm tensions in especially contentious areas.[16] But soon, reports of violence against Catholic clergy across the Bordelais were again on the increase and, in June 1561, the *parlement* was forced to remonstrate with Burie over his policy. Interestingly, it seems that, the previous month, Lange had offered the *lieutenant du roi* the services of over four thousand Catholics to assist in the policing of the town, presumably composed of *confrères*, *basochiens* and local militia.[17] Burie had rejected the offer then, wary no doubt of the divisive nature of such a force. Now, though, the court urged Burie to reconsider, arguing that this additional manpower would allow professional troops to be released from guard duty, and thus to be deployed to counter the troubles ravaging the countryside.[18] The magistrates also expressed concern at the activity of one of Burie's local gendarmes, the Protestant noble, the *sieur* de Savignac de Thouars, who seemed to be dispensing particularly harsh punishments to Catholic communities across the region, while showing inappropriate leniency to reform centres.[19] When Roffignac and Malvin confronted Burie directly over this issue, alleging that Savignac had created a vigilante force over two thousand strong, the *lieutenant du roi's* reply – that Savignac's force was operating in the *sénéchaussée de l'Agenais*, and thus outside Bordeaux's official jurisdictional boundaries – did little to appease Catholic ire at his inactivity.[20]

November 1561 would prove a nadir for Catholic fortunes in Guyenne, with numerous communities across the Bordelais and Agenais coming under intense pressure from roving gangs of reformers. In one incident, assailants razed the convent of the Cordeliers at Marmande to

---

[15] AMB, ms 767, fo. 746.
[16] See for example AMB, ms 767, fos 747–8.
[17] Devienne, *Histoire de la ville de Bordeaux*, I, p. 134.
[18] AMB, ms 767, fo. 495.
[19] AMB, ms 767, fos 693–700.
[20] AMB, ms 767, fos 711–12.

the ground, with the loss of several lives,[21] while at Fumel, the Catholic baron, François de Fumel, was savagely murdered by a Protestant mob in his own home.[22] Bordeaux was not exempt from such disturbances. On 21 November, Protestant forces attempted an assault on the château Trompette, the impressive fort that guarded the north-east approaches to Bordeaux.[23] The move was tactically astute, as the château was known to be the key to the town's defences. For Dupré, this was a seminal moment for Catholicism in the region: if the château fell then so would Bordeaux, with the likelihood that many lesser Catholic satellites of the region would quickly follow. Potentially, the Protestant forces could have sealed victory over the south-west with this one gambit.[24] But the fort held firm, thanks to the stubborn resistance of its captain, Vaillac, and his garrison.

Perturbed by events at Marmande, Fumel and the château Trompette, and by ever increasing numbers of reports alleging escalating Protestant violence across the region, Catholics finally lost patience with the political process at Bordeaux. In early December, militants within the *parlement* met to decide upon their riposte. The result was the formation of a syndicate of *avocats* and *procureurs* of the court, ostensibly a hybrid of confraternal and *parlementaire* militancy that drew on cooperative relations forged during the ceremonial and functions of the Confraternity of Saint-Yves, to be headed by Lange and located within the environs of the *palais de l'ombrière*.[25] Aptly the birth of the syndicate was made public during one of Lange's frequent harangues before the court, on 18 December 1561.[26] This tirade, however, was more explosive than usual. Commencing with a now mandatory indictment of Burie's management of the province, Lange then lambasted the crown's policy of accommodating Protestantism, arguing that the frequent synods and consistories were hampering effective local government and serving as breeding grounds for discontent and disunity. Lange was joined in this outburst by his Catholic cohort, Thomas de Ram, who also launched a fierce condemnation of Burie's leadership, asserting that the *lieutenant*'s inactivity had encouraged Protestants to rebel, leaving Catholics with little option than to take independent measures to defend themselves. Ram continued by presenting the court with fresh evidence, garnered by syndicate members, that a number of officials of Bordeaux were frequenting local *prêches*, despite recent interdictions, and that

---

[21] AMB, ms 768, fos 184–5.

[22] AMB, ms 768, fos 202–4.

[23] The assault was reported before the *parlement* on 24 November 1561. See AMB, ms 768, fos 133–40.

[24] Dupré, 'Projet de ligue catholique à Bordeaux', p. 373.

[25] Lecler, 'Aux origines de la Ligue', p. 193. Burie alerted the king to the presence of a syndicate in Bordeaux on 16 December 1561: AMB, ms 768, fo. 346.

[26] For Lange's speech, see AMB, ms 768, fos 369–96.

witnesses had seen weapons being taken from the town hall and distributed among the Protestant community, all under the nose of Burie.[27]

Condemnation of the *lieutenant du roi* was not universal, though, as two Protestant speakers, Dubois, a *jurat*, and Bichon, a *conseiller*, rebutted Catholic accusations. After defending Burie's reputation, they countered by claiming that it was Lange and the syndicate who were the divisive forces in Bordeaux; Catholic machinations were already under-mining effective governance within the town's institutions, while its militia force, now vastly outnumbering the town guard, proved to be a disruptive element on the streets.[28] But these voices were in the minority, and in the subsequent vote Lange and Ram carried the day, securing permission to draft a remonstrance to the crown urging that Catholic troops be sent to the province immediately to quell the unrest, and requesting permission to coopt greater numbers of Catholic militia into the guard to bolster the town's defences in the meantime.[29]

It should be noted, however, that the syndicate's success in this debate owed much to the absence from proceedings of the *premier président* of the *parlement*, Jacques-Benoît de Lagebâton. Lagebâton would be a constant thorn in the side of Catholic militants at Bordeaux, his moderate politics and desire to adhere to crown policy regardless of confessional complaints infuriating Lange, Roffignac et al. throughout the 1560s. On his return from consultations with the *conseil privé*, in January 1562, Lagebâton entered the fray at Bordeaux. After reviewing the minutes of the contentious debate, the *premier président* deemed the proceeding to have been illegitimate. He therefore rescinded the remonstrance to the crown, berated the syndicate for agitating within the court and rebuked fellow moderates for acceding to Catholic demands.[30] Lagebâton then turned on Lange, censuring the *avocat* for using inappropriate rhetoric before the court, and for employing improper pronouncements in his harangue against Burie, irregularities that contravened the technicalities of language permitted to an *avocat* before the *grand'chambre*.[31] Despite appeals from several Catholic *présidents*, Lagebâton refused to absolve Lange, and his reprimand was formerly entered into the *registres*.[32]

---

[27] AMB, ms 768, fos 399–403.

[28] AMB, ms 768, fos 444–7; 477–9.

[29] AMB, ms 768, fos 448–62.

[30] AMB, ms 768, fos 685–99.

[31] Powis has examined the irregularities in this speech to the *parlement*, and supports Lagebâton's claims that Lange's language directly infringed on the privileges of the court, and that his claim to represent the Catholic populace was in derogation of the rights of the *jurade*, which claimed sole representation of the corporation of the city: Powis, *The Magistrates of the Parlement of Bordeaux*, p. 266.

[32] AMB, ms 768, fos 685–99.

It seems ironic that the divisive debate over Catholic efforts to militarize and secure Bordeaux had taken place against a backdrop in which the crown was attempting to settle confessional tensions by forcibly disarming urban populaces. The edict of Saint-Germain (July 1561), for example, had imposed a strict ban on the carrying of all weapons within the towns of France, a proscription that even extended to the nobility, whose weaponry had traditionally been seen as a sign of their elite status. At Bordeaux, the edict met resistance on two levels. Firstly, the town fathers complained that it compromised the municipal charter, which placed matters pertaining to the security of the town in their, not the crown's, hands. Secondly, Catholics argued that disarming their militia would leave the town at the mercy of nearby Protestant forces. Indeed, during the first reading of the edict Catholic *parlementaires* disrupted proceedings to such an extent that Lagebâton was forced to adjourn the session pending guidance from the royal council.[33] When, in July 1561, Lange delivered a petition containing over three thousand signatures to the court, demanding that the edict be rejected, the *premier président* dismissed the appeal by claiming Lange was agitating against the crown.[34] Lagebâton was supported in this matter by Burie, who remarked that recent violence at Toulouse had been the result of a similar flawed policy by the town's governors – that is, allowing the militia to remain armed – and should be avoided at Bordeaux.[35] The two moderates won the day on this occasion, and the edict was duly registered in late July.[36]

Within weeks, however, the Catholic party had returned with a further petition, this time signed by many of the local clergy, arguing that Bordeaux should be deemed exempt from the terms of the edict because of its position as 'a frontier and maritime town'.[37] This traditional entreaty of border provinces of France would become a common ploy of Catholics throughout the wars: in March 1562, Monluc would try to exempt Bordeaux from having to site a *prêche* near its walls by citing a clause within the edict of January that allowed 'frontier towns' to ban such assemblies within their jurisdiction for reasons of security;[38] in September 1563, the governor of Bordeaux, d'Escars, attempted to secure similar immunity, this time referencing exclusion terms within the edict of Amboise;[39] while three months

---

[33] BMB, ms 369, II, fos 297–303.
[34] Lagebâton to Catherine de Medici (July 1561), BN, ms français, 15 875, fo. 442.
[35] BN, ms français, 22 372, fo. 949.
[36] AMB, ms 767, fos 614–22.
[37] Ruble, *Jeanne d'Albret*, p. 47.
[38] BN, ms français, 3186, fo. 60.
[39] D'Escars to Catherine de Medici (6 September 1563), BN nouv. acq. français, 20 598, fos 191–6. One month later, d'Escars repeated his request, claiming that an English force, recently landed at La Rochelle, threatened to move into Guyenne unless local Catholics were allowed to arm themselves and join the king's forces arrayed against the enemy: d'Escars to Charles IX (15 October 1563), BN nouv. acq. français, 20 598, fos 199–201.

later, the clergy of Bordeaux urged the crown to allow Catholic citizens to arm themselves so as to resume its traditional role as a buffer between the kingdom of France and its enemies of Spain, Navarre and England.[40] Guyenne's Catholic neighbours were no less willing to try this manoeuvre, with the provincial governor of Languedoc, Henry de Montmorency-Damville, arguing in December 1563 that his territory deserved exemption from the provisions of the recent edict, given that Languedoc 'is a frontier province just like Picardy, Burgundy, Brittany, Provence and others'.[41]

The August 1561 petition at Bordeaux failed, however, angering the clergy who were particularly aggrieved at the rising levels of violence against their churches. They claimed that, should Catholics be forced to disarm, the number of assaults would increase dramatically.[42] In this they were supported by the archbishop of Bordeaux, Antoine Prévôt de Sanssac, who appeared before the *parlement* to chide the magistrates over their inability to counter the recent disorder.[43] With Sanssac and the clergy now more prominent in affairs, Catholic policy switched tack. If Catholics were to be forced to lay down their weapons, and Catholic troops were not to be on hand to defend the countryside, then measures should be taken to ensure that all Protestants were disarmed too, and their communities policed regularly to prevent further assaults.[44] Demands for the surveillance of Protestant activities thus became the new focus of Catholic attention at Bordeaux. Lange and Roffignac wasted little time in marshalling manpower, with Catholics everywhere urged to observe and report any suspicious behaviour. Among the first to submit a report was a *commissaire* of the Confraternity of Saint-Yves, Beraud, who informed the *parlement* in late 1561 that a stranger, 'dressed as a nobleman', had made numerous visits at night to the house of a known reformer in Bordeaux.[45]

---

[40] 'Remonstrance faicte au Roy par le clergé du pays de Bourdeloys' (4 December 1563), BN, ms français, 15 878, fos 294–5.

[41] Damville to Charles IX (18 December 1563), *HGL*, 9, *Preuves* X, p. 507.

[42] AMB, ms 767, fos 692–3.

[43] AMB, ms 767, fo. 396. In March 1561, a representative of the clergy of Agenais, Dunoyer, had also demanded that the *parlement* do more to arrest and condemn those 'mutiners, heretiques, schismatiques et seditieux' currently terrorizing the Catholic clergy of the province. See AMB, ms 768, fos 419–26.

[44] These developments can be found in two appeals dispatched to the crown at this time. See Sanssac and Catholic clergy to Charles IX (19 June 1561), BN, ms français, 3186, fo. 153; Clergy of Bordeaux to Charles IX (19 June 1561), BN, ms français, 3159, fo. 72.

[45] AMB, ms 767, fos 719–24. The *registres* show that Catholic officials were particularly suspicious of Protestants who moved about the town dressed in 'robes longues ou courtes', presumably from fears that such clothing could conceal weapons, and gave their spies permission to stop and search anyone so attired at any time: *Registres du parlement de Bordeaux* (29 June 1562), BN, ms français, 22 372, fo. 1045.

The court dispatched several *conseillers* to investigate, but before the visitation could arrive, the two men fled to the safety of Béarn.[46] Ducourneau suspected that the men were warned by sympathetic *jurats*, concerned about the victimization of their co-religionists, but also irritated by the usurpation of this tool of the *jurade* by Catholic magistrates.[47] As stated above, the searching of houses traditionally fell within the category of policing the town, and as such was a prerogative of the civic authorities, not the *parlement*.

The expanding Catholic intelligence network soon had its first big-name victim, though, with the arrest of Mathieu le Berthou, the captain of the guard at Bordeaux, in September 1561. Berthou was accused of allowing several Protestant prisoners to escape from prison, and was arrested and imprisoned on the order of the *parlement*. His trial was delayed for several months, however, as the court worked through a backlog of cases. But when Berthou finally came before the *grand'chambre*, in April 1562, he must have despaired as he looked up and saw that the presiding judges were none other than those Catholic stalwarts, Roffignac and Malvin. It was of little surprise, then, when the captain was subsequently reprimanded and removed from all duties.[48] The most prominent and audacious case came in May 1562, when Catholic magistrates ordered that the house belonging to Lagebâton be searched for hidden arms.[49] To intrude into the sanctum of the *premier président* was a risky move. It can be construed as a reflection either of the confidence felt by Catholics at Bordeaux at their rising authority, or of their desperation to remove this belligerent impediment to their designs at any cost. Certainly, such a weighty duty had to be undertaken by a high-ranking official, and Roffignac selected his trusted lieutenant, Malvin, for the job. Despite his hard-line credentials, however, Malvin revealed a shrewd side to his character, requesting that witnesses accompany him in his task, keen no doubt to obviate, or at least diminish, any possible recriminations.[50]

Although the search proved fruitless, Catholics continued to press their adversaries. In September 1562, the court was forced to investigate claims made by the Catholic *procureur-général*, la Ferrière, that the wives of Protestant *conseillers* had been seen attending a nearby *prêche*.[51] The

---

[46] AMB, ms 767, fo. 725.

[47] Ducourneau, *La Guienne historique et monumentale*, II, p. 192.

[48] AMB, ms 768, fo. 751.

[49] ADG, 1B 247, *Arrêt du parlement* (21 July 1562), fo. 153. See also AMB, ms 769, fo. 582.

[50] Malvin selected Jehan Gauteille, a *clerc du greffe* of the court, as his witness: ADG, 1B 247, *Arrêt du parlement* (21 July 1562), fo. 153.

[51] AMB, ms 769, fo. 746.

question of whether officials at Bordeaux should be censured if their families were seen attending illegal assemblies had actually long dominated court proceedings. In September 1561, for example, two *commissaires* of the Confraternity of Saint-Yves, Sauvanelle and le Bouhet, had petitioned the court to demand that any such official be severely sanctioned.[52] Their case was strengthened the following month, when a *prêche* held near the church of Saint-Michel in Bordeaux degenerated into violence, leaving many killed and numerous more injured or arrested.[53] This episode became a *cause célèbre* for Catholics, especially when the widow of Menault de la Grave, one of the deceased Catholic noblemen, laid the blame for her husband's death squarely at the feet of Lagebâton, who, she claimed, had allowed numerous armed Protestant officers and their wives, not to mention his own spouse, to attend the *prêche*. The widow demanded that the court determine and divulge the religious affiliation of its magistrates and their wives, and that it declare the number of its officials who regularly attended such assemblies.[54]

A similar case, in late December 1561, made for quite entertaining theatre. When the *parlement* granted a new injunction preventing all officials of Bordeaux from attending the *prêches*, it was immediately contested by two lesser officers of the court.[55] These men, Moreau, a *procureur*, and le Blanc, an *avocat*, claimed that, as at least sixty other officials had expressed a desire to continue to attend such assemblies, the injunction should be rescinded.[56] Lange, speaking on behalf of the newly-formed syndicate, challenged their claim, stating that, if there was indeed such strong sentiment within the court, it should be presented in written form. So, on 10 December, Moreau and le Blanc returned to the *parlement* with a *requête*, signed by forty officials, confirming their wishes. But it was a trap. La Ferrière, an ally of Lange, interjected, stating that every *avocat* and *procureur* had sworn an oath promising to be 'bons Catholicques' and to observe the constitutions of the Catholic church on taking office. By signing the new declaration they had contravened the terms of their contract, and, as such, should be suspended until the court decided their punishment.[57]

The syndicate had gained a significant victory, but moderate hackles were now raised, and over the following months questions over the legitimacy of this Catholic confederation within the *parlement* began to surface. One major bone of contention concerned the validity of the

---

[52] AMB, ms 767, fo. 756.
[53] AMB, ms 767, fo. 755.
[54] AMB, ms 767, fos 755–6.
[55] AMB, ms 768, fo. 293.
[56] AMB, ms 768, fos 301–9.
[57] AMB, ms 768, fos 313–18.

syndicate's militia. At inception, Lange had divided the syndicate's membership into six quasi-military units, corresponding roughly to the six administrative *jurades* of Bordeaux. Each of these districts was to be supervised by a Catholic syndic, who would report directly to Lange, with captains appointed to command each sub-division of *quartier* and *paroisse*.[58] The combatants of the Confraternity of Saint-Yves, who during 1561 had numbered over four thousand, according to Lange, were then assigned to each syndic to make up the bulk of the syndicate's militia. The *Histoire ecclésiatique* asserts that Catholics even had plans to incorporate the suburban peasantry into this enterprise, though there is little evidence to support this.[59] Such initiatives were not novel, of course. Similar measures had been implemented recently by the *écoliers* of the *collège de Guyenne* and the synod of Clairac, and an analogous scheme had even been introduced by the *parlement* in June 1561, whereby eight *conseillers* were designated to serve as deputies to the eight parishes of Bordeaux so as to maintain order and prevent unrest before it escalated.[60] Interestingly, seven of the eight deputies appointed were known Catholic zealots, although the sole moderate *parlementaire*, de Ferron, was assigned to the largest parish of Saint-Michel.[61]

In order to combat the potential of the syndicate and its militia, Lagebâton and Burie launched a two-pronged assault on the Catholic corpus. In March 1562, the *premier président* ordered a formal investigation into the activities of the syndicate, with its findings dispatched to the *conseil privé* for deliberation.[62] Burie, meanwhile, re-examined the *lettres-patentes* that had confirmed the syndicate the previous year, suggesting that, as they had not yet been fully registered before the *parlement*, Lange's organization, was in effect little more than an illegal assembly, and thus should be banned, as per the terms of the edict of January.[63] Lagebâton's

[58] Gaullieur, *Histoire de la réformation à Bordeaux*, I, pp. 311–25. Court records also refer to this infrastructure: 'les Catholicques de ladicte ville ont créé six syndics d'entre eulx'. (*AHG*, 10, p. 320).

[59] [Bèze], *Hist. eccl.*, I, p. 872.

[60] AMB, ms 767, fos 536–8.

[61] The Catholic deputies were Malvin (parish of Saint-Projet), Vergoing (Saint-Pierre), Anselin (Saint-Éloy), de Nort (Sainte-Maxance), de Monehn (Sainte-Colombe), Guilleragues (Sainte-Aulaye) and d'Alesme (Saint Rémy): AMB, ms 767, fos 536–8. Even when the *parlement* tightened its hold within the parishes the following December by providing each deputy with a list of two hundred parishioners eligible to be mobilized for active duty should the need arise, the bias towards Catholic appointees remained at seven to one: Cocula, *Étienne de la Boétie*, p. 134.

[62] AMB, ms 768, fo. 763.

[63] O'Reilly, *Histoire complète de Bordeaux*, II, p. 206. For further details of Burie's attempts to censor the syndicate, see Gaullieur, *Histoire de la réformation à Bordeaux*, I, pp. 412–17; Ducourneau, *La Guienne historique et monumentale*, II, p. 192.

initiative drew first blood, however, when the *conseil privé* returned its verdict on 12 April, demanding the immediate cessation of all syndicate activity, declaring any and all resolutions passed by its leadership to be null and void.[64] On the face of it, this was a triumph for the moderates at Bordeaux. But events soon forced the court to rethink its decision. On 26 June 1562, the château Trompette was once more besieged by Protestant forces, this time led by the leading military captains in the south-west: Duras, Pardaillan and Langoiran.[65] Seemingly, the reformers had colluded with two captains serving in Burie's company, gaining assurances that the gates would be opened under the cover of darkness to allow Protestant soldiers to enter unopposed. Crucial to this plan was the assumption that the castle's Catholic commander, Vaillac, the saviour of the château in 1561, would remain neutral during this new assault – a rational if optimistic scheme, given that the captain had recently married into the Protestant Pardaillan family. When Vaillac remained constant in his duties, and ordered the gates to remain locked, however, Duras's forces were denied and the plan failed.[66]

This had been a close call for the Bordeaux authorities, and Catholics used it as evidence of the paucity of the town's defences since the suspension of the syndicate. With confessional tensions raised again, Roffignac and Malvin urged the court to require all officials to give a public declaration of their faith,[67] while Monluc, newly arrived to bolster the town's security, called upon the Catholic population to 'spare neither their goods nor their blood in the service of the king and the defence of the true Catholic church'.[68] Meanwhile, Burie, who had been embarrassed by the complicity of his men in the attempted coup, was called upon to stem the increasing number of violent outbursts within Bordeaux. The formal outbreak of war in April 1562 had stretched the *lieutenant*'s resources to breaking point, so much so that the *parlement* was forced to assign its own Catholic officers to permanent guard duty to augment the town's defences.[69] As the syndicate had not yet been dismantled, hundreds of its armed militia were also enlisted to patrol the streets at night, under the command of Catholic syndics.[70] But as this was still proving inadequate

[64] *AHG*, 46, p. 268.

[65] For events surrounding the attempt on the château Trompette of 26 June 1562, see Bordeaux *parlement* to Charles IX (4 July 1562), *AHG*, 17, p. 269; AMB, ms 769, fo. 662; ADG, B, *Arrêt du parlement* (13 January 1563), fo. 92.

[66] Boscheron-Desportes, *Histoire du parlement de Bordeaux*, I, p. 151; Ducourneau, *La Guienne historique et monumentale*, II, p. 193.

[67] AMB, ms 769, fo. 427.

[68] [Monluc], *Commentaires 1521–1576*, p. 515.

[69] BMB, ms 369, II, fo. 421; BMB, ms 370, fo. 654.

[70] BMB, ms 369, II, fo. 359.

by the following month, the *parlement* instructed Lange and la Ferrière to initiate a count of all Catholics of fighting age across the Bordelais, in case an emergency force was needed,[71] while, in the meantime, three hundred Catholic soldiers were levied from neighbouring *ressorts* to solve the town's immediate security problem.[72] To finance this, the Catholic governor of Bordeaux, Antoine de Noailles, proposed a tax on Protestant citizens, a move opposed by Burie, who wanted Catholics and members of the clergy to contribute.[73] A compromise was reached whereby Catholics would contribute a lesser sum, but would be exempt from lodging external troops within their homes, a recourse Noailles was determined should be reserved for Protestant homes as punishment for the recent troubles. This was soon amended to include residences belonging to the *jurade*, with each *jurat* now required to accommodate two soldiers.[74] Such a punitive measure was almost certainly an act of revenge by Catholic hierarchs against a body that had been overtly sympathetic to the Protestant cause over recent months, and was probably the enterprise of Roffignac, who had waged a private campaign against the *jurade* for several years.[75]

The volume of violent episodes across Bordeaux was becoming unmanageable. Breaking point was reached in late June 1562, when a major disturbance erupted in the parish of Saint-Rémy.[76] Burie was forced to dispatch his personal troops to restore order, but, with the syndicate's militia no longer available as cover, the remaining town defences were weakened considerably. As reports of unrest continued to filter through, the *lieutenant du roi* had little option other than to permit Catholics to arm and defend themselves as appropriate. The level of desperation reached is evident from the fact that Burie then authorized the *sénéchal* of Guyenne to permit Catholics to establish a new corporation, to be administered as an adjunct of the *parlement*, with the remit of

---

[71] ADG, 1B 245, *Arrêt du parlement* (8 May 1562), fo. 66.

[72] BMB, ms 370, fo. 644.

[73] AMB, ms 768, fo. 875.

[74] BMB, ms 369, II, fo. 385.

[75] In April 1559, Roffignac secured backing from the Constable, Anne de Montmorency, for the removal of a number of the *jurade*'s civic powers: Roffignac to Montmorency (28 April 1559), *AHG*, 13, p. 119. Then, in June 1561, he lobbied successfully to deny anyone suspected of affiliation to the reform movement the holding of office on the *jurade*: AMB, Carton II, 17, *Election des jurats* (29 May 1561). This injunction was only revoked on 2 July 1564, in keeping with the terms of the edict of Amboise, which allowed municipal authorities to elect candidates 'sans avoir égard de la diversité des religions': AMB, Carton II, 17, *Election des jurats* (2 July 1564). In April 1562, Roffignac countersigned an *arrêt* requiring all *jurats* to live within the walls of Bordeaux and to attend Catholic services within their local church: AMB, ms 768, fos 816–19.

[76] BN, ms français, 22 372, fos 1070–4.

serving on the town guard and reporting violent incidents to the court only.[77] Moderates were understandably wary of such a move, and demanded that five *conseillers* liaise with this corporation, with its movements to be validated by the *procureur-général*, Lescure.[78] This most surprising development reveals the extent of the predicament faced by Burie. Rejuvenating Catholic power so soon after securing its termination could only have been considered as a last resort, but the security and stability of the town came first, and Burie needed competent militia to stave off the threat of widescale insurrection.

If Burie saw this as a simple expedient, Catholics viewed it as a prime opportunity to re-establish their syndicate. On 20 July 1562, one of Lange's fellow *avocats*, Melon, petitioned the *parlement* to register this new body as a 'sindicat',[79] seconded by Malvin, no less, with former syndicate members Lescure, La Ferrière and Lahet confirming that Melon had 'the full support of the clergy and the majority of the bourgeoisie and Catholics of the town'.[80] Accepting the necessity of this, Burie counter-signed the *requête* the same day,[81] though not before informing Monluc that the syndicate's duties would comprise 'the guarding of the town, but nothing else'.[82] While some moderate magistrates admitted that they found this new syndicate 'useful and necessary',[83] the *jurade* were far from happy at the regeneration of such a potent force within Bordeaux politics, especially the ceding of jurisdiction over guard duties to Melon, which one *jurat* described as 'novel'.[84] But it would not take long for Burie to backtrack over this issue, or for Lagebâton to rouse the moderates from their torpor and oppose Catholic plans. Within the week, the *premier président* had called a special séance of the *parlement* to debate the new syndicate. Remarkably, given recent Catholic victories within the administrative corpus, when Melon's application was put to a vote it was rejected by a narrow margin. Lagebâton detailed three grounds for this rebuff: firstly, such a confessional assembly was 'contrary to the will of the king and his edicts'; secondly, the concerns of the *jurade* over the infringement of jurisdictional prerogatives were valid – experience had shown that such a prominent, well-supported entity would establish a competing body of power within the administration, and could only

[77] BN, ms français, 22 372, fos 1070–3.

[78] BN, ms français, 22 372, fos 1072–4.

[79] AMB, ms 769, fo. 504.

[80] AMB, ms 769, fos 514–16. See also Boscheron-Desportes, *Histoire du parlement de Bordeaux*, pp. 154–62 for resurgence of the syndicate under Melon at Bordeaux.

[81] BMB, ms 370, fo. 661.

[82] BN, ms français, 22 369, fo. 137.

[83] AMB, ms 769, fo. 523.

[84] BN, ms français, 22 372, fos 1074–5.

prove divisive to the government of the town; thirdly, if the court accepted an official Catholic corpus within the political framework of Bordeaux, it would be difficult to reject demands from Protestants to establish their own version, and with two such bodies active within the town, the *parlement* foresaw only conflict and contestation.[85]

Melon threatened to go over the head of the *parlement* and appeal directly to the crown over this slight.[86] Sensing that Catholic ire might bring the machinery of government at Bordeaux to a grinding halt at such a delicate time, Burie attempted to calm matters by stating he would honour his commitment to allow the confraternity's *commissaires* licence to present minor denunciations concerning policing matters before the lower court for the foreseeable future, so as to give Catholics more of a role in the security of the town.[87] But Lagebâton would have none of this, stating that there was no need for syndics to make such denunciations as appropriate machinery to deal with lesser claims already existed within the court structure; if Catholics wanted justice, he added, they should pursue it through civil suits.[88] The debate closed with Lagebâton and Burie agreeing that it would be wise to remove all powers from the syndicate and its officials, and to prohibit further Catholic association within the town.[89]

Such was the brief but influential life of the Catholic syndicate at Bordeaux. Despite a short duration and dual identity, its impact on the political map of the region was profound, revealing how a number of dedicated lesser officials could influence policy in support of their cause, so long as they received the backing of like-minded patrons. Here, the list of supporters was impressive: from leading Catholic magistrates of the court, to the clergy and local nobility of the Bordelais, to the Confraternity of Saint-Yves and the Catholic populace of Bordeaux. This wide cross-section reflects the disenchantment felt by Catholics of all social strata at ineffective crown and local policy. But it also reveals the extent to which decades of communal activism had permeated the Catholic psyche; the syndicate may have been established as a direct result of events of November 1561, but it clearly emerged from a milieu in which Catholic patience with the aggressive tactics of the reformers had finally run out.

That the syndicate had its roots in the quintessential Catholic forums of the Saint-Yves ceremonial is clear, for its first luminaries were *confrères*

---

[85] AMB, ms 769, fos 514–16.
[86] AMB, ms 769, fo. 551.
[87] AMB, ms 769, fo. 539.
[88] AMB, ms 769, fo. 551.
[89] AMB, ms 769, fos 551–2.

and patrons of the confraternity. Undoubtedly, their experience of confrontations with evangelicals on the streets of Bordeaux during the 1540s and 1550s was harnessed in the creation of the syndicate in 1561. So was Lange's corpus also a counter to the escalating machinations of the *écoliers*, and a response to the division of the *collège* into military cadres? And were the four thousand Catholics offered by Lange to augment the town guard in May 1561, months before the syndicate's inception, the very militants who had fought these battles over the previous decades? The formal cadre of November 1561 should be seen as an escalation – if not a culmination – of decades of Catholic anxiety and anger, and not simply as a response to the events of that month. But Lange and the syndicate also generated vociferous opposition from Protestants and moderates within the administration of Bordeaux, the latter marshalled by leading royal officials, Burie and Lagebâton. Both men were determined that crown dictate would prevail over personal and confessional conviction, and so set about suppressing Catholic and Protestant militancy in accordance with the royal edict. When this demanded that the syndicate be dismantled, and that formal Catholic organization be prohibited, the defence of Catholic interests required a new mechanism, a new set of protagonists, to carry it forward. Enter the Catholic nobility of the Bordelais, who would take up the baton from Lange and the *confrères*, and assume the role of patrons of Catholic hegemony in Guyenne for the coming year.

CHAPTER FOUR

The Nobility of the Bordelais

With the censoring of the syndicate in July 1562, moderates within the *parlement* and *jurade* at Bordeaux sought a fresh approach to consensual and equitable government of the town. Relations between the faiths would now be characterized by conciliation rather than sectarianism, with the crown's policy of accommodation, soon to be defined explicitly by the terms of the edict of Amboise (March 1563), laying out the preferred demeanour of confessional relations within the communities of the south-west. Without access to a legitimate outlet for their grievances, Catholic militants such as Lange, Melon and d'Escars should, in theory, no longer have been able to influence or interrupt this agenda. Such optimism neglected to account for the Catholic nobility of the Bordelais. Already an active force across the countryside, Catholic gentlemen such as Candalle, Terride, Tilladet and Negrepelisse had assumed the mantle of 'defenders of orthodoxy' almost before the syndicate had been terminated, and, much to the chagrin of the moderate party, took Catholic activism to new levels of organization and intensity over the next decade. Isolating the driving forces behind the Bordelais nobility's intervention has long divided historians. Analysis of the numerous petitions dispatched by these men to the *parlement* reveals that confessional and social grievances were often blurred, with violent assaults, for example, construed at times as Protestant outrages, and at others as attacks against a landholder and his property. For many, the Gabelle riots at Bordeaux in 1548, and particularly the murder of the Catholic *lieutenant du roi*, Tristan de Moneins, by a rampaging mob, were still fresh in the mind.[1] Powis believes this event had a profound effect on the Bordelais nobility, shaking the very foundations of their social structures: 'if such a high-ranking officer, a symbol of the king's authority, could be overthrown, then the nobility's own standing, whether as royal officers or as provincial notables – in short as members of the ruling class – could not long survive'.[2]

---

[1] Moneins was the *lieutenant du roi* in Guyenne in the absence of the king of Navarre. His other offices at this time were governor of Navarrenx and *sénéchal* of Béarn. For the 1548 Gabelle riot, see Boscheron-Desportes, *Histoire du parlement de Bordeaux*, esp. Chapter 3; S.C. Gigon, *La révolte de la gabelle en Guyenne, 1548–1549* (Paris, 1906), pp. 73–84.

[2] Powis, *The Magistrates of the Parlement of Bordeaux*, p. 62.

Throughout 1560, tensions had risen dramatically across the Bordelais, with violent confrontations becoming the norm rather than the exception. Confessional relations moved to breaking point, then shattered in the summer of 1561, as a brutal seven-month period commenced in which Catholic nobles were hounded from their property, assaulted and murdered. The first attacks occurred in August, with the *seigneur* de Levignac forced to flee his château after an attack from around two thousand 'thieves', while his neighbours, the *sieurs* de Lestelle and de Thouars, also fell victim to aggressive gangs who raided and ransacked their homes.[3] Over the following months, numerous Catholic *gentilshommes* reported being maltreated by their vassals, with some of the most violent episodes occurring on the Bordelais–Agenais border.[4] Here, the *sieur* de Rouillac was besieged at his home at Saint-Mézard, in February 1562, following an attempt to prevent an armed mob from damaging the church on his land. In fact, Rouillac would have his throat cut, as did his neighbours, the *sieurs* de Cuq and de la Monjoye, from nearby Astaffort, when they tried to intervene and save their compatriot.[5] Even the renowned general, Blaise de Monluc, would find himself confined to his home at Estillac in June 1561 by 'five to six hundred men of the countryside', a legacy of his intervention against the Protestant coup at Agen.[6]

The most significant attack on a Catholic noble, however, occurred in late November 1561, when the baron de Fumel was murdered in his own home by an armed mob, seemingly intent on destroying his residence and pillaging his estate.[7] This crime scandalized the Catholic community. Fumel was a major landholder in Guyenne, a prominent lawyer well known at court, and a former ambassador to Constantinople during the 1550s.[8] He was also renowned for his dislike of Calvinist ministers preaching on his lands, a loathing that may have contributed to his downfall. Labenazie, the prior of the *collège d'Agen*, certainly thought so, stating that Fumel was killed by a mob of angry Protestants, seeking

---

[3] Courteault, *Blaise de Monluc. Historien*, p. 408; Ruble, *Jeanne d'Albret*, pp. 141–2.

[4] Crouzet, *Les guerriers de Dieu*, I, pp. 515–23.

[5] [Monluc], *Commentaires 1521–1576*, p. 483.

[6] 'Jurade d'Agen sur les enterprises des Prétendus Réformés' (4 June 1560), *AHG*, 29, p. 11. Monluc also claimed to be the target of an assassination plot, forged by a secret council of Guyenne reformers, an assertion that Burie would later validate before the *parlement* 'Les réformés avoient formé le projet de l'assassiner, et que leurs ministres excitoient le peuple à la révolte', Burie to *parlement de Bordeaux* (17 January 1562), Devienne, *Histoire de Bordeaux*, p. 138.

[7] For three contemporary descriptions of the events at Fumel in November 1561, see AMB, ms 768, fos 202–4; *AHG*, 8, pp. 207–21; J.A. de Thou, *Histoire universelle* (London, 1734), IV, pp. 369–71.

[8] See Pierre Miquel, *Les guerres de religion* (Paris, 1980), p. 226.

vengeance for the baron's continual violation of their *prêches*: 'Fumel was cruelly killed ... he died in agony, stripped naked and tied to his bed, before being shot through the heart by arquebusiers, who cried: Vive l'Evangile!'[9]

Historians, however, have not been so sure about this account, and have posited quite different theories about the role played by confessional tensions in the murder of Fumel. Janine Garrisson-Estèbe, for example, portrayed Fumel as a tyrant, his murder 'une révolte populaire, spontanée, sanglante'.[10] For Garrisson-Estèbe, the killing of Fumel was an act perpetrated by oppressed workers attempting to liberate themselves from social subjugation, embittered by the consequences of a pervasive economic decline. Jules Andrieu, on the other hand, saw both social and religious motivations behind the assault, suggesting that, while Fumel's employees 'profoundly detested him', and may well have wanted him dead, his flagrant disregard for the sanctity of Protestant worship (the baron was known to ride his horse through reformed gatherings) may have been the specific trigger for his murder.[11] Mack P. Holt has followed this line, asserting that, as several hundred Catholic peasants had joined in the assault, 'it is clear that religion was not the foundation of the revolt ... [and] that religious tensions had been overtaken by longstanding social and economic complaints'.[12] Georges Weill, meanwhile, claimed that it was the capricious nature of the reformers of the south-west that had led to this escalation, and highlighted the propensity of popular elements within the province, 'more volatile than their counterparts across France', to turn defiance into disorder.[13] Géralde Nakam concurred, adding that the ruthless treatment meted out to malefactors by the forces of law and order in Guyenne, and the harsh conditions under which the poor were forced to survive, contributed to this volatility. At Bordeaux, for example, it was commonplace for 'les gahets' to be singled out and forced to wear a red piece of cloth on their chest, precluding most from entering the town's shops.[14]

---

[9] Labenazie, *Histoire de la ville d'Agen*, I, p. 248.

[10] Garrisson-Estèbe, *Les Protestants du midi*, pp. 166–7.

[11] Andrieu, *Histoire de l'Agenais*, I, p. 218. Andrieu seems to have borrowed here from De Bèze, who wrote that Fumel was 'détesté à cause de sa crauté', and that his death was revenge for continued disruption of Protestant services on his lands: Bèze to Calvin (12 December 1561), Théodore de Bèze, *Correspondance de Théodore de Bèze* (26 vols, ed. H. Aubert, Geneva, 1960–2002), III, pp. 235–8.

[12] Holt, *French Wars of Religion*, p. 50.

[13] Georges Weill, *Les théories sur le pouvoir royal en France pendant les guerres de religion* (Paris, 1891), pp. 75–6.

[14] See Nakam, *Montaigne et son temps*, p. 46. For the broader debate of the role of class struggle, religion and political relations in the French Wars of Religion, see Mack P. Holt,'Putting Religion Back into the Wars of Religion', *FHS*, 18 (1993), pp. 524–51; H. Heller, 'A Reply to Mack P. Holt', *FHS*, 19 (1996), pp. 853–61.

For Denis Crouzet, though, these events were no 'brief social war', but were emphatically religious riots. Crouzet argued that Garrisson-Estèbe's statement that Protestant labourers marched 'as peasants not reformers' during the revolt is too rigid, as much of the violence of the early 1560s was explicitly Protestant against Catholic, not at all the socially or economically disadvantaged against their superiors.[15] He supported this supposition by analysing the social composition of the assailants: of those arrested in relation to the unrest at Fumel, only sixty-three (less than 11 per cent) were from the town of Fumel or its jurisdiction. If this had been inspired by social or economic grievances, he argued, one would expect the majority to be disgruntled locals or tenants complaining against their landlord. Instead, the bulk of those arrested hailed from neighbouring towns: seventy-four lived at Tournon de l'Agenais; thirty-one at Penne de l'Agenais; with others from Monflanquin, Cuzorn, Sauveterre and other nearby centres. These were all areas well known for their adherence to the reform movement, and for episodic violence against Catholics.[16] Yet Garrisson-Estèbe's eagerness to place the 'lower classes' at the forefront of agitation in Guyenne during the 1560s is not without corroboration from contemporary accounts. In December 1560, for instance, Fronton de Béraud, *conseiller* of the *parlement* of Bordeaux, observed that the reformed doctrine had infiltrated 'most of the people of the Agenais and the Bazadais, even rustics and labourers',[17] a sentiment that was echoed by the court itself the following year: 'in the town of Périgueux, those who assemble are mostly artisans and tradesmen ... we fear such popular emotion'.[18] At Agen, meanwhile, the town's bishop, Janus Frégose, informed the *états de l'Agenais* in early 1561, that 'the nobility is indignant at the revolt of the peasantry ... the king can count on our devotion in this matter',[19] while Monluc rather ominously noted: 'and so began the furtive war against the nobility'.[20]

Such apprehension resonates through much of the counsel given by Monluc to local magistrates throughout the wars, in which he urged them to stamp out deviancy and delinquency at its first appearance, so as to avoid repeating the 'error of leniency' made by the *parlement* on the eve

---

[15] Crouzet, *Les guerriers de Dieu*, I, pp. 516–17.

[16] Crouzet, *Les guerriers de Dieu*, I, p. 518. The figures here are contentious. The *Histoire ecclésiastique* claimed that over two thousand gathered to protest against the baron de Fumel, whereas Monluc's *arrêt* of March 1562 noted that only two hundred and twenty-three had been present. See [Bèze], *Hist. eccl.*, I, p. 885; [Monluc], *Commentaires 1521–1576*, pp. 483–7.

[17] Fronton de Béraud to Cardinal de Lorraine (4 December 1560), *AHG*, 13, p. 143.

[18] AMB, ms 767, fo. 789.

[19] BN Dupuy, 588, fo. 106; Tholin, 'La ville d'Agen', XIV, p. 446.

[20] [Monluc], *Commentaires 1521–1576*, p. 483.

of the Gabelle riots: 'if you give people licence … they will take author-ity'.[21] For Henri Hauser, though, any correlation between class-based stereotypes and confessional affiliation is contentious. He concluded that the peasantry of France were rarely pro-reform in any great numbers, and largely neutral in the sectarian confrontations of the 1560s, while most were often more concerned with protecting their traditions, and strug-gling with the harsh realities of life, than with involving themselves in confessional disputes.[22] Although Hauser predicated this thesis on national rather than province-specific evidence, his conclusions were viewed as relevant for the south-west by Paul Courteault, whose work on the *paysans* of the Bordelais construed that this was not a confessionally homogenous unit, while his study of the participation of the peasantry in the creation of a commune at Montségur in 1560 revealed that 'labourers and the illiterate … were attracted to reform doctrine more out of ig-norance, simplicity and curiosity than malice' – hardly the united revolu-tionaries of Garrisson-Estèbe's texts.[23]

Courteault did, however, identify the collection of obligations and taxes as a major flash point between Catholic nobles, their tenants and the peasantry during this period. Refusal to pay was often accompanied by physical violence against the collector, many of whom were lesser Catholic *gentilshommes* of the region. This became especially frequent after 1560, as the reformers started to divert traditional tariffs into their own coffers.[24] The authorities, of course, were strict in dealing with such non-payment. The *lieutenant du roi* for Guyenne, Burie, saw to it that all instances reported to him were investigated fully, while the Bordeaux *parlement* also came down hard on evasion, even suspending the reformed church at Montauban in October 1561 for refusing to pay its obligations.[25] Some contemporaries claimed that many were embracing the reform movement simply as a means of avoiding taxes, rents and other dues: the correspondence of Armand de Gontaut, baron de Biron, a leading Guyenne nobleman, for example, noted a propensity among local *seigneurs* to convert to Calvinism in order to free themselves of their fiscal

---

[21] [Monluc], *Commentaires 1521–1576*, p. 578.

[22] See Henri Hauser, 'The French Reformation and the French people in the sixteenth century', *AHR*, (January 1899), pp. 222–6.

[23] Courteault, *Histoire de Gascogne et de Béarn*, p. 218.

[24] See James B. Collins, *The Fiscal Limits of Absolutism* (Berkeley, 1988), pp. 3–4.

[25] Kingdon, *Geneva and the Coming of the Wars of Religion*, p. 43. It should be noted that these issues were by no means specific to the south-west of France; a royal ordinance, issued at Dieppe in August 1563, reported that 'plusiers personnes … tant gentilshommes que autres tenant terres et possessions des prélats et gens d'église de nostre Royaume et autres charges de dixmes, champarts, cens, rentes et devoirs, sont refusants et dilayants de leur payer': Henri Forneron, *Histoire de Philippe II* (2 vols, Paris, 1887), I, p. 269.

duties,[26] although he also suggested that economic hardship brought about by rising inflation, bad harvests and loss of earnings due to a decline in military sponsorship should be considered in this regard.[27] Monluc took a sarcastic view of Protestant justification for non-payment, relating the story of a rent collector whose demand for payment from his tenant was met with the retort: 'Show me where it says in the Bible that I should pay?'[28]

The controversy, then, over whether the murder of Fumel was viewed as a 'crime against the establishment' or a 'confessional outrage' has yet to be resolved. That the Catholic nobility were energized into forming associations for mutual protection as a result of such episodes is somewhat less contentious. Certainly, these events impelled Catholics at Bordeaux to create their syndicate as a means of countering Protestant violence and defending Catholicism across the province. Less well known, perhaps, is the fact that Burie, the archetypal liberal at this time, was roused to respond in a similar manner at Fumel's murder, personally heading an association of local Catholic nobles in order to track down and bring to justice the perpetrators. This 'ligue nobilaire', as Burie referred to it in a missive to the king of Navarre, included the *sieur* de Negrepelisse and many from the nobility of Quercy, Armagnac, Rouergue, Comminges, Périgord and Agenais.[29] In fact, it proved a most effective vehicle, for many of the main culprits were subsequently tracked down and taken into custody by these *ligueurs*. Once it had achieved its purpose, however, Burie severed his affiliation and returned to Bordeaux, never to associate himself with *ligue* ethos again. Burie's actions here are complex. The threat posed by unruly mobs across Guyenne was undoubtedly multifaceted, encompassing confessional, political, social and economic motivations. Yet Burie chose to ally himself with a Catholic association rather than step up police patrols in the area. If this was the

---

[26] Biron to Catherine de Medici (31 October 1560), Armand de Gontaut, Baron de Biron, *The Letters and Documents of Armand de Gontaut, Baron de Biron, Marshall of France (1524–1592)* (2 vols, ed. S. Ehrman and J. Thompson, Berkeley, 1936), I, pp. 8–11.

[27] For arguments over economic downturn and its consequences, see Zeller, *Les institutions de la France*, pp. 15–16; Henri Hauser, *La prépondérance espagnole, 1559–1560* (Paris, 1948), pp. 197–203.

[28] [Monluc], *Commentaires 1521–1576*, p. 487.

[29] Burie to Navarre (November, 1561), BN ms français, 3186, fo. 62. The *Histoire ecclésiastique* asserts that this *ligue nobilaire* was also headed by Lalande, the Catholic leader at Agen, and three of Monluc's captains: Monts, Terride and d'Aussun: [Bèze], *Hist. eccl.*, I, pp. 885–7. Crouzet, though, can find no evidence to support this claim: Crouzet, *Les guerriers de Dieu*, I, p. 378. For evidence that Catholics at Bordeaux were aware of Burie's anger at events at Fumel and the perceived threat to the Bordelais nobility, see Antoine de Noailles to Gilles de Noailles (1561), BN ms français, 6910, fo. 138.

reaction of a model moderate and conciliator, then how would the more hard-line nobles react when violence was visited upon their own households and communities? To explore this further, an overview of the exploits of one of the leading Catholic elites in the region, the *comte* de Candalle, will be made to reveal the integral role played by the nobility of the Bordelais in securing the territory, taking the fight to the reformers and assuming the mantle of champions of Catholic activism following the demise of the syndicate.

Frédéric de Foix, *comte* de Candalle, had long been a controversial figure within provincial politics of the south-west, largely owing to the determined efforts of the house of Foix to frustrate the designs of Antoine de Bourbon, the governor of Guyenne, during the 1550s. This rivalry reached its low point in 1558, when Candalle's heroic defence of Dax against besieging Spanish forces was rewarded with an invitation to the royal court and entry into the elite circle of the Guise. Both gifts seemed to antagonize Antoine, as Candalle reported in a letter to the cardinal of Lorraine in October 1558: 'it is not possible to disguise the hatred shown by the king of Navarre ... his correspondence reveal a great vehemence towards me'.[30] Yet Candalle would be equally adversarial in his dealings with Burie and Lagebâton during the late 1550s, frequently attacking Burie's mismanagement of the province,[31] and repeatedly crossing swords with Lagebâton – another bitter rivalry that would run throughout the decade.[32] His first telling contribution to the Catholic cause at Bordeaux came during the first religious war, on 12 December 1562, with the presentation of a remonstrance before the *parlement*, in which he vilified the activities of local reformers, 'those most bellicose rebels', especially their practice of guarding *prêches* with armed soldiers, paid for by 'tributes' from churches and nobles alike. He concluded his tirade by urging loyal Catholics to arm and assemble so as to disperse these illegal gatherings, and to guard against complacency: 'the [Protestant] enterprise seeks nothing less than the ruin of all Catholics ... if the seditious succeed they will cut all to pieces'.[33]

---

[30] Candalle to Cardinal of Lorraine (16 October 1558), *AHG*, 24, p. 13.

[31] As early as 1558, Candalle accused Burie of negligence and then incompetence. See Candalle to Henry II (16 October, 1558), *AHG*, 24, p. 11.

[32] The first recorded clash between Candalle and Lagebâton occurred in December 1554, with Candalle being barred from the *parlement* for refusing to lay down his weapon while appearing before the *grand'chambre*: BMB, ms 370, fos 343–5. A similar clash occurred four years later, in August 1558: BMB, ms 370, fo. 428.

[33] For Candalle's remonstrance, see AMB, ms 771, fos 129–44.

In early March 1563, Candalle wrote to his old friend, Louis de Lur, *vicomte* d'Uza, the *sénéchal* of Bazadais, for advice on how best to co-ordinate the local Catholic nobility in the war effort.[34] The two met in Bordeaux several days later, joined by d'Escars and leading notables of the Bordelais, where d'Uza suggested that Candalle convoke the *états de la noblesse de Guyenne* so as to ensure greater consensus among Catholic elites before any plans to confront the reformers were made.[35] Candalle concurred, and submitted the *lettres* of convocation before the *parlement* later that week.[36] That the sponsor of this application was none other than Blaise de Monluc reflected the close relationship that had been forged between the two over the past years; Candalle had served with distinction in Monluc's forces during mid-1562, and had even acquired a similar reputation for over-zealous treatment of Protestant captives after an incident at Castelvieil in January 1563.[37] Monluc's triumphant entrée into Bordeaux, on 10 March, confirmed this bond, as Candalle took his place in the ceremonial guard of honour alongside Catholic hard-liners such as Roffignac, Malvin, Baulon and Lange.[38]

Catholic fortunes seemed to be in the ascendant at this moment, a position confirmed the following day with news that the crown had decided to divide the lieutenancy of Guyenne between Monluc and Burie, with Monluc given charge of the western province, which included authority over Bordeaux and Agen, while Burie was left to administer the countryside east of the river Lot.[39] To many, this appeared to constitute a promotion for Monluc, and a demotion for Burie. The Catholic advantage was soon pressed home, as Candalle presented the 'Requête de la part de la noblesse de Guyenne' before the *grand'chambre* on 17 March 1563.[40] This incendiary document offered a damning indictment of Lagebâton's presidency. It opened by accusing the *premier président* of having long held affection for the Protestant faith, of twisting the recent edicts to favour the reform movement, and of showing repeated bias in his deliberations. It continued by condemning Lagebâton for failing to reprimand certain perpetrators of unrest while aiding others to avoid punitive

---

[34]   Candalle to d'Uza (5 March 1563), *AHG*, 19, p. 314.
[35]   BMB, ms 369, II, fo. 458. Convoking the *états de la noblesse de Guyenne* had been a prerogative of the house of Foix since the previous century.
[36]   BMB, ms 370, fo. 708–12.
[37]   The *lieutenant-juge* at Castelvieil complained to the Bordeaux *parlement* that Candalle had proved 'over-zealous' in his repression of disorders in the town: ADG, 1B 254, *Arrêt du parlement* (11 January 1563), fos 71–2.
[38]   BMB, ms 369, II, fo. 455. Moderates such as Burie, Lagebâton and de Ferron were conspicuous by their absence from this most triumphal Catholic event.
[39]   AMB, ms 771, fo. 593.
[40]   For 'Requête de la part de la noblesse de Guyenne', see AMB, ms 771, fos 635–41.

justice, and even of sheltering some in his home. Meanwhile, it claimed, Catholic suspects were continually spied upon, and were fined and incarcerated more frequently than Protestants. Its most damning charge, though, alleged that the *premier président* had been seen armed and mounted in the *grand rue des fosses*, in the company of Protestant captains and fugitives, some of whom were wanted for complicity in the attack on the château Trompette in mid-1561. This was a perilous step, which historians have asserted could only have been possible had Candalle had the full backing of Roffignac and the leading Catholic magistrates of the court.[41] This was certainly the case here, as the two men seconding Candalle for the presentation of the *requête* were Malvin, Roffignac's lieutenant, and Charles Dada, a *procureur* who had represented *commissaires* of the Confraternity of Saint-Yves on numerous occasions, and who was a client of one of the leading Catholic – and anti-Lagebâton – families of the region: the Pontacs.[42]

Lagebâton's response was typical of the man. He countered by attacking the legitimacy of the *requête*, drawing the court's attention to several irregularities. Firstly, if the *requête* had been written on behalf of the nobility of Guyenne, why did it feature just two signatures, those of Candalle and a *gentilhomme* named Vignac? Where were the names of the other Catholic nobles who supported the *requête*, and who was this Vignac character – as far as the *premier président* was aware, this was 'a man totally unknown and without quality or expression'.[43] Secondly, if Candalle had indeed assembled the Catholic nobility to prepare this document, then the gathering would have been illegal, as it contravened numerous royal edicts, and so its resolutions were invalid. Lagebâton therefore ordered the *requête* to be dismissed, and that Candalle be censured for his 'excesses'.[44] Catholics leapt to Candalle's defence. Jean de Mabrun, another *conseiller* whose family was involved in a long and bitter dispute with Lagebâton, argued that, as magistrates were precluded

---

[41] See Devienne, *Histoire de la ville de Bordeaux*, I, p. 144; O'Reilly, *Histoire complète de Bordeaux*, II, p. 224; Powis, *The Magistrates of the Parlement of Bordeaux*, p. 276.

[42] For Dada's representation of *commissaires* of the Confraternity of Saint-Yves against Protestant accusations in June 1562, see AMB, ms 769, fos 204–9. Jean and Jaccques II de Pontac were notorious Catholic zealots, both serving as *conseillers* of the Bordeaux *parlement*. Jacques II also served as *greffier* to the Confraternity of Saint-Yves, dean of the cathedral of Saint-André, and was a co-author of a remonstrance drawn up by the clergy for the Bordeaux *états* in June 1561, warning of the imminence of violent unrest and the need to suppress the reform movement in Guyenne. See BN Dupuy 588, fos 19–35; BN ms français, 3159, fo. 72.

[43] AMB, ms 771, fo. 642; BN ms français, 22 369, fo. 145.

[44] For more on this contest, see Devienne, *Histoire de la ville de Bordeaux*, I, p. 144; O'Reilly, *Histoire complète de Bordeaux*, II, p. 225.

from sitting in judgement on litigation that named them personally, the *premier président* should not be moderating this tribunal.[45] Lagebâton's reply was astonishing. He rejected Mabrun's appeal, retorting that he was 'not a child, and knew well enough how to preside over such *requêtes'*.[46] Further, he informed the court that he had recently acquired evidence that Candalle had met Lange, and a 'great number of Catholic gentlemen and *avocats'*, at a house in Bordeaux, on 15 March, at which meeting Candalle and Lange had concocted this attack on his presidency.[47] This claim sent the assembly into uproar, and the *séance* ended with both Catholics and moderates exchanging recriminations.

Historians have tended to award this contest to Lagebâton, deeming Candalle's *requête* to be invalid largely owing to the dispute over Vignac, '*l'homme inconnu'*, the presumption being that, if this nobleman was nothing more than a figment of Candalle's imagination, then the *requête* must be attributable to the *comte* alone, as it lacked any other authentic signatures. Yet a document held within the departmental archives at Agen reveals that one 'Gaston du Vignac, *jurat de la ville de Cadillac'*, was among the delegates attending the local *états* in November 1561.[48] As Cadillac was Candalle's home town, only 45 kilometres south-east of Bordeaux, and as the *comte* was known to frequent the meetings of the *états*, it is reasonable to assume that he would have been well acquainted with this *jurat* and local delegate. Was this notable the Vignac who co-signed Candalle's *requête*? If so, his existence would negate one of Lagebâton's main arguments in dismissing the Catholic allegations against him.

Given the hostility of the exchanges, it is remarkable that the debate was contained within the *grand'chambre*. After all, Candalle's armed supporters were gathered outside the court, while Lagebâton had ordered the *huissiers* onto full alert just in case they were needed. Yet both sides seemed content to bide their time, confident perhaps that desperate measures were not yet required. This suggests that both had some form of contingency plan to fall back on which would strengthen their position. For Lagebâton, this may well have been the peace of Amboise, which reached Bordeaux in late March, a treaty designed not only to end hostilities across France but to censure radical activities such as those recently employed by Candalle and the Catholic hierarchy. As *premier président* of the *parlement*, it is probable

---

[45] AMB, ms 771, fos 644–68. Mabrun's brother served as a company commander in Catholic forces in 1562 under another nemesis of the *premier président*, Antoine de Noailles. For the Mabrun family's confrontations with Lagebâton, see Powis, *The Magistrates of the Parlement of Bordeaux*, p. 278.

[46] AMB, ms 771, fo. 648.

[47] AMB, ms 771, fos 646–50.

[48] 'Procès-verbal fait par les députés aux états de la généralité de Guyenne en la ville d'Agen, les 16 et 17 novembre 1561'. ADLG, E Sup. Agen, CC 65 (17 November 1561).

that Lagebâton would have known of the edict's imminent arrival, and he was thus biding his time until the arrival of legislation that would allow him to censor freely such Catholic rhetoric. For Candalle, it may well have been the knowledge that he would shortly establish a formal mechanism with which to defend Catholicism in the region: an oath-bound league, launched from his base at Cadillac, and boasting support from the Catholic nobility of the region.[49]

Little is known about the structure of this association. Historians suggest that it was pyramid-shaped, with Candalle as supreme chief, assisted by a council chosen from delegates of the *états*. Below this, local members commanded agents across the region, who in turn governed Catholic cells within the *sénéchaussées*, districts and parishes.[50] There is a wealth of debate about the nascence of Candalle's league, though. Some commentators speculate that it was a direct response to the controversy between Candalle and Lagebâton, thus placing its inception some time in late March 1563. Ruble, however, believes it to have been a consequence of the meeting between Candalle, d'Uza and other Catholic nobles at Bordeaux on 13 March, a theory that suggests Catholics intended to establish an organization regardless of the *premier président's* subsequent obstinacy over the *requête*.[51]

The timing is significant, because in late March the edict of Amboise arrived in Bordeaux, declaring all such divisive associations to be illegal.[52] Were Catholics caught out by this peace, or did they go ahead and establish their league despite crown dictate? In one sense the point is moot as, despite the edict being registered at Bordeaux on 10 April, Candalle made no move to dismantle his association.[53] Such obstinate and illegal behaviour

---

[49] The league at Cadillac would be the third such noble-led association of the region, following on from similar bodies at Agen and Toulouse. These are dealt with at length in subsequent chapters.

[50] For Candalle's league at Cadillac, see Lecler, 'Aux origines de la Ligue', pp. 195–8; Thompson, *Wars of Religion*, pp. 213–17; Théodore Agrippa d'Aubigné, *Histoire universelle* (10 vols, ed. A. de Ruble, Paris, 1886–1909), II, p. 213; Jouanna et al., *Histoire et dictionnaire*, pp. 151–2; [Condé], *Mémoires de Condé*, VI, pp. 290–306; Arlette Jouanna, *Le devoir de la révolte. La noblesse française et la gestation de l'état moderne, 1559–1661* (Paris, 1989), pp. 181–3.

[51] [Monluc], *Commentaires et lettres*, IV, pp. 206 note and 214. A later copy of the 'articles' for the association at Cadillac gives no clue as to its inception date. See BN ms français, 15 875, fo. 491.

[52] For the peace of Amboise (19 March 1563), see André Stegmann, *Édits des guerres de religion* (Paris, 1979), pp. 32–7. For a detailed analysis of the registration of the edict at Bordeaux, see Hauchecorne, 'Le parlement de Bordeaux', pp. 329–40.

[53] The peace edict was registered at Bordeaux on 10 April 1563, but not fully ratified until ten days later, on 20 April 1563: ADG, 1B 257, *Arrêt du parlement* (20 April 1563), fo. 163; BN ms français, 22 369, fo. 146.

outraged reformers, who claimed that the league was a destabilizing element within Guyenne. On 15 April 1563, the Protestant noble, the *sieur* de Pardaillan, informed Catherine de Medici that 'the grandees of Guyenne have formed an assembly that has a common treasury ... and has nobles, captains and soldiers to carry out its evil deeds. I think it is favoured by many among the magistrates of Guyenne'.[54] Lagebâton dispatched a similar communiqué to Catherine, urging the crown to compel Monluc to intervene and terminate this union.[55] This left Monluc with a problem: to act against his Catholic confederates or to defy the crown. Typically, he chose the expedient route, bending the truth by assuring the regent that 'since the new peace there have been no signs of any illegal associations in the region'.[56] The Catholic clergy of Bordeaux also seemed to contract a propitious bout of amnesia when questioned on the matter, reporting that 'no such associations exist within the region'.[57]

As ever, it fell to Lagebâton and the moderates to act. Candalle was duly summoned before the *parlement* to explain himself, appearing on 4 May 1563, with his close confidant, la Rivière, the acting mayor of Bordeaux, at his side as sponsor. Lagebâton immediately dismissed la Rivière, though, stating that, as the acting mayor was 'a known Catholic fanatic and signatory of Candalle's illegal association', he had forfeited his right to give evidence before the court.[58] The *premier président* then turned on Candalle, levelling a charge of subversion against the noble for contravening the will of the king.[59] Candalle countered by presenting a second *remonstrance* before the magistrates, this time in the name of the *états de la noblesse*, expounding further grievances against Lagebâton.[60] The document also set out the justification for recent Catholic activities and demanded that the *parlement* legitimize the league at Cadillac rather than censure it, as it represented the only body capable of defeating the enemies of the crown, and of defending the Catholic religion, in Guyenne.

---

[54] Pardaillan to Catherine de Medici (15 April 1563), *AHG*, 17, fo. 289.

[55] *Lettres de Catherine de Medici*, I, pp. 551–3.

[56] Monluc to Catherine de Medici (11 April 1563), [Monluc], *Commentaires et lettres*, IV, p. 206; Monluc to Charles IX (15 April 1563), ibid., p. 214.

[57] Clergy of Bordeaux to Catherine de Medici (15 April 1563), [Monluc], *Commentaires et lettres*, IV, p. 214.

[58] For Lagebâton's dismissal of La Rivière, see Lagebâton to Charles IX (27 May 1563), [Condé], *Mémoires de Condé*, V, p. 186.

[59] AMB, ms 771, fo. 783.

[60] See AMB, ms 771, fo. 777; BN ms français, 22 372, fo. 1132. Copies of the *remonstrance* were sent by Candalle and the Catholic nobility to the crown as justification of their league at Cadillac: Catholic nobility at Cadillac to Catherine de Medici (20 May 1563), BN ms français, 15 875, fo. 491; Candalle to Catherine de Medici (20 May 1563), BN ms français, 15 875, fo. 495.

The clashes between Lagebâton and Candalle threatened to choke effective government at Bordeaux once more, so the crown moved to intervene, ordering its royal commissioners in the region, Antoine Fumée and Jehan Angenoust, to investigate the matter.[61] But the two made little headway, as hostility from Catholic magistrates and nobles precluded any effective inquiry. Their final reports to the crown, in August 1563, thus lacked any definite conclusions on the presence or otherwise of Candalle's league, and were also surprisingly vague on the state of confessional tensions within the province.[62] This is remarkable given that the commissioners were present at a number of contentious episodes during their stay in Guyenne. On 22 June 1563, for example, Candalle's second-in-command, the *vicomte* d'Uza, launched yet another vitriolic attack on the incompetence of moderates at Bordeaux. Taking the form of an open letter to the king, d'Uza's *requête* lambasted Lagebâton's aptitude, and urged that the royal council redeploy the *premier président* 'outside the province'.[63] It also attacked the March edict, claiming that Catholics were still being attacked and their churches ransacked, yet no longer had confidence in receiving justice from the courts. The closing paragraph should have caught the attention of the commissioners, as d'Uza admitted that high levels of Protestant violence had forced the nobility of Guyenne to form a confederation to 'protect their lives and goods', but that the terms of the association had been presented to and agreed by Monluc so as not to contravene royal dictate. The *vicomte* added that the league had since been terminated, however, 'in such fashion as if it had never existed'.

None of this information found its way into the report made by the commissioners. Nor indeed did the contention surrounding death threats made by anonymous Protestants against Candalle, de Lauzan and the marquis de Trans, the leaders of the Cadillac league, in July 1563. This despite the threats becoming a *cause célèbre* within the *parlement*, with Roffignac taking them seriously enough to assign two of his most trusted Catholic *conseillers*, Jean d'Alesme and Charles Malvin, to investigate the claims, and providing permanent armed escorts for the nobles' visits to Bordeaux.[64] Nor for that matter was a further contretemps between Candalle, Lange and Lagebâton reported, despite its having considerable resonance for the crown. The dispute took place within the *grand'chambre*, on 30 July, with Candalle aggrieved that the *premier président* had

---

[61] BN ms français, 15 876, fo. 201.
[62] Fumée and Angenoust to Catherine de Medici (20 August 1563), BN ms français, 15 878, fo. 112.
[63] *Vicomte* d'Uza to Charles IX (22 June 1563), BN nouv. acq. français, 20 598, fos 170–80.
[64] AMB, ms 772, fo. 12.

indicted the Catholic nobility of the Bordelais before the *conseil privé* for 'falsities, imposture, lies, pillaging and thievery'.[65] Candalle's first attempt to have Lagebâton arraigned over this matter failed, but a second, co-signed by d'Uza and the Catholic nobles, made more progress as it pointed out that the *premier président* had included Lange in his indictment. As an officer of the *parlement*, Lange was within his rights to call Lagebâton to account before the *grand'chambre* over his accusation.[66] Yet, as notorious as these episodes were at Bordeaux, and as relevant to any analysis of sectarian affairs in post-Amboise Guyenne, they somehow failed to be included in the commissioners' reports – hardly the most perceptive study of provincial confessional relations made during this period.

The matter of the inquiry was far from over, though. On 6 September 1563, d'Escars, now governor of Bordeaux, came before the court to accuse Lagebâton and the commissioners of concocting certain evidence against leading Catholics of Guyenne.[67] Lauded as 'a stalwart of Catholicism in Guyenne',[68] d'Escars was another of those who listed themselves as long-time adversaries of the *premier président*. Powis has traced the roots of their enmity back to the 1550s, when d'Escars, then a high-ranking official in the government of Antoine de Bourbon, was reproached by Lagebâton during an investigation by the crown into the affairs of Navarre.[69] Mutual animosity had marked their meetings ever since, and d'Escars was not prepared to hold back on this occasion. Lagebâton was incensed at the charge of 6 September, but had little option other than to hear the accusation before the *grand'chambre*. He could, however, order the *huissiers* to deny d'Escars access to the parquet until he and his bodyguard had removed their swords. This would be a calculated slight against d'Escars' honour, as the governor had dispensation from Burie to go anywhere within the *parlement* building fully armed.[70] The ploy worked, for d'Escars refused to disarm, and the séance was postponed. When they attempted to reconvene in December, the governor found he had been banned from entering the palace.[71] This caused a major furore, and forced the crown to intervene, as such a high-profile dispute was damaging to the image of sovereign government in the

---

[65] AMB, ms 772, fos 72–7.

[66] AMB, ms 772, fos 79–81.

[67] D'Escars to Catherine de Medici (6 September 1563), BN nouv. acq. français, 20 598, fo. 197.

[68] De Trans to d'Escars (12 January 1564), BMB, ms 369, II, fo. 549.

[69] Powis, *The Magistrates of the Parlement of Bordeaux*, p. 140.

[70] BMB, ms 369, II, fos 506–15. D'Escars had been named governor of Bordeaux following the death of Antoine de Noailles on 24 May 1563. *AHG*, 55, p. 50.

[71] BMB, ms 369, II, fos 534–9.

south-west. Lagebâton's manoeuvrings were thus ended as the crown found in favour of d'Escars, who received authorization to enter the court at will, fully armed, with his bodyguard at his side if appropriate.[72]

With a moral victory over their nemesis, other Catholic bodies moved to confront the *premier président*. Throughout 1564, Lagebâton had repeatedly accused Candalle, Monluc, Lange, de Trans and others of reconstituting the league at Cadillac, and of promoting armed resistance across the province in defiance of the royal edicts.[73] By August, Lagebâton was including the clergy of Guyenne in his allegations, asserting that they were guilty of inciting this militancy, and singling out the archbishop, Prévôt de Sanssac, as the key provocateur.[74] In December, the clergy reacted to this chiding. In a brash outburst that was far from a denial, and directed as much against moderates within the *parlement* as it was to the crown, representatives of the clergy confirmed that many of their number had indeed supported the Catholic associations throughout the previous years. But, they argued, this had been necessary as Protestant violence against Catholic communities, and especially against the clergy and churches of the province, had been excessive and relentless. And while they acknowledged the peace edict, they asked that the crown compare the nature of the confessional organizations in Guyenne: the Catholic bodies had been defensive associations, designed to protect Catholics from assault, whereas the Protestant synodal confederations had been subversive in nature, aggressive in tone, and violent in assaulting, pillaging and committing numerous sacrileges.[75]

When the clergy's remonstrance came before the Bordeaux *parlement* for debate, however, the archbishop, Sanssac, found himself barred from entering the chamber. Again, Lagebâton was adamant that he would not hear testimony from anyone still in collaboration with militants such as Candalle and Lange.[76] Fearing another embarrassing squabble, the crown dispatched a *maître des requêtes*, the *sieur* de Vouzan, to oversee conciliation between the two parties, allowing each to voice their opinion

---

[72] Powis, *The Magistrates of the Parlement of Bordeaux*, p. 170; O'Reilly, *Histoire complète de Bordeaux*, II, p. 226.

[73] See 'Délibération du sieur de Candalle et autres de sa ligue contre le Roy et ses edits faits au mois d'août 1564', [Condé], *Mémoires de Condé*, V, pp. 170–6; 'Ligue, confédération et alliance du sieur de Candalle et autres sieurs papistes de Guyenne, bons fideles sujets du Roy catholique, voulans vivre et mourir en la religion ancienne Romaine et Catholique, au mois d'août 1564', [Condé], *Mémoires de Condé*, V, pp. 177–81.

[74] Lagebâton to Charles IX (20 August 1564), [Condé], *Mémoires de Condé*, V, pp. 182–5; Lagebâton to Charles IX (28 August 1564), BN ms français, 15 880, fos 246–7.

[75] Clergy of Bordeaux to Catherine de Medici (December 1564), BN ms français, 15 881, fo. 381.

[76] *AHG*, 13, p. 179.

without fear of rebuke or recrimination.[77] By May 1565, however, Sanssac had still not been permitted to present his case before the *grand'chambre*, and so complained that the pace of proceedings was too slow. A new petition was drafted, with Lange appointed as prosecuting *avocat* for the archbishop, while Candalle acted as his second for the proceedings. The new remonstrance was blunt: Lagebâton should be removed from office for malpractice, and all libellous claims against Catholics should be withdrawn.[78] Lagebâton, though, remained unfazed by this Catholic triumvirate and stopped the procedure in mid-flow, informing Vouzan that the *séance* would be suspended while five technicalities relating to Sanssac's application were investigated. Firstly, as the honour of the *premier président* of the *parlement* was being challenged, the presence of 'so many renowned and intimate friends' of the archbishop was inappropriate. The forum was too open and partial, and so would be rescheduled for a private sitting devoid of all interested parties except litigants. Secondly, Lagebâton refused point blank to be questioned by Lange: 'if it is not reasonable that a captain be confronted by a soldier, then neither a *président* by his *avocat*'. Thirdly, this should be a debate, not a trial, and as such all challenges should be submitted in writing, to be read out by the clerk of the court in the accustomed manner, not delivered by a long-time ally of the plaintiff. Fourthly, Lagebâton was equally adamant that Candalle should play no part in the proceedings, as the court was technically still investigating his participation in the various Catholic associations of the previous year. Finally, the *premier président* informed Vouzan that, as Sanssac was known to be a 'confidante' of *président* Roffignac and *conseillers* Mabrun, Gaultier, La Ganne, Vergoing and Belcier, these magistrates must abstain from proceedings as a matter of protocol. In one fell swoop, Lagebâton had removed the leading Catholic activists from playing a part in the affair, devastating Sanssac's chances of winning the case. The archbishop had no alternative other than to withdraw his *requête* and leave the chamber, though not before adding that he would take his case before the crown and, if nothing came of that, he and his brother, the *sieur* de Lanssac, would 'take revenge themselves'.

Although Sanssac, Candalle and Lange were to make one final attempt to arraign Lagebâton in August 1566, they were again outmanoeuvred.[79] It is this political skill and dexterity that characterized Lagebâton's

---

[77] *AHG*, 13, pp. 179–83.

[78] This process is to be found in 'Procès-verbal du différand entre l'archevêque de Bordeaux et le premier président du parlement' (1565), BN ms français, 15 881, fos 157–60.

[79] 'Requête de la clergy et noblesse de guienne et maires et jurats de Bordeaux contre le premier président' (August 1566), BMB, ms 369, III, fo. 99.

performances during the early 1560s, explaining his longevity in the office of *premier président* in the face of prolonged invective from Catholic agitators. For the moment, Lagebâton and the moderate party had maintained control over the militant and hostile nobility of the Bordelais, who were supported in their machinations by officers of the court and the provincial clergy. But matters were soon to change, as the recommencing of open war in 1567 saw a more determined Catholic consensus emerge at Bordeaux; one that would stop at nothing to remove the *premier président* from office, to defeat the moderate faction within the government and to secure Catholic hegemony within the region.

CHAPTER FIVE

Catholic Consolidation at Bordeaux

By 1565, political and confessional relations at Bordeaux had reached stalemate. While moderates maintained tacit control of the *parlement*, the simmering hostility of Catholic magistrates, silenced temporarily, but still a majority within the court, loomed large. Catholic militancy may have been suppressed by the edict of Amboise of March 1563, but the networks and alliances formed during the first war remained intact, and their leaders continued to be vocal in political debate. The crown was well aware of the tentative nature of this détente, and realized that some form of equitable settlement for both Catholic and Protestant communities was imperative to prevent sectarian violence proliferating across Guyenne once more.

Yet matters were being further complicated by the involvement of external powers in the affairs of the south-west. Throughout 1563 and 1564, Spain, the papacy and leading Protestant and Catholic grandees from France and northern Europe had begun to exert varying degrees of influence over the region. Central in much of this manoeuvring was the hostility between Catholic powers and Jeanne d'Albret, the Calvinist queen of Navarre. Fears over Jeanne's religious orthodoxy had flared during the mid-1550s, with rumours of her covert adherence to the new religion culminating in evidence of overt affiliation after 1557.[1] This tension was exacerbated with the removal of the unitary duchy of Albret from the remit of the *sénéchaussée* of Guyenne, and the growing influence of Jeanne's commissioners at the courts at Nérac, Tartes and Casteljaloux.[2] In October 1558, the governor of Languedoc, Anne de Montmorency, felt compelled to respond to the religious disturbances in neighbouring Béarn by sending his *lieutenant du roi* at Toulouse, George, Cardinal d'Armagnac, into the region to restore order and re-establish ecclesiastical discipline.[3] Further efforts to pressurize Jeanne followed in November 1559, with the cardinal of Lorraine urging the military captains of the south-west, Monluc and de Termes, to cooperate fully with the Spanish viceroy to Navarre in his attempt to unite the Catholic forces of the region in opposition to the queen's scheming.[4]

---

[1] Bryson, *Queen Jeanne*, pp. 101–8.

[2] Powis, *The Magistrates of the Parlement of Bordeaux*, p. 251.

[3] Cardinal Armagnac to Montmorency (15 October 1558), Tamizey de Larroque, 'Lettres inédites du Cardinal d'Armagnac', pp. 99–102.

[4] Marthe W. Freer, *The Life of Jeanne d'Albret* (London, 1862), p. 107.

On 19 July 1561, though, Jeanne d'Albret formally legalized the reform movement in Béarn, Navarre and her *comtés* of Foix and Armagnac, ordering all Catholic practices to desist with immediate effect.[5] When churches across the region began to be commandeered and stripped bare for use as Protestant temples, Catholic communities had little recourse other than to appeal to their French neighbours for help. Condemnation of Jeanne's activity from the *parlements* at Bordeaux and Toulouse and the Catholic nobles of the south-west was swift. Complaints flooded into the courts demanding that the queen revoke her orders, and calling for military intervention should she refuse. Then, in November 1562, Blaise de Monluc warned Jeanne that, if she continued in her dalliances with the reform movement, he would 'pass into Spain and ask the Catholic king to enter Béarn at the head of his army and overthrow her rule'.[6] To back up his threat, Monluc moved several companies of Spanish troops to the border with Béarn. But Jeanne was one step ahead, and had already complained to the crown about this intimidation, securing royal backing for the withdrawal of Monluc's Catholic troops.[7] Jeanne's supporters at court, among them the leading Protestant grandees, Admiral Coligny and Odêt de Châtillon, bishop of Beauvais, petitioned the crown to reproach Monluc for his insolence, and the captain was duly reprimanded in June 1563 and ordered to proceed with care in dealing with the queen of Navarre, 'without offending or irritating her'.[8]

This was the opening gambit of a clash between the two that quickly reached vendetta-like proportions. In October 1563, Jeanne, now widowed following the death of her husband, Antoine de Bourbon, at the siege of Rouen the previous November, raised the stakes considerably by accusing senior Catholics of collusion against the crown. The allegation charged Monluc, Damville, Armagnac, Pierre d'Albret, bishop of Comminges, and two of Monluc's senior captains, Negrepelisse and Terride, of plotting with Spain to overthrow her government.[9] Jeanne claimed that a secret meeting had been held at the town of Grenade to finalize these plans, and that Monluc's son, Jean, had been dispatched to Madrid to secure Spanish troops for this purpose.[10] Monluc's response

---

[5] Bryson, *Queen Jeanne*, p. 132; Greengrass, 'The Calvinist experiment in Béarn', p. 125. Jeanne had officially converted to the reformed church on Christmas Day 1560: Bryson, *Queen Jeanne*, p. 113.

[6] Courteault, *Blaise de Monluc. Historien*, p. 470.

[7] Charles IX to Monluc (May 1563), BN nouv. acq. français, 6001, fos 7–8; Bryson, *Queen Jeanne*, p. 154.

[8] Charles IX to Monluc (June 1563), BN nouv. acq. français, 6001, fos 42–3.

[9] Courteault, *Blaise de Monluc, Historien*, p. 478.

[10] Courteault states that Jean had recently visited Spain, but merely as a staging post on his journey to Malta. See Courteault, *Un Cadet de Gascogne*, p. 210.

clearly aimed to rally local Catholic audiences more than to placate crown indignation. He rejected Jeanne's 'lies' out of hand, and asserted that it was the Protestant queen who was destabilizing the region and promoting disharmony among the faiths, not the Catholic nobility.[11] In two subsequent letters, Monluc bemoaned this slighting of the good name of Guyenne Catholics, and argued that their exemplary behaviour and loyal devotion to the crown should be commended, not doubted.[12]

Yet moves to discredit the Catholic leadership continued. In February 1564, a Protestant captain, Marchastel, baron de Peyre, delivered six articles before the crown, each countersigned by Jeanne d'Albret and leading Protestant dignitaries of the south-west, alleging that a Catholic cartel was now active in Guyenne, intent on handing the province over to the king of Spain.[13] Courteault has shown that Marchastel came upon such information in a quite convoluted manner: the accusations were based on the testimony of the *sénéchal* de Quercy, François Séguier, *seigneur* de la Gravière, who claimed to have overheard Monluc discussing the cartel's activities while the commander and his party lodged in his house. Séguier had then dispatched Rapin, a captain in Marchastel's company, to inform his superior of these events.[14] Those Catholics accused were outraged. Monluc rejected the allegation outright, adamant that he had never had any dealings with the king of Spain or any other prince concerning the 'sale' of Guyenne,[15] as did Cardinal d'Armagnac, who urged that Catherine should not tolerate such calumnies against honest servants of the king and crown.[16] The

---

[11] *Mémoires et instructions de Monluc* (November 1563), [Monluc], *Commentaires et lettres*, IV, pp. 294–301.

[12] Monluc to Charles IX (27 December 1563), [Monluc], *Commentaires et lettres*, IV, pp. 302–5. Monluc to Catherine de Medici (27 December 1563), ibid., pp. 305–7.

[13] Those accused by Marchastel were Monluc, Damville, Terride, Armagnac, Negrepelisse and d'Albret, plus the *vicomte* d'Orthe and Charles, *comte* de Luxe, two of the leading Catholic militants in the Languedoc and Béarn theatre in the late 1560s. See Pierre d'Albret to Philippe II (15 April 1564), in Ritter, 'Jeanne d'Albret et les troubles de la religion', p. 82.

[14] Courteault, *Un Cadet de Gascogne*, p. 214.

[15] Monluc to Catherine de Medici (5 March 1564), BN ms français, 15 879, fo. 111.

[16] Cardinal d'Armagnac to Catherine de Medici (5 March 1564), BN ms français, 15 879, fo. 112. Interestingly, both Monluc and Armagnac would confirm in other correspondence that a meeting of Catholic notables had taken place at Grenade in late 1563, but neither made any reference to subversive compacts being agreed upon there. In fact, Armagnac would inform Catherine that the meeting had witnessed nothing more sinister than the funeral obsequies for the baron de Clermont, and the marriage of the son of Mirepoix to Terride's daughter, presided over by the bishop of Comminges. See, for example, Monluc to *protonotaire* of Sainte-Gemme (5 March 1564), [Monluc], *Commentaires et lettres*, IV, p. 331; Cardinal d'Armagnac to Catherine de Medici (5 March 1564), BN ms français, 15 879, fo. 112.

parlements at Bordeaux and Toulouse sided with the Catholic nobles in this matter, disputing Jeanne's testimony and calling those behind the accusations to explain themselves before the court.[17] When Jeanne complained to the *conseil privé* that provincial courts had no right to challenge her evidence, the crown decided that mediation was called for, and dispatched two of its commissioners to intervene. But they had hardly left Paris before further remonstrations reached the court, in May 1564, this time from Catholics reiterating outrage that their loyalty and service were being brought into question by 'heretics and seditious types'.[18] Ominously, their tone suggested that Catholics were unwilling to let these insinuations go unchallenged, with one letter, penned by Catholic nobles following a meeting at the abbey of Belleperche, near Montauban, threatening to seek reparations for such 'libel and slander'.[19]

The mention of litigation alarmed the crown, who saw its policy of conciliation being frustrated by a Gordian knot of allegation and counter allegation. Matters were certainly not helped by the partiality of the sovereign courts of the region, who asserted that suspicions against the regional Catholic nobility would be taken as slights against the *parlementaires* themselves.[20] The dispute was also adversely affecting existing wrangling within the court, and even entered the contest between Lagebâton and the Catholic militants at Bordeaux, in August 1564, with the archbishop, Prévôt de Sanssac, and Lange attempting to secure the condemnation of the falsehoods of Jeanne d'Albret and her conspirators, only for the *premier président* to deny their request for a formal hearing within the *grand'chambre*.[21] With its commissioners still inactive, the crown decided that, instead of being dragged into yet another dispute, it would remain neutral in this instance, and allow what was ostensibly a local feud to run its course devoid of external mediation, perhaps aware that previous endeavours at arbitration had been unsuccessful.

An intriguing footnote to these developments concerns Henry de Montmorency-Damville, the newly appointed governor of Languedoc. Although named in several Protestant allegations, Damville declined to

---

[17] When Rapin refused, a warrant was issued for his arrest and he was subsequently held in prison at Toulouse for several months before being questioned before the *parlement*. See Courteault, *Un Cadet de Gascogne*, p. 211.

[18] Monluc to Catherine de Medici (5 May 1564), BN ms français, 15 879, fo. 113. See also Armagnac to Catherine de Medici (15 May 1564), *HGL*, 9, *Preuves* 13, p. 512; Terride to Catherine de Medici (27 March 1564), BN ms français, 15 880, fo. 11; Terride to Charles IX (27 March 1564), BN ms français, 15 880, fo. 13.

[19] Joint letter of Armagnac, Monluc, Negrepelisse, Mirepoix and Terride to Charles IX (15 May 1564), Tamizey de Larroque, 'Lettres inédites du Cardinal d'Armagnac', p. 37.

[20] See for example Daffis to Charles IX (17 May 1564), *HGL*, 9, *Preuves* 14, pp. 512–14.

[21] Devienne, *Histoire de la ville de Bordeaux*, I, p. 154.

participate in the collective remonstrations of the Catholic nobility, preferring to clear his name through private correspondence with the crown.[22] His insistence that he had been absent from the region at the time of the alleged meeting at Grenade, and so could not have been complicit in Catholic machinations, is curious, as he was known to have been touring the province during these months as part of his duties. Also strange is a paragraph within Damville's letter that notes the arrival – incognito – in Avignon of Chantonnay, the Spanish Ambassador and a key player in relations between Monluc and Madrid. Was Damville attempting to prove his loyalty by betraying information to the crown? And while the governor denied being present at the Grenade meeting, it is significant that he made no attempt to refute the allegations of collusion levelled against the Catholics of Guyenne. Was this the moment at which Damville started to distance himself from his former militant compatriots of the south-west?

The allegation made by Jeanne d'Albret, that Catholic activists in the south-west were 'in league' with the king of Spain, merits closer attention. While the peace of Cateau-Cambrésis (1559) ended decades of conflict between France and Spain, it failed to re-establish amicable relations. Madrid continued to be perturbed by the evolving confessional situation in France, and complained frequently at the leniency shown by the French crown to its Protestant population. For Philip II religious plurality was anathema, and religious toleration should be opposed unreservedly. Forneron stated that the Spanish king formulated a plan as early as 1561 to combat France's conciliatory stance, aiming to bypass Catherine de Medici who, according to Madrid, lacked 'a fixity of ideas', and instead encourage the practices of Monluc and the Catholics of the south-west.[23] Courteault, though, has suggested that the French crown was well aware of this hostility and that, in appointing Monluc as *lieutenant-général* to Guyenne in December 1561, it had one eye on reassuring Philip, and thus forestalling Spanish military intervention in the south-west.[24] If this is correct, the ploy seemed to have worked, for Chantonnay informed his master that, in Monluc, 'Guyenne has found its saviour'.[25]

For the moment, Philip seemed content to menace France rather than intervene directly, though he continued to give financial rewards to the Triumvirate, the Catholic cabal featuring Antoine de Bourbon, Francis,

---

[22] Damville to Catherine de Medici (30 May 1564), BN nouv. acq. français, 6013, fo. 31.

[23] Forneron, *Histoire de Philippe II*, I, p. 327.

[24] For Monluc's role in reassuring Philip, and his relations with Spain during this early period, see Courteault, *Un Cadet de Gascogne*, pp. 208–12.

[25] Chantonnay to Philippe II (December 1561), in Roelker, *Queen of Navarre*, p. 193.

duke of Guise, and Marshal St André, with Spanish gold.[26] The Spanish ambassador was the driving force behind this alliance. He saw the Triumvirate as far more than an anti-Protestant force in France, envisaging a pan-European Catholic army, funded and provisioned by Rome and Madrid, and directed by his master, Philip II.[27] Chantonnay thus worked tirelessly to ensure that enmity and jealousy were not allowed to splinter the union, and it was largely through his personal efforts that the papacy agreed to ratify the Triumvirate as *une grande ligue*, and to dispatch 2500 soldiers, together with sufficient funds to hire several companies of Swiss and German mercenaries, to the duke of Guise in mid-1562.[28] The Spanish king was more than willing, though, to offer sizeable military reinforcements to boost Catholic garrisons in France during the early 1560s. This would prove especially important for Catholic fortitude in Guyenne, where Spanish troops under Don Carbajal played an important role in Monluc's successes at Castelvieux (3 July), Penne (August), Realville (9 September), Lectoure (2 October) and at the battles of the Dordogne (5–8 October) and Vergt (9 October).[29] Indeed, the Catholic hierarchy at Bordeaux were so keen to secure further reinforcements that the French ambassador at the Spanish court, Saint-Sulpice, was inundated with requests for additional manpower, retorting irritably to one request: 'men of war are not assembled as easily as canons in the chapterhouse'.[30]

---

[26] Jacques d'Albion, *sieur de* Saint-André, *maréchal* of France since 1547, was a long-time acquaintance of Monluc, having supported his nomination to the governorship of Siena in 1554. See Ian Roy, *Blaise de Monluc* (London, 1971), p. 234. The list of prominent Catholics involved in supporting the Triumvirate was impressive, including the duke of Montpensier, the cardinal of Tournon and the marshals Brissac and Termes. For a general history of the formation of the Triumvirate, see Jouanna et al., *Histoire et dictionnaire*, p. 100; De Lamar Jensen, *Diplomacy and Dogmatism. Bernadino de Mendoza and the French Catholic League* (Cambridge, MA, 1964), p. 16.

[27] The English ambassador to France was in no doubt of the main powerhouse behind the Triumvirate: 'the enterprise is pushed forward by the Spanish ambassador and by Spanish threatenings'. See *Recueil des choses mémorables passées et publiées pour le fait de la religion et état de la France* (Strasbourg, 1566), in Jensen, *Diplomacy and Dogmatism*, p. 51.

[28] Edouard Frémy, *Essai sur les diplomates du temps de la Ligue, d'après des documents nouveaux et inédits* (Paris, 1873), esp. Chapter 1, pp. 1–56. See also Holt, *French Wars of Religion*, p. 56; Louis Pierre Anquetil, *L'esprit de la Ligue, ou histoire politique des troubles de France pendant les XVIe et XVIIe siècles* (2 vols, Paris, 1818), I, pp. 77–81. In fact, the scale of support from Rome for the Triumvirate led Nicola Sutherland to paint Francis of Guise as a *knight-errant* of the papacy, rather than as a religious appellant of France. See Sutherland, *The Huguenot Struggle for Recognition*, p. 144.

[29] [Monluc], *Commentaires 1521–1576*, pp. 517–69.

[30] Saint-Sulpice to Burie (20 July 1562): Edmond Cabié, *Ambassade en espagne de Jean Ébrard, seigneur de St. Sulpice de 1562 à 1565* (Albi, 1903), p. 53. For requests from Burie, Monluc and Noailles for additional Spanish troops, see Cabié, *Guerres de religion*, pp. 8–15; Cabié, *Ambassade en Espagne de Jean Ébrard*, pp. 61, 84–6.

But early in 1563, Spanish foreign policy toward France received two setbacks. First, its attempts to prevent further concessions being granted to the reformers failed, as the peace of Amboise enshrined explicit – if limited – rights of worship to Protestants within French law. Chantonnay condemned this edict outright, and warned of the consequences should Protestant powers across Europe interfere in French politics: 'if the heretics obtain all that they desire, and are assisted by the English queen ... Catholics will rise in turn, supported by the king, my master, and the Catholic princes; for their cause is just'.[31] Second, when the Council of Trent closed in January 1563, promises of reform and revitalization of Catholicism were forthcoming from all European affiliates; all, that is, except the Gallican delegates, who refused to register its dictates or to accept its ideological development within France.

Spain now faced a conundrum. Should it invade to prevent Protestantism becoming irrevocably established within the kingdom that bordered its northern reaches, and intervene to force the Tridentine decrees upon France? One possible course of action lay in offering aid to the numerous Catholic associations that had recently sprung up across the south-west. This would allow Madrid to apply pressure on the crown from within. The obvious protagonist in such a policy was Monluc, whose military reputation and Catholic zeal were undeniable, and who had recently been promoted to the lieutenancy of south-west Guyenne. Courteault, Forneron and Ruble are convinced that it was now, as a result of these developments, that Monluc became an agent of Philip, and quote his voluminous correspondence with Spanish intermediaries such as Jean de Bardaxi, a Spanish agent living in Guyenne, during late 1563 and early 1564 as evidence.[32] Courteault reports that at one meeting between the two, in February 1564, Bardaxi enquired as to how his king could gain the confidence of Damville, and whether the Catholic nobility of Guyenne would support Spanish attempts to oust Jeanne d'Albret from her capital at Pau. He added that great rewards, including safe haven and a pension from the Spanish crown, were to be

---

[31] Forneron, *Histoire de Philippe II*, I, pp. 276–7.

[32] See Courteault, *Un Cadet de Gascogne*, pp. 13–14; Forneron, *Histoire de Philippe II*, I, pp. 293–330; [Monluc], *Commentaires et lettres*, IV, pp. 317–71; V, pp. 76 and 77 notes. Bardaxi had gained the confidence of the *lieutenant du roi* in the late 1550s through his cousin, Felipe, who had served for two decades as a loyal captain in Monluc's Italian company. During their campaign at Saragossa in 1558, Felipe had been accused of blasphemy by the Inquisition, and was only cleared when Monluc intervened and secured the rescinding of all charges. Felipe was still hung in effigy at Saragossa, though, in October 1563, his name only cleared from the warrant book of the Inquisition in 1567 on the orders of the king of Spain. See [Monluc], *Commentaires et lettres*, IV, p. 318 note 1.

offered as a safety net should any Catholic involved in this campaign fail.[33]

Opinion is divided within the historiography as to Monluc's role in this affair. Protestant contemporaries such as Jeanne d'Albret and Louis, prince of Condé, clearly saw intent to cede French soil to Spain in return for military assistance,[34] while historians such as Thompson have described Monluc as 'the military agent of Philip's purpose', with Catholic activity in the south-west 'little more than a tool of Spanish ambition'.[35] Judging Monluc by his correspondence with Madrid alone is problematic, for while certain letters do detail the state of affairs in Guyenne, they hardly prove collusion.[36] Historians have also had to battle against eighteenth- and nineteenth-century portrayals of the Catholics of the south-west as conspirators in the secret meeting with Spanish officials at Bayonne in 1565 which was believed to have been at the root of the Saint Bartholomew Day massacres of 1572. Indeed, this tradition dates back at least as far as de Thou, who perceived a progression from the 1558 Compact of Péronne – an attempt to secure an alliance between Spain, the papacy and the Catholic grandees of France to ensure the triumph of Catholicism across Europe – through the machinations of Philip and Monluc in 1564, to the meeting at Bayonne in 1565, and on to events at Paris in August 1572.[37]

But the recent debunking of the 'Spanish plot' as the genesis of the 1572 massacres has left much of this as little more than speculation, to be enjoyed as fragmentary and ambiguous anecdote, if disregarded as substantive history.[38] Similarly, the myth surrounding Monluc's 'treason-

---

[33] Courteault, *Un Cadet de Gascogne*, pp. 13–14. While Courteault's narrative is speculative at best, a letter from the Spanish king in 1566 thanks Monluc personally for his cooperation during this period. Philip II to Monluc (13 September 1566), see Pierre Honoré Champion, *Charles IX, la France et le contrôle de l'Espagne* (2 vols, Paris, 1939), I, p. 33.

[34] For Condé's accusation, see Courteault, *Blaise de Monluc, Historien*, p. 470, note 4.

[35] Thompson, *Wars of Religion*, p. 351.

[36] See, for example, Monluc to Philip II (February 1564), [Monluc], *Commentaires et lettres*, IV, pp. 319–27; Monluc to Philip II (March 1564), ibid., pp. 333–7.

[37] Freer, *The Life of Jeanne d'Albret*, p. 247.

[38] For the debate surrounding Catholic meetings at Bayonne in 1565 and discussions over the premeditation of massacre, see Denis Crouzet, *La nuit de la Saint-Barthélemy. Un rêve perdu de la renaissance* (Paris, 1994), pp. 142–78. For wider discussions of the Saint Bartholomew's massacres, see Sutherland, *The Massacre of Saint Bartholomew*; Géralde Nakam, *Au lendemain de la Saint-Barthélemy. Guerre civile et famine* (Paris, 1975); Alfred Soman (ed.), *The Massacre of Saint Bartholomew. Reappraisals and Documents* (The Hague, 1974); Robert M. Kingdon, *Myths about the Saint Bartholomew's Day Massacre 1572–1576* (London, 1988); Jean-Louis Bourgeon, *Charles IX devant la Saint-Barthélemy* (Geneva, 1995), pp. 181–84.

able activities' also needs to be reviewed; the response of the French crown is perhaps the most telling piece of evidence here, as it never once moved to demote or oust its general from power in Guyenne. The reality was that Monluc had secured and now maintained peace in a province notorious for faction and confessional strife. The crown was not about to remove the main buttress preventing Guyenne from exploding into uncontrollable civil war, and risk allowing Protestant forces to capture and control the south-west, while allegations against the Catholic general remained just that: allegations. Even when Bordeaux reformers convinced the *conseil privé*, then resident in the town as part of the king's grand tour of 1565, to indict Monluc for participating in recent militant activity alongside Candalle and Lange, nothing came of the subsequent investigation.[39] It appears the general was an asset the crown was not yet ready to part with. Besides, as Jean-Charles Sournia points out, the whispers against Monluc were as nothing compared to the allegations of high treason levelled against Coligny and Condé for conspiring to deliver Le Havre to Elizabeth of England: 'Coligny delivered a territory of France to a stranger, Monluc wrote correspondence that had no historical consequence'.[40]

If confessional relations in the south-west were fractious during this period, at least there had been no major confrontations on the scale of those of 1562. This would change dramatically in September 1567, however, following a failed bid by Protestants to kidnap the king during his sojourn at Meaux. Suspecting Condé's involvement in the affair, the duke of Guise urged Catholic communities across France to rally to the defence of the crown. In the south-west, the speed with which Catholic militants answered the call shocked many, with those who had assumed that the 1563 edict had fatally weakened Catholic resolve dismayed as earlier structures and hierarchies were reconstituted overnight. Within days, militants had seized control of strategic offices at Bordeaux, Agen and Toulouse, and were busy ordering their captains and confederates to make preparations for armed combat.

Monluc was, as ever, a pivotal figure in this regeneration. His promotion to the office of *lieutenant du roi* for all Guyenne, in June 1565, following the death of Burie, afforded enormous influence over a

---

[39] See Samazeuilth, *Histoire de l'Agenais*, II, p. 126; O'Reilly, *Histoire complète de Bordeaux*, II, pp. 236–9; Charles Weiss, *Papiers d'état du Cardinal de Granvelle (1516–1565)* (9 vols, Paris, 1841–52), VIII, p. 632.

[40] Jean-Charles Sournia, *Blaise de Monluc. Soldat et écrivain (1500–1577)* (Paris, 1981), pp. 293–4.

province still devoid of legitimate grandee governorship.[41] Such unchallenged authority, combined with a résumé that boasted numerous successes in securing Catholic communities against Protestant threats, made Monluc the obvious choice as chief arbiter of Catholic interests in Guyenne. It was a role he assumed with verve. *Arrêts* were issued by the Catholic hierarchy at Bordeaux banning all Protestant activity and restricting movement within the town,[42] while Monluc ordered all members of the *jurade* and *parlement* to profess their faith before their peers; those failing to do so, or who admitted to being 'of the reformed faith', were ejected from office.[43] Monluc was supported in this by Sanssac, the archbishop of Bordeaux, who proposed that reformers be excluded from all public office,[44] and by the Catholic chapter of Saint-André, who informed the *lieutenant du roi* that he had the 'full support of all Catholics in his endeavours'.[45] The clergy, however, wanted more stringent measures enforced, especially a crackdown on the activities of the wives and families of Protestant officials, many of whom had benefited from immunity from prosecution because of their familial ties.[46] They also urged that Protestant residents be forced to pay the costs of preparations for war, as compensation for the culpability of their co-religionists.[47] Monluc agreed to both demands, ordering the *jurade* to initiate collection of this tax and requiring all *gens de guerre* arriving in Bordeaux to be garrisoned in Protestant homes.[48]

The ease with which Catholic authorities were able to implement such controversial legislation can be explained by the absence of the *premier président* from the court at this time. According to rumour, Lagebâton had fled Bordeaux at the outbreak of war and was now in hiding. Keen to take advantage of the situation, the clergy requested an emergency session of *parlement* to indict the *premier président* for desertion, and thereby remove him from office, the standard procedure for officials absenting themselves from duty in a time of crisis.[49] They also enjoined the court to

---

[41] The seat of governor to Guyenne was still vacant as its rightful holder, Henry of Navarre, the young son of Antoine de Bourbon, was still a minor and so unable to assume office. For Monluc's promotion to the office of *lieutenant du roi* of Guyenne, see Charles IX to Monluc (11 June 1565), *AHG*, 55, pp. 59–62.

[42] *AHG*, 13, p. 399.

[43] Monluc to *jurats* of Bordeaux, ADG, G 42 (4 November 1567).

[44] ADG, G 42 (30 October 1567).

[45] ADG, G 287, fos 249–51.

[46] 'Remonstrance du clergé de Bordeaux au Blaise de Monluc', ADG, G 42 (November 1567).

[47] Clergy of Bordeaux to Monluc, ADG, G 42 (November 1567).

[48] Monluc to *jurade* of Bordeaux, ADG, G 42 (November 1567).

[49] Clergy of Bordeaux to Monluc, ADG, G 42 (4 November 1567); Clergy of Bordeaux to Monluc (4 December 1568), *AHG*, 24, p. 454.

dismantle the safe refuges that had been created for Protestants at Bergerac, Mussidan, Sainte-Foy and Montauban following the peace of 1563, claiming they were being used as bases from which rebels would strike at Catholic forces patrolling the area.[50] Monluc relayed these accusations to Paris and informed the king that he had formed an emergency military council at Bordeaux to coordinate its defence.[51] He and Roffignac were to head its executive committee, with *parlementaires* Malvin, Alesme, Vergoing, d'Escars, la Ferrière, Lahet and Roux, and delegations from the clergy of Bordeaux, the *sénéchaussée* of Guyenne, the two *châteaux* of the town, and the bourgeoisie invited to compose the deliberating corpus. In contrast to the situation in 1562, however, the crown was in no position to object to the existence of such a militant Catholic body. The Protestant attempt to seize the king had not only failed in its objective, it had allowed Guise policy to influence crown dictate. The king thus had little option but to sideline attempts to introduce toleration for the time being, and to support Catholic activists across France so as to defeat Condé's forces. So at Bordeaux, with Lagebâton absent, and crown authority weaker than at any period since 1561, Monluc and the Catholic hierarchy were free to manage their affairs with a degree of impunity.

Despite securing a truce in March 1568, matters failed to improve for the crown. The peace of Longjumeau may have ended this second war, but it satisfied neither faith. Catholics were incensed that Protestant forces had been granted substantial concessions, despite suffering heavy military reverses in the latter months of the conflict – a grievance that echoed complaints at the Amboise compromise five years earlier, which also followed a series of Protestant defeats. Equally galling to Catholic sensibilities was a clause ordering acts of violence committed by Protestant forces to be 'played down' for the sake of future confessional relations. Guyenne had suffered more than most at the hands of Protestant armies during this last campaign, and military leaders were especially vocal in reproving the crown's conciliatory moves. Labelling the edict 'the most unjust law ever made by a prince', Monluc condemned as unforgivable the manner in which Catholic victims were being neglected, with little or no chance of receiving reparations for damages and loss.[52]

At Bordeaux, the Catholic hierarchy snubbed the peace agreement entirely, moving to bolster its control of the town despite the edict's insistence on non-confrontation within urban settings. On 27 March 1568,

---

[50] Clergy of Bordeaux to Monluc, ADG, G 42 (27 November 1567).
[51] Monluc to Charles IX, ADG, G 42 (November 1567).
[52] [Monluc], *Commentaires 1521–1576*, pp. 658–9.

just three days after Longjumeau, Monluc appointed a Catholic military governor to oversee the defence of the town.[53] The appointee, François de Cassagnet, *sieur* de Saint-Orens, known as captain Tilladet, was one of Monluc's most trusted captains, having held this same office temporarily during the crisis of 1562. He was also known as a leading Catholic activist, and had been a prominent supporter of the associations of Lange and Candalle during the first war. His first act as governor, on 5 April, reflected this reputation: the removal of jurisdiction over town security from the *jurade* of Bordeaux.[54] This provoked furious challenges from the *jurats*, who argued that control of policing, and of the keys to the gates, were traditional prerogatives of the city councillors, a privilege that could be traced back to English rule in the thirteenth century.[55] Monluc, however, rejected these protests out of hand, asserting that current instability required that military expediency take precedence over convention.[56]

The loyalty of the *jurade* had, in fact, long been suspect to Catholic leaders at Bordeaux, with many known to sympathize with the reform movement despite having sworn an oath of office that required all officers to 'live as Catholics according to the Roman Church'.[57] Steps were thus taken to curb their powers in April 1568, with Tilladet ordering all officials caught assembling under arms in support of the reformers to be arrested and punished as traitors.[58] Meanwhile, loyal Catholics were rewarded for their support with influential posts within the Bordeaux administration. In May 1568, Lange was promoted from *avocat* to *conseiller*, a major boost to Catholic authority within the *parlement*,[59] while the *sieur* de Lanssac, brother of the archbishop, Sanssac, was assigned to the office of mayor, with a remit to bolster the town security: Monluc and Tilladet were still to be consulted over general policy, but day-to-day policing now fell to Lanssac, who no doubt welcomed the additional four thousand Catholic soldiers enlisted by Monluc to augment the town guard.[60] Catholic hegemony over regional defence was complete when the *vicomte* d'Uza, Candalle's associate from Cadillac, was given charge of the royal navy docked at the port of Bordeaux in November,[61] and Vaillac, the governor and, in Catholic eyes, the saviour,

---

[53] ADG, 1B 307, *Arrêt du parlement* (27 March 1568), fo. 255.

[54] Devienne, *Histoire de la ville de Bordeaux*, I, p. 154.

[55] These privileges were reaffirmed by Louis XII in 1511. O'Reilly, *Histoire complète de Bordeaux*, II, p. 241.

[56] ADG, 1B 308, *Arrêt du parlement* (24 April 1568), fo. 231.

[57] AMB, ms 768, fo. 642.

[58] ADG, 1B 308, *Arrêt du parlement* (27 April 1568), fo. 237.

[59] Tamizey de Larroque, 'Jean Lange, conseiller', pp. 687–8.

[61] ADG, 1B 314, *Arrêt du parlement* (5 November 1568), fo. 4.

of the château Trompette, was appointed commander of the Garonne's major seaports.[62]

These latter appointments took place with Catholic and Protestant communities once more at odds. Anger at the Guise's continuing ascendancy at court had forced Condé to issue a fresh manifesto, in August 1568, attacking the crown for failing Protestants. The response of the Catholic-dominated *conseil privé* was simple: it revoked the Longjumeau edict and rescinded all clauses legitimizing toleration. So, in September 1568, the country slid back into war. The Catholic leadership at Bordeaux, however, was well prepared for such an outcome, having not accepted the peace in the first place. It moved seamlessly to a heightened level of security, requiring all Catholic 'bourgeoisie, merchants and habitants' to present themselves for duty in the guard, without exception, with all vagrants and strangers ordered to leave the town within twelve hours or face arrest.[63] A curfew followed, forcing Protestants to remain indoors between 6pm and 6am,[64] augmented by a complementary law requiring them to carry a passport when moving about the town in daylight hours.[65]

In December 1568, Monluc replaced Tilladet as governor of Bordeaux with the ultra-Catholic baron de Montferrand.[66] Tilladet had done nothing wrong, but in Montferrand Catholics now had a town governor of substantial noble rank. His first task was to deal with the thorny problem of the continuing absence of the *premier président*, which had rumbled on for months without resolution. Montferrand duly revisited the *requête* posted by the clergy calling for Lagebâton to be exiled in perpetuity from the *parlement* for vacating his post and, in a deliberation that reflected Catholic unanimity at Bordeaux, endorsed the request.[67] With such a cavalcade of Catholic protagonists holding high office, potential threats to the governance and security of Bordeaux were alleviated. Consolidation of authority and defence could now commence in earnest, and the *parlement* wasted little time in tackling its most troublesome opponents. Baulon was charged with removing all suspect officials from town council deliberations,[68] while Roffignac and Malvin were to vet the *jurade* to ensure that only 'true

[62] ADG, G 42 (29 January 1569), no folio.
[63] ADG, 1B 313, *Arrêt du parlement* (8 September 1568), fo. 198.
[64] ADG, 1B 313, *Arrêt du parlement* (10 September 1568), fo. 201.
[65] ADG, 1B 315, *Arrêt du parlement* (11 November 1568), fo. 55.
[66] For Montferrand's appointment, see ADG, B 38, fo. 74. Indeed, Montferrand would head the six companies of soldiers that massacred Protestants at Bordeaux in October 1572. See Benedict, 'The Saint Bartholomew's Massacres', pp. 205–25.
[67] BMB, ms 369, III, fo. 118.
[68] ADG, 1B 314, *Arrêt du parlement* (22 November 1568), fo. 39 and (25 November 1568), fo. 50.

Catholics' served the town.[69] Soon all offices of Bordeaux were held by Catholics, although three prospective candidates had to be disqualified from a ballot for election to the *jurade* in August 1569 after an investigation proved they had links to the reform movement.[70] As a result, all candidates were now required to prove their Catholicity before Roffignac and Malvin before even being permitted to apply for posts.[71]

Montferrand then moved to tighten the restrictions on personal freedoms in Bordeaux. Vagabonds, strangers and potential troublemakers were to be ejected summarily from the town, as were those apprentices who refused to serve their Catholic masters, and anyone caught sheltering itinerant reformers.[72] In October 1569, the *procureur-général* was commissioned to compile a report on the activities of all Protestants still resident within the town, with the result that over one hundred suspects, including many former military, administrative and clerical personnel of Bordeaux, were ordered to appear before the *parlement* to be questioned.[73] Montferrand also turned his attention to the Catholics' longstanding nemeses, the *régents* and *écoliers* of the *collège de Guyenne*, passing legislation that rigorously curtailed the movement and behaviour of all staff and students within and without the walls of the *collège*.[74]

Provincial grievances were also addressed at this time. In January 1569, Roffignac and Baulon stipulated that any Catholic of Blaye who had been chased from their home during the rioting of the previous year could take possession of property belonging to absent Protestants in Bordeaux, adding that resident Protestant families would be evicted to make room for homeless Catholic refugees should vacant accommodation become scarce.[75] In March, the *parlement* ended the jurisdictional arguments raging at the *présidial* court at Bézas, simply by dismissing all Protestant magistrates and replacing them with known Catholic *conseillers*,[76] while at Castillon, Lamerque and Guitinières, town councils were ordered to disarm their Protestant populations and distribute the collected weaponry among their Catholic inhabitants.[77] Monluc, too, was active here, advising the council at Casteljaloux of the necessity to keep firm control over its town guard, and

---

[69] ADG, 1B 317, *Arrêt du parlement* (31 January 1569), fo. 185.

[70] ADG, G 287, fo. 275.

[71] ADG, 1B 324, *Arrêt du parlement* (8 August 1569), fo. 76.

[72] ADG, 1B 318, *Arrêt du parlement* (10 February 1569), fo. 69; ADG, 1B 325, *Arrêt du parlement* (24 September 1569), fo. 140.

[73] ADG, 1B 326, *Arrêt du parlement* (29 October 1569), fo. 110.

[74] ADG, G 287, fo. 267.

[75] 'Arrêt du parlement de Bordeaux en faveur des Catholicques de Blaye' (15 January 1569), *AHG*, 12, fos 77–80.

[76] ADG, 1B 319, *Arrêt du parlement* (12 March 1569), fo. 74.

[77] ADG, 1B 319, *Arrêt du parlement* (19 March 1569), fo. 88.

to ensure that its membership was trustworthy and well organized. Should they require extra manpower, he added, the council was to contact him immediately and reinforcements would be dispatched forthwith from Bordeaux.[78] Catholic domination of Bordeaux was now complete, as evidenced by the lavish ceremony that welcomed the arrival, on 9 October 1569, of the baron de la Garde, whose fleet of eight galleons was stacked high with supplies of food and armaments for the town. On mooring, de la Garde was greeted by a committee consisting of Montferrand, Roffignac, d'Escars, Sanssac, Vaillac, Malvin, Baulon and Lange, with the remaining Catholic officials of Bordeaux forming an honorary guard to escort the baron to a reception at the *maison de ville*. This was quite a welcome, and reflected a renewed sense of Catholic confidence and optimism following the travails of the previous decade. Only Monluc was missing, his arrival delayed by continuing military operations in Béarn.[79]

A final, intriguing footnote to the Catholic success story concerns the return of the Jesuits to Bordeaux. Even though Catholics had consolidated control over political and administrative functions in Bordeaux by 1569, reform ideology still flourished within its three academic institutions: the *collège de Guyenne* and the chapter *collèges* of Saint-André and Saint-Seurin. This left the town without a major Catholic school, a lacuna that Catholic *parlementaires* viewed as an affront.[80] In early 1570, Baulon moved to correct this, proposing that a number of Jesuits be invited to return to Bordeaux to establish and oversee a Catholic school, to be supported by the local clergy, but out of reach of the *collège de Guyenne* and those remaining moderates within the *parlement*.[81] A consortium of Catholic magistrates was thus formed to coordinate this endeavour, led by Baulon and Lange, both of whom had been in contact with Jesuit dignitaries during the previous months. Lange, in fact, had played host to François Borgia, *général* of the Society of Jesus, and cardinal Alexandre, nephew and papal legate to Pius V, on their recent visit to Bordeaux in 1569, and had subsequently been commended to Rome by the delegation as 'wise and eloquent, a man of strong Catholic zeal'.[82]

---

[78] J.-F. Samazeuilth, *Histoire de l'Agenais, du Condomois et du Bazadais* (2 vols, Auch, 1847), II, p. 149.

[79] *AHG*, 13, p. 266.

[80] Even at the height of the sectarian struggle in 1563, the Bordeaux *parlement* seemed aware of the importance of the *collège de Guyenne* for the town, granting additional payment for its upkeep despite its continuing problems with Protestant *écoliers*: ADG, 1B 262, *Arrêt du parlement* (22 September 1563), fo. 207.

[81] Gaullieur, *Histoire du collège de Guyenne*, pp. 291–2.

[82] Darnal, *Chronique Bordelais, Supplément*, p. 81. Lange was also cited by Arnauld de Pontac, bishop of Bazas, as one of the 'bons catholiques' of Bordeaux, in a letter to Rome concerning the possibility of a Jesuit college being established in Bordeaux in 1569 (ibid.).

What was remarkable about the composition of this consortium was that it echoed almost exactly the faction that helped establish the Catholic syndicate nine years earlier: Roffignac, Malvin, Lange, Baulon and Cazeaux, with Sanssac and his nephew, Charles Dusault, second *avocat-général* to the *parlement*, lending support.[83]

Sanssac, in fact, would be instrumental in persuading the leading Jesuit theologian in the south-west, Edmond Auger, to leave Toulouse to head this new college at Bordeaux, which was to be created within the archbishop's palace.[84] Baulon secured an initial *rente* of 2000 *livres* to facilitate Auger's move, and soon acquired an additional 24 000 *livres* to finance his annual keep.[85] The Catholic consortium, however, had yet to inform the crown of their plans, no doubt wary of the traditional mistrust between the French monarchy and the Jesuit order. It would take two years before such a request was forthcoming, only for Catherine de Medici to reject Baulon's petition within the week.[86] Tradition histories thus paint this as a failed enterprise, with the Jesuits having to wait until the 1580s, under the auspices of the Catholic League, before returning to Bordeaux in any formal capacity.[87] The archives suggest a less conclusive verdict, however. Certainly, the proposal to re-establish the Jesuits had been denied by the crown, but it seems that on 20 May 1572 the Bordeaux *parlement* agreed to allow Baulon to continue with his scheme regardless.[88] Shortly afterwards, Auger and several of his followers are recorded as having arrived within the town, and to have founded a small hospice for the poor and a refuge for pilgrims.[89] Worthy of consideration, here, is the date: 20 May 1572, the day after the feast day of Saint-Yves. It is interesting to note that, just as the ceremonial that accompanied the confraternity's festivities had underpinned initial Catholic militancy, allowing *basochiens*, *confrères*, officials and magistrates to mix freely, and had provided the forum from which activists went on to establish the syndicate in 1561, so this same environment would be chosen as the host for the re-establishment of that most Catholic of sixteenth-century militant groups: the Jesuits.

---

[83] Gaullieur, *Histoire du collège de Guyenne*, p. 296.

[84] The Jesuit Edmond Auger was also known in the south of France as Charles Sager. See Dom Devienne, *Histoire de l'église de Bordeaux* (Bordeaux, 1862), p. 95.

[85] ADG, H 2512, fo. 5. It would later transpire that these funds had not, as Baulon claimed, been collected from Catholic benefactors, but had instead been diverted from the *parlement*'s financial expenditures.

[86] ADG, H 2380, liasse 68–2, *Actes de Grandes Personnages* (4 May 1572).

[87] See, for example, Devienne, *Histoire de l'église de Bordeaux*, pp. 95–6.

[88] BMB, ms 828, 5, fo. 32. See also ADG, H 2512, fos 1–4.

[89] ADG, H 2380, liasse 68–2, *Personnel* (August 1572); ADG, H 2380, liasse 68–2, *Collège de Jesus* (17 November 1572).

CHAPTER SIX

Coalition and Consensus at Agen

A second arena of Catholic militancy in Guyenne centred on the town of Agen and its environs, the Agenais. Situated 110 kilometres south-east of Bordeaux, Agen was in many respects a miniature version of its provincial capital. Its population, around 7000 in 1560, was less than one-seventh that of Bordeaux, but its robust walled defences, stout gates and dominant position on a bend of the river Garonne mirrored the architecture and geography of its neighbour quite closely.[1] As with Bordeaux, such advantages meant that Agen would be prized as a command centre by both faiths throughout the 1560s. For Catholics, the town's location, equidistant from its sister bastions of Bordeaux and Toulouse, made it an important staging post for the distribution of troops, munitions and resources across the region, and a hub for communication between dispersed Catholic communities. For Protestants, the capture of Agen would sever this umbilical cord and establish a significant satellite for its own forces instead. Indeed, the strategic importance of the town is witnessed by the fact that numerous military commanders, including Blaise de Monluc, Henry of Navarre and marshals Biron, Villars and Matignon, made Agen their headquarters during campaigns of the religious wars.

Why Agen and not the capital? Historians suggest that Agen's compactness made it easier to defend with limited forces than the sprawling first city, a fact made all too obvious to Burie during the early 1560s, while Bordeaux's large Protestant population always posed a threat to internal security, and so hampered the ability of a commander to be certain of the integrity of his defences in times of crisis.[2] But if Agen could compete in military terms, it could not rival Bordeaux's political authority, and regularly deferred contentious matters to the *parlement* there. This meant that local authorities enjoyed only limited participation in provincial government. Their input became more restricted as confessional tensions rose during the 1550s, as the *parlement* urged regional officials to cede civic prerogatives in favour of centralized, standardized legislation. The logic behind this was clear. By restricting urban councils from implementing independent agendas, the *parlement* hoped to maintain a uniform policy

---

[1] Boutrouche, *Bordeaux de 1453 à 1715*, p. 243.

[2] Courteault, *Blaise de Monluc, Historien*, pp. 404–5. See also Powis, 'Order, religion and magistrates', p. 192.

vis-à-vis the growing reform movement and thus prevent confessional appeals from obstructing court business. The council at Agen seemed content to be so guided at first, and confirmed all relevant *arrêts* during the late 1550s.[3] The *jurade* at Agen also supported this policy, gaining wider powers to confront illegal reformed activities in return for accepting new extradition procedures, which required all locally incarcerated heresy suspects to be transported to Bordeaux for trial and punishment.[4] Thus, when in August 1559 Antoine de Tholon, *lieutenant-criminel* of the *sénéchaussée d'Agenais*, was ordered to make an example of those reformers caught profaning Catholic images in a local church, he acted under the joint jurisdiction of the Agen and Bordeaux authorities.[5]

Significantly, consensus between the two centres was also reached over the censuring of disorderly communal assemblies. The Bordeaux *parlement* had successfully imposed legislation against unrest at feast day celebrations and public gatherings such as burials, processions and the *charivari* during 1558, but at Agen, such violent incidents remained largely unchecked. In March 1559, though, the *jurade* petitioned for and was granted permission to amend a standing *arrêt* to make it illegal to hold Protestant gatherings, *charivaris* and other unruly assemblies, on pain of a 10 000 *livres* fine.[6] But when news of this reached the provincial governor, Antoine de Bourbon, his reservations over the legitimacy of the *parlement's* ruling were made clear to all. Orders were dispatched for the immediate suspension of all heresy trials and associated legislation until his return to the province, with the governor further charging Tholon and Bernard d'Aspremont, *lieutenant-particulier* of the *sénéchaussée*, to ensure the compliance of the *jurade* in this matter.[7] This certainly pleased a young Cordelier named Melchior, who had recently found himself incarcerated at Agen on heresy charges, but who was now freed from prison into Tholon's custody until further notice.[8]

Antoine's involvement here can be explained on two grounds. Although the king of Navarre would later be an integral member of the triumvirate – the Catholic coalition formed to oppose the Protestant

---

[3] See, for example, the *arrêt du parlement* of July 1558 banning any *prêches* that had failed to secure royal or episcopal consent: ADLG, E Sup. Agen, BB 30, fo. 26ᵛ.

[4] Such was the case for Pierre Lachèze, a *cordonnier* at Agen, who had been arrested in December 1558 for having broken a crucifix with a large stone. Where Agen magistrates would previously have interrogated Lachèze themselves, under the new agreement he was now dispatched to Bordeaux for trial: ADLG, E Sup. Agen, BB 30, fo. 31.

[5] 21 April 1559. ADLG, E Sup. Agen, BB 30, fo. 43.

[6] ADLG, E Sup. Agen, BB 30, fo. 20.

[7] Antoine de Bourbon to *jurade d'Agen* (24 March 1559), Marquis de Rochambeau, *Lettres d'Antoine de Bourbon et de Jehanne d'Albret* (Paris, 1877), pp. 175–76.

[8] Rochambeau, *Lettres d'Antoine de Bourbon*, p. 176.

prince of Condé – his religious inclination during the late 1550s was far more equivocal, tending towards moderate Catholicism rather than the evangelical Calvinism practised by his wife, Jeanne d'Albret, or the zealous orthodoxy of many magistrates of the *parlements*. Secondly, Navarre may simply have been asserting his prerogative as governor over Guyenne, making it clear that the various over-mighty councils of the region should consult him fully before publishing such contentious legislation. Catholics, though, were exasperated at the governor's stance, especially as it coincided with a most dramatic period of Protestant expansion across the region, with complaints of rising levels of intimidation, unrest, illegal armed gatherings and violence against priests, churches and communities flooding into the courts.[9] In February 1560, events at nearby Montségur did little to alleviate Catholic concerns, as weeks of insurrection left the town in ruins, with the self-proclaimed ruling commune severing all trade links with surrounding centres.[10] Rumours that rebel partisans were also active at Agen saw the *jurade* seek permission from the governor to put the guard on high alert in case Protestants troops attempted to take advantage of the situation and besiege the town. In this instance, Antoine acceded.[11]

The deteriorating situation across the Agenais forced the authorities to address the defence of Catholic interests as a matter of priority. Determined leadership was called for, and two prominent Catholic councillors, Martial de Nort, *consul* of the *jurade*, and Clément de Lalande, canon of the church of Saint-Caprais, stepped forward to direct the Catholic response. Their first success was in persuading the *jurade* to enlist Monluc, then at his château at nearby Estillac, to act as advisor on military security. Arriving at Agen in late-February 1560, Monluc promptly identified civil stability as a primary concern, urging each *jurat* to take a turn guarding the gates, and advising Catholics on the town council to maintain a watchful eye over the town so as to pre-empt agitation and unrest.[12] The council further determined to reclaim its prerogative to impeach heresy suspects, recently ceded to Bordeaux, so as to allow greater scope in prosecuting Protestant rebels across the Agenais.[13] But progress here was slow, and when a local schoolmaster, Philippe Levi,

---

[9] The *registres du parlement* at Bordeaux highlight the numerous reports of illegal *prêches* and illicit and armed assemblies. See AMB, ms 766, fos 1–68 for November 1559; fos 69–77 for December 1559; fos 178–256 for January 1560; fos 257–326 for February 1560; fos 327–73 for March 1560; fos 374–427 for April 1560; fos 428–554 for May 1560; fos 555–632 for June 1560; fos 633–707 for July 1560; and fos 708–89 for August 1560.

[10] See Nakam, *Montaigne et son temps*, p. 46.

[11] Andrieu, *Histoire de l'Agenais*, I, p. 211.

[12] Courteault, *Blaise de Monluc. Historien*, p. 388.

[13] ADLG, E Sup. Agen, BB 30, fo. 55.

was arrested for holding secret *prêches* in private houses at Villeneuve, the Agen authorities were unsure as to whether they could employ local judges to try and sentence Levi, or whether the standard procedure of transferring him to Bordeaux for punishment was to be followed.[14] Without consultation, they chose the former option, and awaited complaints from Bordeaux over this infringement. When these failed to materialize, the *jurade* presented an application to the king requesting that jurisdiction be formally transferred back to the council. To augment their request the council proffered detailed interrogation techniques to show their competence in this matter, and included a case report on the successful trial of Pierre Brune, a Protestant charged with possessing the banned book, *La Légende Dorée*, to confirm their zeal.[15]

But the *jurade* would soon find that authority over confessional trials could be a double-edged sword. In May 1560, two high-profile Calvinist ministers, Jean Voisin and Jacques Lafontaine, were arrested for 'over-zealous' preaching and for inciting followers to assault members of the *présidial* court of Agen.[16] Once they had been incarcerated, the jail became the focal point for demonstrations demanding the ministers' release, with Lalande and de Nort forced to deploy Catholic guards to maintain order as more and more armed reformers gathered to protest. In the inevitable furore, both ministers managed to escape, although Lafontaine was quickly recaptured. Monluc led his forces to quell the unrest, and soon found himself appointed to adjudicate over the controversial imprisonments. When he found in favour of the original judgement – the inflammatory rhetoric of the two had clearly contravened a recent royal edict – the mob turned on Monluc and besieged his home at Estillac.[17] Monluc's decision also roused the wrath of the provincial governor, who reported the captain and the *jurade* of Agen to the king for acting outside their jurisdiction. Monluc saw this as a serious rift between himself and the governor, noting in his *Commentaires* that he long awaited some form of retribution from the king of Navarre for this transgression.[18] Yet despite Antoine's diatribe, the Agen council proceeded with the prosecution of the ministers, pending clarification from the crown on proceedings.[19] On 10 June, however, the matter was taken out of their hands, with Lafontaine ordered to be transported to Bordeaux for trial before the *parlement*.[20] It is doubtful that the

---

14 ADLG, E Sup. Agen, FF 13 (16 March 1560).
15 ADLG, E Sup. Agen, FF 31 (1 June 1560).
16 [Monluc], *Commentaires, 1521–1576*, p. 473.
17 Tholin, 'La ville d'Agen', XIV, p. 435; [Monluc], *Commentaires, 1521–1576*, p. 473.
18 [Monluc], *Commentaires, 1521–1576*, p. 473.
19 Tholin, 'La ville d'Agen', XIV, p. 435.
20 ADLG, E Sup. Agen, BB 30, fos. 67ᵛ-8.

Agen authorities were too concerned at this, as the minister was rapidly becoming a *cause célèbre* for Protestants of the region.

While the prevalence of anti-Protestant legislation may indicate the presence of a pro-Catholic consensus within the patriciate at Agen, no formal corpus existed as such. This would change in June 1560, as the *jurade* received intelligence that a Protestant force from Nérac was approaching the town, intent on gaining entry and desecrating the churches and cathedral of Agen.[21] Officials of the *jurade* and *présidial* decided that an urgent meeting of all Catholic notables of the region should be held to determine a response. As de Nort and Lalande had already begun to assume greater authority over council meetings, they were nominated to chair this assembly, which convened at the *maison commune* on 4 June 1560.[22] Monluc was again called to attend, as were prominent Catholic officials of the *jurade* and *sénéchaussée*, including Antoine de Nort (Martial's son), Tholon, d'Aspremont and Pierre Redon, with Nadal and Lobatery, senior canons of the cathedral of Saint-Étienne, representing the clergy.[23]

George Tholin saw this congress as a pivotal moment for local confessional relations at Agen, as explicit cooperation between secular and clerical institutions helped realize the creation of a pan-Agenais coalition of Catholic delegates that would define Catholic activism in the region for the coming decade.[24] As will be seen, this is a sustainable assertion. The first directive issued by the coalition was the formation of a *conseil militaire* to oversee the defence of Agen.[25] *Conseil* members were drawn from the attending delegates, with Lalande appointed leader. Its remit was concise: based within the *maison commune*, the *conseil* would oversee the surveillance of all Protestant activity within Agen. Meanwhile, the coalition would make available a sizeable force of Catholic townsfolk, to be deployed by Lalande in emergencies, with experienced Catholic captains appointed to command these units, and arms and artillery made available from the town arsenal.[26] These measures clearly contravened the recent royal edict that prohibited the carrying of firearms, a consequence of the recent Conspiracy at Amboise, but evidently the coalition felt the scale of the Protestant threat justified such an expedient.

Monluc and Lalande, however, were mindful of crown sensitivities to such a development, and dispatched d'Aspremont to the royal court to

21   ADLG, E Sup. Agen, FF 31 (1 June 1560).
22   ADLG, E Sup. Agen, FF 31 (4 June 1560).
23   ADLG, E Sup. Agen, FF 31 (4 June 1560).
24   Tholin, 'La ville d'Agen', XIV, p. 435.
25   ADLG, E Sup. Agen, FF 31 (4 June 1560).
26   ADLG, E Sup. Agen, FF 31 (4 June 1560).

seek permission for their initiatives.[27] The replies from Francis II and the Cardinal of Lorraine, thanking the authorities for their zeal in tackling sedition across the region, and for their defence of Agen against the threat of insurrection, arrived in early June 1560. However, they stopped short of fully supporting the coalition.[28] The crown, it seemed, intended to explore conciliatory measures, such as the implementation of dual-faith council chambers (or *chambres mi-parties*) before falling back on local interest groups to maintain order.[29] This appeared to catch the Agen authorities off guard, and they were suddenly inundated with demands from Protestants for a *mi-partie* chamber within the town. The coalition procrastinated as long as possible, wary to make any concessions yet, but their refusal to follow the crown's lead angered local Protestants. Accusing the Catholic leadership of bias and provocation, they took to the streets, attacking Catholic homes and forcing their way into the church of Saint-Fiary to destroy its statues.[30] François Raffin, the *sénéchal de l'Agenais*, struggled to restore order with his limited resources, and advised the coalition that such large-scale unrest could be contained effectively only by an experienced military force, and recommended they recall Monluc to take command of the situation.[31]

Monluc, who still held no official position within local or crown government, returned to Agen in February 1561. His first act was to deploy the *consuls*, attired in their formal robes of office, to guard the gates.[32] This was far more than a mere gesture. By employing the elites as well as the citizens in the defence of a town, and by making them conspicuous to all by wearing their dress of office, Monluc was reminding everyone of the symbolism and traditions of the town, and emphasizing the value of collective responsibility and communal defence.[33] The coalition, meanwhile, moved to expand the militia, arming new recruits from the arsenal, before dividing them into smaller units, each headed by Catholic consuls when patrolling the

---

[27] Andrieu, *Histoire de l'Agenais*, I, p. 212. Simultaneously, the coalition registered the disarmament edict as a precaution: ADLG, E Sup. Agen, BB 30, fo. 60.

[28] Francis II to *Consuls d'Agen* (20 June 1560), ADLG, E Sup. Agen, BB 30, fo. 67; Cardinal of Lorraine to *Consuls d'Agen*, ibid., fo. 67ᵛ.

[29] For a detailed analysis of the *chambres mi-parties* of France during the religious wars, see Eckart Birnstiel, 'Les chambres mi-parties: les cadres institutionnels d'une juridiction spéciale', Jacques Poumarède and Jack Thomas (eds), *Les parlements de province. Pouvoirs, justice et société de XVe au XVIIIe siècle* (Toulouse, 1996), pp. 121–38.

[30] *AHG*, 29, p. 22.

[31] Raffin had served 'with honour' under Monluc at Thionville, in June 1558. See Courteault, *Blaise de Monluc, Historien*, p. 363.

[32] ADLG, E Sup. Agen, FF 31 (no folio).

[33] For similar requirement of Bordeaux magistrates to wear their formal robes while on guard duty in June 1562, see BMB, ms 369, II, fo. 421; BMB, ms 370, fo. 654.

streets.[34] Lalande, who had personally established a garrison at the collegial church of Saint-Caprais the previous year, was able to deploy these troops to guard the numerous churches of Agen, while members of his entourage began to remove the treasures of Agen's cathedral and other decorated churches for safekeeping at his nearby château.[35] Once the town had been secured, the coalition launched an attack on the reformers, blaming the incendiary organizational reforms implemented by the Synod of Clairac for encouraging such belligerence, and singling out the *abbé* of Clairac as the architect of the recent insurrection.[36] There is little doubt that the synod's division of the region into colloquies had strengthened the military potential of Protestant forces in Guyenne, with the fact that the Agenais now had nineteen distinct centres of military control, by far the largest number designated during the reforms, making it an extremely well defined and well prepared combative entity.[37]

The crown responded to this unrest by imposing a general truce. At first, it was accepted with little complaint. Raffin agreed to stand down the militia in Agen, Protestant delegates were allowed to attend meetings of the *jurade* and *présidial* once more, and Monluc withdrew with his men to Estillac. The coalition, however, were unhappy at the inclusion of an amnesty within the truce which ordered the release of all prisoners held for 'religious offences', of which there were many within the Agen jails, and at the renewed demands by Protestants for the instigation of a *mi-partie* chamber at Agen. In response, Catholics revived their *conseil militaire* and forwarded a document to the crown detailing continuing illegal assembly by armed reformers, and stating that *mi-partie* government at Agen would be impossible while such transgressions continued.[38]

---

[34] ADLG, E Sup. Agen, FF 31 (no folio).

[35] Tholin, 'La ville d'Agen', XIV, p. 444; Abbé Joseph Labrunie, 'Abrégé chronologique des antiquités d'Agen', *Revue de l'Agenais et des anciennes provinces du sud-ouest,* XV (Agen, 1888), pp. 174–7.

[36] BN Dupuy, 588, fo. 106. Intriguingly, while Courteault and Ruble both suggested the *abbé* in question was the *protonotaire* Geoffrey de Caumont, the *Mémoires de Condé* claimed it was Gerard Roussel, the former bishop of Oloron, which would suggest a link between the disturbances and the court of Jeanne d'Albret. See [Monluc], *Commentaires, 1521–1576,* p. 489; [Monluc], *Commentaires et lettres,* IV, p. 118; [Condé], *Mémoires de Condé,* III, p. 186.

[37] The seven colloquies were Condommois, les Landes, Béarn, Agenais de la Garonne, Agenais vers Sainte-Foy, Bourdellais et Bazadois, and Quercy et Rouergue. The nineteen constituent towns of the Agenais were Agen, le Port, Tonneins, Marmande, Gontaud, Grateloup, Saint-Barthélemy, Verteilh, Laparade, Monclar, Montflanquin, Villeneuve, Castelsegen, Cassenel, Sainte-Livrade, Castelmoro, Laffite, Clayrac and Lemousin-sur-Lades: ADLG, E Sup. Agen, GG 201, fo. 1.

[38] Paul Courteault, 'Notes et Variances', in [Monluc], *Commentaires 1521–1576,* p. 1178 note 3; *Jurade d'Agen* to Charles IX (17 February 1561), ADLG, E Sup. Agen, BB 30, fo. 72ᵛ; ADLG, E Sup. Agen, BB 30, fo. 79ᵛ.

The crown had little option other than to accede to this evidence and, on 14 May 1561, validated an ordinance that banned all *prêches* and large gatherings at Agen under pain of a fine and imprisonment.[39] Protestant demands for *mi-partie* representation were thus buried under the weight of Catholic remonstrations to Paris.

Complaints of illegal assemblies and armed assaults against Catholics continued to dominate court affairs at Agen, though. In August 1561, the crown was forced to intervene once more, instructing Herman de Sevin, *juge-mage* of the *présidial*, and Gratien Delas, *procureur du roi*, to issue an *ordonnance* banning the carrying and use of firearms in the *sénéchaussée d'Agenais*, even those used for hunting.[40] Burie was also ordered into the region, a move that initially placated Catholic anxieties.[41] Tholin suggests that the coalition fully expected Burie to exact 'exemplary justice' against the rebels, and Lalande certainly anticipated a major disarmament of Protestants, as he organized a special task force to expedite the confiscation and storage of illicit arms within the *maison de ville*.[42] But Burie had his own, very different agenda. Instead of proceeding directly to Agen, he criss-crossed the Agenais, halting frequently for talks with representatives of both faiths, not arriving at the town until 3 October. Accompanied by Etienne de la Boëtie, an up-and-coming councillor from Bordeaux, Burie counselled conciliation rather than confrontation and, where direct intervention was necessary, he ensured that it was the forces of the *sénéchal d'Agenais*, Raffin, that were deployed, rather than his own, perhaps mindful that both communities continued to accuse the crown of intervening on behalf of their opponents.[43]

This approach encountered two problems. Firstly, Catholic patience with Burie's ineffective policy was evaporating, as increasing numbers of churches and priests came under attack. Secondly, Burie had made a major diplomatic blunder in appointing a renowned local Protestant captain, the *sieur* de Mesmy, to head one of his patrols. Mesmy was so despised by Catholics across the region that many communities rejected his intervention out of hand, accusing the *lieutenant du roi* of inflaming, not calming sectarian tensions by this measure. Indeed, so hated was Mesmy that, when he was captured, fighting in Béarn during the war of 1562, he was summarily executed by order of the Bordeaux *parlement*.[44]

---

[39] ADLG, E Sup. Agen, BB 30, fo. 79ᵛ.

[40] Tholin, 'La ville d'Agen', XIV, p. 448.

[41] ADLG, E Sup. Agen, BB 30, fo. 83ᵛ.

[42] Tholin, 'La ville d'Agen', XIV, pp. 449–50; ADLG, E Sup. Agen, BB 30, fo. 75.

[43] Estienne de la Boëtie, *Mémoire sur la pacification des troubles* (ed. M. Smith, Geneva, 1983), pp. 11–12.

[44] Andrieu, *Histoire de l'Agenais*, I, p. 217.

Burie's efforts to pacify and accommodate were thus failing badly, as violence across the Agenais intensified. By August 1561, communities at Clairac, Tonneins, Montflanquin and Sainte-Livrade had all reported that local Catholic priests had been chased from their parishes, while at Villeneuve, Penne and Nérac the orders of Cordeliers had been evicted from their monasteries, which had now been transformed into sites of reform worship.[45]

Rather than bolster its military presence to deal with this upsurge in violence, the crown gambled on pursuing its policy of accommodating both faiths within government to settle the impasse. It thus directed the council at Agen to install *mi-partie* chambers immediately. The order was met with disbelief by Catholics, who refused point blank, threatening to paralyse the town's administration instead. Burie was dispatched to negotiate a settlement, which, surprisingly, he managed after only ten days of arbitration.[46] The acquiescence of the coalition here is puzzling, especially considering the high levels of violence endured by the Catholics of the Agenais. Also unexpected was the coalition's acceptance that the *mi-partie* chamber would fall under the jurisdiction of the *sénéchaussée*, and not the *jurade*, although it can be argued that Catholic domination of both bodies was equally extensive. So, on 20 October 1561, after two years of continually refusing all appeals regarding *mi-partie* government at Agen, the motion before the council was passed by a majority verdict.[47]

Whatever the rationale behind Catholic compliance, it became clear over subsequent months that their cooperation had been tacit at best. By 27 December 1561, leading members of the *jurade* and *présidial* felt compelled to protest to the king that the reformers were continuing to contravene royal edicts.[48] They also complained that the *mi-partie* experiment was failing Catholics, as the split-chamber was too lenient on Protestant suspects. So, in mid-January 1562, the coalition informed the *sénéchal*, Raffin, that all non-Catholics were to be excluded from serving on the *jurade* or *présidial*, citing the ancient custom and tradition of the town's charter as justification.[49] Raffin concurred, and sanctioned the law whereby only 'loyal and orthodox' candidates would be considered for office: restrictions that were to become the backbone of the Catholic usurpation of government during the 1560s.[50]

---

[45] Andrieu, *Histoire de l'Agenais*, I, p. 213.
[46] ADLG, E Sup. Agen, BB 30, fo. 83.
[47] ADLG, E Sup. Agen, FF 31 (20 October 1561).
[48] ADLG, E Sup. Agen, BB 30, fo. 83ᵛ.
[49] ADLG, E Sup. Agen, BB 30, fo. 84ᵛ.
[50] ADLG, E Sup. Agen, BB 30, fo. 86ᵛ.

It is at this point that a 'second phase' of Catholic activism is identifiable at Agen: the increased involvement of the Catholic nobility of the Agenais. To date, the defence of Catholic prerogatives had been confined largely to the struggle for pre-eminence within town government and regional council, championed by administrators and officials such as Lalande, de Nort, Raffin, Tholon and others. Now the Catholic cause would be bolstered by the participation of local elites, first supporting the coalition government so as to ensure Catholic domination of authority and administration, then moving to form a dedicated oath-bound league to unite and mobilize Catholic militants across the region. The impetus for both measures can be found in the activism of the *états d'Agenais*, an institution dominated by elite Catholic delegates who saw this regional assembly more as a forum for their personal grievances than as the three-tiered congress dedicated to discussion of local issues that it was in most other regions of France.[51] This was significant, for the *états* of 1560 were dominated by complaints of Protestant incursions and the denuding of elite prerogatives across the Agenais, with delegates advocating confrontation with the reformers rather than acceptance of the conciliatory policies being promoted by the crown. Indeed, noble discontent was such that a remonstrance was drafted by the assembly, calling for Catholic reinforcements to be dispatched to defend the region, to be financed by diverting taxes from the royal coffer into a military fund, and requesting a replacement for the ineffective Burie, who, the *états* claimed, was failing the Agenais as he rarely left the security of his base at Bordeaux.[52]

That a second appeal was issued by the *états* in March 1561 suggests that Catholics were far from satisfied with the crown's response to their initial draft. But this second document was more than a simple remonstrance; it laid out the administrative and military counter measures that should be forced upon all Protestant communities involved in civil disobedience.[53] That most of the region's prominent Catholics signed the appeal, including Monluc, the *comte* de Villars, and the *sieurs* de Lauzun, d'Estissac, Caumont, Negrepelisse, Tonneins and Biron, reveals the degree of consensus behind such a militant manifesto. It opened with the standard oath of the period, that all 'Catholic gentlemen' devote their goods, and their lives, to the defence of orthodoxy, and continued by suggesting that the crown would be better served utilizing the local Catholic nobility of the south-west to maintain the peace, rather than continuing with its ineffective policy of legislating for concord. Accordingly, if the king would grant

---

[51] Tholin, 'La ville d'Agen', XIV, p. 213.
[52] ADLG, E Sup. Agen, AA 43.
[53] BN Dupuy, 588, fo. 106.

Monluc – newly appointed as *lieutenant-général* of Guyenne – a company of *arquebusiers*, with full authority to deploy them as necessary against Protestants, the *états* were confident that order could be restored within two to three months.[54]

As such radical demands were impractical at this time, the crown dismissed the remonstrance. But confessional tension across the Agenais continued to worsen through the year, with the months of October and November 1561 witnessing especially brutal violence. One of the most notorious episodes was the murder of the baron de Fumel, in late-November. The significance of this event for Catholic militancy at Bordeaux has been explored above, but its consequences for the Agenais were no less dramatic. When the crown's initial investigation into the affair stalled, Monluc, a lifelong neighbour of Fumel, dismissed the commissioners, claiming they had failed to pursue the crime with sufficient vigour.[55] In order to continue the search for justice, Monluc subpoenaed eight officials from Agen to sit on a specially convened judicial panel. This was no time for *mi-partie* politics, and the eight judges were drawn from the coalition, all staunch Catholics who had each known Fumel personally. Tholon was appointed to preside over the board, with d'Aspremont, Gervais Heraudeau, the *prévôt-général*, and fellow Catholic *présidial* councillors, Robert de Raymond, Jean Jourdan, Florens du Repaire, Antoine de Nort and Saux Dupin serving on the panel. It was no surprise when, in late March 1562, guilty verdicts were returned on all fifteen suspects brought to trial, with Monluc's guard summarily executing the men the same day.[56] Orders were also given that the houses of two hundred others suspected of having taken part in the killing be razed to the ground. The town of Fumel also suffered: stripped of all privileges and ordered to pay an indemnity of 320 000 *livres*, its gates and walled defences were dismantled, as if to warn offenders that there was no place to hide from Catholic ire.[57]

Then, in early April 1562, the prince of Condé raised the Protestant banner at Orléans. Reform communities across France rose in support, and quickly gained control of important centres such as Rouen and Lyon, among many others. Incredibly, given the pre-eminence of the coalition, and the greater involvement of the Catholic nobility, Agen also fell, on 17 April, to a Protestant force that caught the authorities off guard.[58] The

---

[54] BN Dupuy, 588, fo. 106.

[55] [Monluc], *Commentaires, 1521–1576*, p. 488.

[56] [Monluc], *Commentaires, 1521–1576*, p. 489.

[57] Andrieu, *Histoire de l'Agenais*, I, p. 220. For the original sentence of the royal commissioners regarding the murder of Fumel, see *AHG*, 8, pp. 207–21.

[58] ADLG, E Sup. Agen, BB 30, fo. 87[v].

Catholic defeat was almost complete: all coalition officials were arrested and imprisoned, although Lalande managed to escape and flee to his fortified *château*; seventeen churches had been sacked and occupied by the reformers within the first week; all Catholic ceremonial was prohibited, with the cathedral now used as a site for *prêches*.[59] The situation was little better across the Agenais, with Lectoure, Tonneins, Villeneuve-d'Agenais and Nérac all falling to the Protestant generals Caumont and Duras.[60] The town of Condom, however, managed to resist, thanks to the initiative of its *lieutenant-sénéchal*, Dufranc. Dufranc had spent much of March 1562 trying to persuade the crown that wide-scale unrest was imminent. For lack of a response, he had taken the precaution of arming the Catholic elite of Condom in the name of the king, and had closed the gates to all reformers. Such pre-emptive action undoubtedly saved the town from falling to the rebels, a deed which Monluc found particularly impressive. In subsequent years he would often cite Dufranc's initiative at Condom as the model for Catholic governance of a town under threat.[61]

The crown's response to these uprisings was to ensure that Bordeaux was secured first and foremost, with Burie and Monluc ordered to move their troops to defend the capital. In his *Commentaires*, Monluc suggests that the royal orders did not sit well with the nobility of the Agenais, describing how, in May 1562, a delegation of Catholic notables met him at Lafox to urge their commander to stay: 'for if I was to abandon them, then all would be lost'.[62] While military memoirs are prone to such self-important rhetoric, Tholin cautions that Monluc's testimony should not be dismissed lightly, for the petition seemed to work, and Monluc decided to stay and fight alongside his compatriots.[63] After dispatching messengers to inform the king of this change of plan, Monluc set about boosting his troop numbers. Six new commissions were created, while the local nobles willingly placed their private retinues under his command. Next was the creation of a *conseil militaire*, the staple of Catholic militant associations now, so as to forge disparate elements into a concerted and co-ordinated body. Once this was achieved, Monluc assembled his forces at Faudouas, on 22 May, to plan his strategy.[64] One item of note from this

---

[59] A comprehensive Catholic account of the seizure and occupation of Agen by Protestants in April 1562 exists in the records of the *jurade*, written in November of that year. See ADLG, E Sup. Agen, BB 30, fos 96–99.

[60] ADLG, E Sup. Agen, BB 30, fos 88–91.

[61] [Monluc], *Commentaires, 1521–1576*, p. 499.

[62] [Monluc], *Commentaires, 1521–1576*, p. 498.

[63] Tholin, 'La ville d'Agen', XIV, pp. 506–7.

[64] Present at the council were leading *seigneurs*, Bajaumant, Cancon and Montferrand, the *sieurs* de Terride, Tilladet, Besoles, Gondrin, Jean de Narbonne, the *marquis* de Fimarcon, and 'plusieurs autres gentilzhommes'. [Monluc], *Commentaires, 1521–1576*, p. 499.

assembly concerns Monluc's report that the Catholic gentlemen swore to 'faire amis', a pledge of fraternity that would be common in later, larger leagues.[65] This suggests that the 'council of war' was more than an ad hoc arrangement, and that it constituted a formal association.[66]

Monluc's forces moved against the rebels at Agen in August 1562, regaining control of the town and freeing the incarcerated officials with little resistance. With the coalition restored to power, and the noble fraternity providing potent military support, Catholic dominance of the region was re-established. The repercussions were immediate and effective. Lalande was appointed military governor of Agen, and set about implementing a series of reprisals. Under the auspices of Monluc's *prévôt*, Hélie de Penchéry, *sieur* de la Justinie, Lalande ordered that over one thousand Protestant suspects be arrested and tried for insurrection, with around half hanged on town gibbets between August 1562 and March 1563.[67] The coalition then turned its attention to the sequestering of Protestant goods. On 9 September 1562, the *jurade* met to compile a list of prominent reformers whose houses were to be searched, careful to frame the legislation to imitate a recent ordinance promulgated by Burie and Monluc, which authorized the seizure of Protestant rebels' 'harvests' so long as they were taken 'in the name of the king ... and used to repair and fortify the town'.[68] In January 1563, the order was extended to encompass the sale of household furniture and even wine cellars belonging to the reformers.[69] The coalition also revived its policy of expelling suspicious persons from the town, although this became a contentious issue when the edict of Amboise permitted anyone accused of a crime to remain at their place of residence until after their trial.

This final point epitomized the new problems facing Catholic powers at Agen. They no longer faced iconoclasts and Protestant troops, but now had to navigate the labyrinthine legislation promulgated by the crown in its attempt to secure a cessation of hostilities and accommodate faiths across the realm. But a watershed had been reached; from meagre beginnings, Catholic activists had established themselves as a force to be reckoned with. Their ad hoc alliances of disparate factions within government institutions had coalesced into a formal, authoritative coalition party, which had gained the support of the *états* and local nobility. The town of

---

[65] [Monluc], *Commentaires, 1521–1576*, p. 499.

[66] Samazeuilth supports this assumption, noting that all the leading associates at Faudouas would go on to play key roles in Catholic activism across the Agenais over the coming decade: Samazeuilth, *Histoire de l'Agenais*, II, p. 99.

[67] Andrieu, *Histoire de l'Agenais*, I, p. 226.

[68] ADLG, E Sup. Agen, CC 65 (9 September 1562). For a list of prominent victims of this confiscation, see ADLG, E Sup. Agen, CC 304 (Comptes des Consuls).

[69] ADLG, E Sup. Agen, CC 302 (1563).

Agen itself had also been transmuted, emerging from the shadow of its imposing capital, to stand proud, side-by-side with Bordeaux as twin citadels of orthodoxy in Guyenne. These elements were about to fuse and culminate in the formation of an oath-bound, elite-led Catholic league at Agen, an association that threatened to move Catholic militant attitude from a defensive to an offensive posture, and to see the fight taken to the Protestant communities of the Agenais.

CHAPTER SEVEN

The Defence of Agen

The balance of power at Agen had shifted dramatically during 1562. The early dominance of the Catholic coalition had been ended abruptly by the Protestant coup of April, only for Monluc's forces to retake the town and re-establish Catholic authority in August. In response, the crown sought to negotiate a truce between the faiths, determined that conciliation offered the best hope for a lasting cessation of violence. As part of this policy, an amnesty for all religious prisoners was offered in October 1562, on the condition that active military commanders laid down their arms and came to the negotiating table.[1]

In the south-west, however, this move was greeted with outrage by the coalition, who viewed it as wholly biased against their co-religionists, as the majority of prisoners eligible for pardon in Guyenne and Western Languedoc belonged to the reformed faith. This opinion was shared by the *états d'Agenais* who, meeting in January 1563, derided the amnesty as little more than an attempt to appease Protestant grandees at court.[2] The delegates took particular exception to two facets of the crown's declaration. Firstly, they argued that no distinction had been made between Catholic and Protestant participation in the violence, which meant that honest Catholics were being tarred with the same brush as Protestant rebels in many instances. Secondly, they warned that, by pardoning prisoners already held in custody, the victims of their crimes were being denied the right to seek reparations from their assailants. This was especially pertinent to the nobility of the Agenais, many of whom had had their homes and property ravaged, their livestock stolen and their lands burned. To encapsulate their anger and sense of betrayal over the amnesty, the *états* drafted a remonstrance urging the crown to rethink its policy. Yet, perhaps anticipating a less than satisfactory reply, the assembly also voted to by-pass crown restrictions that precluded Catholic authorities from prosecuting Protestant suspects, so as to allow limited confiscation of property and possessions to recommence, and thus facilitate some recompense for Catholic losses.[3]

---

[1] The *lettres de grâce et pardon* were issued by the crown in October 1562. [Bèze], *Hist. eccl.*, III, pp. 48–54.

[2] See 'Procès-verbal des délibérations de l'assemblée des états du pays de l'Agenais' (January 1563), ADLG, E Sup. Agen, GG 201, fo. 2.

[3] For secondary material relating to these deliberations, see *AHG*, 39, pp. 28–9; Tholin, 'La ville d'Agen', XV, pp. 196–7; Courteault, *Blaise de Monluc, Historien*, p. 471.

Delegates then discussed the contentious issue of royal obligations, deciding that all dues owed to the *prévôt-général* of Agenais, an office known to be sympathetic to the reformers, should be diverted into the hands of Monluc's *prévôt*, Hélies de Penchéry, a solid Catholic who had been hand-picked by Lalande to oversee the execution of guilty suspects at Fumel the previous August.[4] This ploy had been first suggested over a year ago by Monluc, who saw the limiting of the judicial powers of the *prévôté* in the Agenais as key to reducing Protestant influence within the region's administration.[5] While a number of dissenting voices, concerned that it usurped jurisdictional prerogatives of the Bordeaux *parlement*, were raised at this measure, Catholic domination of the *états* was such that the proposal was passed by a majority decision.[6]

If unanimity of purpose now existed between coalition, *états* and Monluc's military forces, Catholic hegemony over the region was about to become even more extensive. On 4 February 1563, Monluc established a Catholic confederation at Agen, the first example in this period of an oath-bound association that incorporated provincial nobility, regional clergy and urban bureaucrats within its structures. The oath of association, sworn by all the leading Catholic nobles of the Agenais before the altar of the cathedral of Saint-Étienne at Agen, featured a standard preamble. Adherents swore loyalty to the crown, pledged to defend the province and the Catholic Church with their lives, and condemned the machinations of the reform party.[7] As with the syndicate at Bordeaux, the significance of this confederation has been played down by many commentators, who dismiss it as either a whim of Monluc or a trial run for the more prestigious leagues created at Toulouse and Cadillac the following month. Those who have examined its formation more closely, however, such as Andrieu and Tholin, believe the confederation was both an attempt to imitate and surpass the Protestant infrastructure established by the synods of Clairac and Sainte-Foy and a move to secure Agen without recourse to crown support.[8]

The confederation's ordinance is actually an extremely important document, as it provided a blueprint for subsequent association, and spelt out Catholic political and military organizational strategy in simple but effective regulations: firstly, energize all strata of Catholics – nobles,

---

[4] ADLG, E Sup. Agen, CC 65 (3 January 1563).

[5] ADLG, E Sup. Agen, CC 65 (17 November 1561).

[6] Andrieu, *Histoire de l'Agenais*, I, p. 227.

[7] For the ordinance establishing Monluc's 'Confederation and association between the habitants of Agen and the various towns and jurisdictions of the Agenais', see [Monluc], *Commentaires et lettres*, IV, pp. 190–95.

[8] Andrieu, *Histoire de l'Agenais*, I, p. 227; Tholin, 'La ville d'Agen', XV, p. 198.

clergy, officials and populace; secondly, unite them under a council or leader, in this case Monluc and Lalande; thirdly, combine Catholic institutions, resources and manpower to facilitate cooperative action where none had existed before; fourthly, secure the major urban centres by usurping government and establishing Catholic authority; fifthly, deploy trusted Catholics to guard duty and establish an armed militia ready to act at a moment's notice; and finally, divide the region and the towns into quasi-military cells, each to be administered by experienced captains.[9]

It is evident that Monluc was drawing on a number of recent examples of successful militancy in this blueprint, including the initiatives implemented by the reformed synods, the experiences of the syndicate at Bordeaux and the coalition at Agen, and his personal preference for harnessing the potential of the community rather than relying on external troops to defend a locality, a trademark of his organizational skills during the Italian campaigns of the 1550s. Monluc now ordered the ordinance to be published simultaneously in all neighbouring towns, and soon Quercy, Périgueux, Casteljaloux and Condom had signed an accord promising mutual cooperation. By disseminating the regulations, Monluc was promoting a sense of unification and interdependence among dispersed Catholic communities, thereby creating a quasi politico-military alliance across the region. This is an important point, for, while the edict of Amboise would censure the confederation within two months, its success in circulating the schematics for concerted activism, and in forming connections and defining relations that would allow Catholic militants to draw on a broader support base than ever before, were highly significant achievements. So, while Monluc would dismantle the physical manifestations of the confederation in April 1562, its legacy would remain intact for years, allowing Catholics to defend the Agenais in more depth and with more effectiveness than previously.[10]

To what extent were reformers and moderate royal officials able to resist this inexorable march towards Catholic hegemony at Agen? One option was to promote bipartisan government across the Agenais. This was now a real possibility, as a clause within the Amboise edict dictated that any Protestant *consuls* ejected from office during the wars should be free to return, and that *chambres mi-parties* should be installed within all *présidial* courts. But if this was supposed to usher in a new era of confessional relations, it did quite the opposite at Agen, choking *présidial* procedure and causing bureaucratic chaos as Catholic, moderate and Protestant officials splintered into factions. Competition centred on two

---

[9] [Monluc], *Commentaires et lettres*, IV, pp. 190–95.

[10] Monluc wrote to Catherine de Medici in April 1563 that he had ended the confederation at Agen. See [Monluc], *Commentaires et lettres*, IV, p. 205.

groups: the Catholic party, headed by the *lieutenant-criminel*, Antoine de Tholon, and the pro-reform delegation, led by the *juge-mage*, Herman de Sevin. Their agendas were quite different. Catholics sought to prosecute those guilty of attacks on their clergy and community over the previous months, while Protestants attempted to recoup the sums and property confiscated by the coalition. The result saw little accomplished by either group, as appeals and counter-claims were simply redirected so as to find favour in the judgement of sympathetic *mi-partie* judges.[11]

Relations deteriorated further when Lalande, recently promoted to the governorship of Agen by Monluc, complained to the crown that orderly governance of the town was impossible while Protestant judges continued to deliver biased judgements.[12] Sevin pulled no punches in his retort, reminding Lalande that Catholics no longer monopolized jurisdiction at Agen, and, consequently, the *jurade* should stay out of *mi-partie* affairs. The *juge-mage* then launched an attack on Monluc's confirmation of Lalande as governor, claiming it to have been a clear abuse of power, as the exercising of military prerogatives over civil jurisdiction had been terminated following the March peace edict, and demanded that a new governor be appointed, thoughtfully suggesting several highly placed Protestant nobles for the office.[13] This was not the new era of peace and harmony hoped for by the crown.

In fact, in the immediate months after the Amboise edict, tensions rose quite dramatically across the Agenais, resulting in episodes of sporadic violence between the faiths. In May 1563, Monluc informed Catherine de Medici that he had evidence of a Protestant plot to assault Agen, and urged Lalande to place the guard on twenty-four hour alert as a precaution. Lalande re-formed the *conseil militaire* and alerted the Agenais *états*, who met the following month to discuss the nobility's response to the worsening situation.[14] The minutes of this assembly are revealing. The *états* openly endorsed the administration of Monluc and Lalande, but demanded that an inquiry be held into the bias and mismanagement of Sevin and his Protestant consuls.[15] An investigation was duly launched and found Sevin guilty as charged, though this is hardly surprising given that the prosecutor was Estienne Thibault, a leading force in the Agen coalition over the past year.[16] Tholin suggested that the Catholic party

---

[11] Tholin, 'La ville d'Agen', XIV, p. 217.
[12] ADLG, E Sup. Agen, EE 56 (June 1563). Lalande was appointed governor of Agen on 17 April 1563: ADLG, E Sup. Agen, EE 56 (17 April 1563).
[13] Tholin, 'La ville d'Agen', XIV, p. 217. See also ADLG, E Sup. Agen, FF 32 (no folio).
[14] [Monluc], *Commentaires et lettres*, IV, pp. 255–62.
[15] ADLG, E Sup. Agen, EE 56 (28 June 1563).
[16] ADLG, E Sup. Agen, GG 201, fo. 3.

had no option other than to move against Sevin at this point so as to protect Lalande, whose governorship was continually being questioned by Protestant remonstrations.[17] That Catholics pooled and employed their full resources to effect this decision is reminiscent of affairs at Bordeaux, where Catholic magistrates united to minimize the attacks by moderate voices within the *parlement* on Lange and the syndicate. By contrast with Bordeaux, though, where Lagebâton had successfully deflected Catholic attacks, the Agen coalition, now supported by Monluc and the *états*, was victorious.

But Sevin had fled to Paris long before the verdict was delivered, and so escaped punishment. In his absence, contention within the chambers of the *jurade*, *présidial* and *sénéchaussée* was minimized, and the Agenais experienced a temporary lull in confessional tensions. The only major incident stemmed from the decision of the reformed synod of the Agenais in mid-1565 to employ full-time ministers for its temples at Sainte-Foy, Clairac, Tonneins and Nérac. Lalande argued that such appointments were illegal and, fearing they would raise the temperature across the province, recalled Monluc to Agen as a precaution.[18] When a large arms cache was discovered at Tonneins, and numerous skirmishes were reported across the countryside, Catholic leaders were forced to consider their next move carefully.[19] The coalition spent September and October weighing up their options, before settling on a plan of action. Lalande determined that, as Agen was the priority both for Catholics and for Protestants, any major confrontation would be centred on the town. He thus set about bolstering its defensive strength. Monluc's captain, Jehan Gasc, was recalled and appointed as military governor,[20] while the *conseil militaire* was charged with securing the town gates and searching all Protestant houses for hidden weapons.[21] As it turned out, however, the expected assault failed to materialize. Whether Protestant forces ever intended such a plan of action is unclear, although the coalition's pre-emptive posturing may well have deterred opposing generals from attacking at this time.

A stalemate thus ensued at Agen, lasting nearly two years, with neither Protestant nor Catholic forces pushing to gain an initiative. As at Bordeaux, the dynamic changed in September 1567, as formal hostilities

---

[17] Tholin, 'La ville d'Agen', XIV, pp. 213–16.
[18] ADLG, E Sup. Agen, BB 30, fo. 138.
[19] ADLG, E Sup. Agen, FF 32 (25 August 1565).
[20] ADLG, E Sup. Agen, FF 32 (16 November 1565).
[21] ADLG, E Sup. Agen, FF 32 (24 November 1565).

recommenced across France. When Condé ordered the Protestant army of the south-west into the field, under the *comte* de Montgommery, the crown wasted little time in ordering Monluc to marshal his forces and to convoke the Agenais *arrière-ban*.[22] At Agen, the governor, Lalande, drew up a rota of twenty-four trusted consuls to accompany the nightly patrol of the town,[23] while guards manning the gates were instructed to admit only those with valid identification passes or vouched for by Catholic residents.[24] By integrating the *consuls* with the town guard, the Agen authorities revealed that they had learnt from their experiences during 1562: the gates would not be opened surreptitiously in the dead of night on this occasion. These moves came just in time, as the Agenais was soon in open rebellion. The towns of Bergerac, Montauban, Moissac and Fronton fell cheaply to Protestant forces, although Catholic defences at Agen, Casteljaloux and Lectoure held firm.[25] Lalande convened the *conseil militaire* once more, and urged Monluc to mobilize the nobility of the Agenais.[26] Monluc's *Commentaires* describe how he, Antoine de Nort and Gratien Delas, together with a scribe and two secretaries, sat up all night writing and signing the two hundred dispatches containing the orders for this mobilization, while Pierre de Naux, Antoine's elder brother, searched for a sufficient number of messengers to deliver them.[27] Copies were also dispatched to the *parlements* at Bordeaux and Toulouse to inform their Catholic allies of their plans.

The coalition then turned to the financing of this war effort. The sequestration of Protestant goods and property had become the most effective means of fundraising for Catholic authorities, as it allowed instant accumulation of capital. On 8 October 1567, the coalition began seizing the assets of those reformers who had deserted the town to join their co-religionists at Montauban and Bergerac,[28] and two days later imposed a one-off fine of 500 *écus* on all wealthy Protestants of Agen.[29] The total raised from these impositions was significant. Between October and December 1567, the sum raised from the sale of sequestered goods amounted to 1178 *livres*,[30] while the confiscation of grain and wine real-

[22] ADLG, E Sup. Agen, BB 30, fo. 194.

[23] Barrère, *Histoire religieuse et monumentale du diocèse d'Agen*, I, p. 305.

[24] ADLG, E Sup. Agen, BB 30, fo. 147.

[25] Labenazie, *Histoire de la ville d'Agen*, I, p. 263.

[26] Labenazie, *Histoire de la ville d'Agen*, I, p. 264.

[27] [Monluc], *Commentaires, 1521–1576*, p. 606. For transcript of the letter, see Paul Courteault, *Douze lettres inédites de Blaise de Monluc, publiées et annotées* (Toulouse, 1898), pp. 12–17.

[28] Ordinance of 8 October 1567. ADLG, E Sup. Agen, GG 202, fo. 2.

[29] ADLG, E Sup. Agen, GG 202, fos 2ᵛ–5.

[30] ADLG, E Sup. Agen, GG 202, fos 2ᵛ–5.

ized 1014 *livres*.[31] Sevin would later claim that much of this money was diverted into the pockets of Catholic generals. However, records confirm that the majority went towards the strengthening of the town's fortifications.[32] Unfortunately, the sources do not detail the totals raised from the fining and taxation of Protestants, although the fact that the *jurade* was able to vote a gift of 200 *écus* to Monluc in December 1567 for 'services to the Catholic cause' suggests that the coalition had access to a fairly substantial sum.[33]

The confiscations also allowed the coalition to increase the number of troops garrisoned at Agen, which rose by 80 per cent over this three month period, and to pay experienced captains to command them.[34] On occasion, the policy of taxing Protestants and stockpiling troops proved problematic. At Francescas, for example, a one-off tax on Protestant residents generated sufficient funds to pay for a large force of Catholic troops to be garrisoned within the town, ostensibly to secure the main road south from the Agenais to Béarn. Within two months of its arrival, however, the Catholic council at Francescas was pleading with Monluc to remove the troops, claiming that the soldiers were causing havoc in the town. The town fathers seemed unconcerned at losing the financial advantage the policy had offered, they simply wanted order restored. In the end, they were forced to buy back the town's liberty, informing Monluc that, should the garrison be withdrawn, they would continue to collect the tax and forward it to Lalande at Agen.[35] At Casteljaloux, meanwhile, a different problem faced the town council. At the introduction of the punitive tax on Protestant residents, the reformers withheld their contribution to the *gages* in protest. This severely compromised the town's administrative budget and again forced a policy rethink.[36]

The boon of such financial expedients came to an end, however, with the peace of Longjumeau, in March 1568. With Catholic authorities

---

[31] ADLG, E Sup. Agen, CC 302 (1567).

[32] The accounts reveal that engineers were instructed to begin a survey of the state of the town's fortifications, and that a great deal of work had to be done to reinforce dilapidated sections of the defences: ADLG, E Sup. Agen, GG 202, fos 2–5. The destination of sequestered funds was also a contentious issue at Bordeaux. Here, Monluc claimed repeatedly that the receipts from the sale of sequestered property had been used to bolster the defence of the province and to pay his armies, whereas many moderates within the *parlement* accused the Catholic captains of simply diverting sums to their own pockets. For these contestations, see, for example, AMB, ms 771, fos 745–54.; BN ms français, 15 879, fos 226–38.

[33] ADLG, E Sup. Agen, BB 30, fo. 195.

[34] ADLG, E Sup. Agen, BB 30, fo. 199ᵛ.

[35] ADLG, E Sup. Agen, 2630 (*jurade* of January 1568).

[36] ADLG, E Sup. Agen, 2386 (1568).

ordered to show restraint towards their Protestant residents, income from emergency taxation and sequestration ceased to be available. Many councils now struggled to find the high level of expenditure needed to maintain garrison forces and continue with fortification works. At Agen, a budget deficit meant that the council was forced to borrow heavily to honour its commissions, although the fact that Catholic towns continued to maintain garrisons and build defences at pre-peace levels – in spite of the truce – says much about the negative perception of the new peace.[37] Both faiths, in fact, seemed dismissive of Longjumeau's ability to secure accommodation and end conflict. The Bordeaux *parlement* ridiculed the treaty as the 'petite' peace, claiming that it resolved nothing,[38] while Monluc dismissed it as nothing more than 'a settlement that allowed one to pause for breath and time to organise for war ... not a peace that would last'.[39]

Protestants were especially concerned at a clause within the edict that declared the crown's willingness to forget past misdemeanours so long as each subject was 'reunited under a single faith'.[40] This suggested that at some point attempts would be made to bring the reform movement back into the Catholic Church, an unacceptable caveat that was rejected by all Protestant theorists. Several historians have even viewed the Longjumeau edict as a catalyst for further conflict, rather than a mediatory event. Mack P. Holt, for example, asserted that by continuing in its adherence to accommodation, the crown was 'fuelling the flames of civil war', as many saw the edict more as a ruse to placate Protestant grandees at court than as a template for peace.[41] Holt continued by noting the burgeoning number of lay confraternities that emerged in the towns throughout the kingdom after Longjumeau, a visible sign of Catholic unease at the course of crown policy.[42] Paul de Félice was similarly damning of any pretensions the peace may have had of resolving the conflict, and also noted a rise in extremism as a result of the edict: 'the war did not stop ... it became a hidden war, one that encouraged the leagues of the ultra-Catholics and divided Protestants'.[43]

---

[37] The Agen council was forced to borrow 1423 *livres* in April 1568. The sum was made up of two loans. The first loan, totalling 1000 *livres*, was obtained from Madame l'Infanta de Portugal: ADLG, E Sup. Agen, BB 30, fo. 199. The second, totalling 423 *livres*, was from a local merchant, Jean de Vaus: ADLG, E Sup. Agen, CC 306 (April 1568).

[38] [Monluc], *Commentaires, 1521–1576*, p. 629.

[39] Monluc], *Commentaires, 1521–1576*, p. 628.

[40] [De Thou], *Histoire universelle*, V, p. 416.

[41] Holt, *The French Wars of Religion*, p. 67.

[42] Holt, *The French Wars of Religion*, p. 68.

[43] Paul de Félice, *Procès-verbaux de la prestation du serment de fidélité au Roi Charles IX par les Huguenots d'Orleans en 1568* (Orleans, 1882), p. 6.

The observation that Catholics were incorporating greater penitential and militant sentiment within their ritual certainly finds resonance at Agen. During March 1568, numerous local Catholic captains were presented with honours for service to the crown and the defence of the Catholic faith. But, rather than simple ceremonies before the *parlement*, the military awards were held in the town's cathedral of Saint-Étienne, attended by all leading coalition members, with Monluc and Lalande bestowing the decorations. Further, the festivities lasted over ten days, with prayers, masses, processions and the full paraphernalia of Catholic pageantry on display throughout.[44] Yet these events did little to prevent the continuing confessional tensions across the region and, by mid-1568, the coalition had become so inundated with complaints from Catholics over continuing Protestant violence that Lalande felt obliged to draft a lengthy remonstrance to the king. In it, he detailed the pillaging and razing of Catholic houses, the destruction of churches, the interruption of services and processions, and the increased frequency of armed assemblies as evidence that the treaty had failed the Catholics of the Agenais.[45] In fact the threat appears to have been so great that the coalition decided not to wait for the crown to respond. On 18 May 1568, it embarked on unilateral action to vet the town guard so that only Catholics were deployed, and to turn away all strangers and Protestants from the gates regardless of their business, in direct contravention of the edict, and of crown requests for moderation.[46] Lalande then ordered that jurisdiction over policing be removed from all *présidial* judges, a response no doubt to the spectre of Sevin.[47] The severing of traditional channels of government to exclude Protestant officials had been used by Catholics at Agen in 1562, but then they had been wartime expedients. Now, the coalition was attempting a similar move during peacetime, and in blatant contravention of numerous royal dictates. It was helpful, therefore, when the Agenais *états* endorsed Lalande's recent pronouncements at its June sessions.[48]

When hostilities resumed in October 1568, such overt shows of mutual support would prove invaluable for Catholics, as Condé assumed personal command of the Protestant forces in the south-west. The most

---

[44] On 9 March 1568, Monluc's right-hand man, Tilladet, and two of his captains, Laussan and Pausas, were awarded *l'ordre du roi* within the cathedral at Agen. The following day, two captains, Cassaniels and Cieurac, received the same honour, while captains Labories and Cancon, and de Berdusan, the *sénéchal* of Bazadois, received their awards on the 18 and 19 March, respectively. See Labenazie, *Histoire de la ville d'Agen*, I, pp. 264–5.

[45] ADLG, E Sup. Agen, EE 56 (1568).

[46] ADLG, E Sup. Agen, BB 60, fo. 210.

[47] The ordinance was revised in July 1568 to include a 1000 *livres* fine for anyone countermanding the order: ADLG, E Sup. Agen, BB 30, fo. 216.

[48] Andrieu, *Histoire de l'Agenais*, I, p. 241.

obvious consequence of this was that Protestant troop numbers now exceeded Catholic units in Guyenne for the first time in the wars, forcing Monluc to review his strategy. He realized that, if he concentrated his troops in an army large enough to meet the enemy in the field, it would leave the towns of the Agenais defenceless. This meant that Catholic centres would have to be organized and taught to defend themselves. To establish a framework for this, Monluc and Lalande divided the region into a number of cells, with small units of experienced soldiers detailed to coordinate local Catholic militias in each sector.[49] Once more, Monluc's predilection for invigorating the community to coordinate localized defence is seen, with the ordinance instructing town fathers to prepare Catholic homes, streets and parishes for all-out war.[50]

Financing such an effort also required innovation, and Monluc granted all Catholics permission to 'kill, massacre and cut to pieces' any reformers, and to 'ransom and take the possessions' of those who surrendered.[51] If this appears to be an act of desperation – the sequestration of Protestant goods had previously been the prerogative of the magistrates only, and Catholics had certainly never been allowed to kill Protestants at will – it was, for Montgommery and his viscounts were sweeping all before them on the battlefields of the south-west. Panic began to set in at many towns, with Lalande reporting that the Agen guard was obliged to prevent merchants and artisans from fleeing the town so as to avert an implosion of the local economy.[52] By mid-1569, with the Protestant forces advancing ever closer, and with no end to the warfare in sight, Monluc made the decision to concentrate his forces and focus on the defence of Agen at all cost. Should this pivotal centre fall, he concluded, the 'domino effect' for towns across the Agenais would be considerable. It would be a loss from which Catholics would struggle to recover.

Placing the main Catholic field army under the command of a trusted general, La Mothe-Gondrin, Monluc headed for Agen with a light complement of troops. He arrived in mid-November 1569 to find a population on the verge of flight. His subsequent actions serve to epitomize the extent to which Catholic unity had been cemented over the previous year, and to highlight the merits of communal defence in the face of overwhelming odds.[53] Immediately, Monluc convened an assembly of nota-

---

49 ADLG, E Sup. Agen, BB 30, fo. 210.

50 ADLG, E Sup. Agen, BB 30, fo. 211.

51 ADLG, E Sup. Agen, BB 30, fos 238–40.

52 [Monluc], *Commentaires, 1521–1576*, p. 739.

53 The account of the securing of Agen in November 1569 is taken from Monluc's own words, see [Monluc], *Commentaires, 1521–1576*, pp. 738–47. Historians such as Paul Courteault and Baron de Ruble accept Monluc's account as accurate.

bles from all sections of society – church, bureaucracy and citizenry – making use of the medieval tradition whereby a leader would appear in person before his audience to confirm his presence among them. He dismissed rumours that the leaders of Agen had deserted the town, urging the populace to be diligent and resolute. To rouse spirits, Monluc swore to 'live and die' alongside the townsfolk in the coming campaign, a pledge that seemed to galvanize the assembly, as spokesmen for the clergy and bourgeoisie then promised their lives to the cause. Martial de Nort, one of Monluc's oldest allies at Agen, completed the avowals, asserting that everyone in the town, rich and poor, women and children, had sworn to contribute 'without reservation'.[54] Monluc had succeeded in his first objective: to energize the community into participating in the defence of the town.

The next move was equally Monlucesque. Eight trusted consuls were selected to form an extraordinary 'council of war' to implement the mechanics of the defence. Ceding authority to an elite council served three purposes: it reduced the number of authority figures to a minimum, thereby obviating delay and miscommunication; it demonstrated to the populace that the town's hierarchy was willing to stand and fight on the front line with them, as each consul was to take their place at the barricades; it freed Monluc to focus on the overall defence of the town and to deploy his trained soldiers independently.[55] The next imperative was to reinforce the town's fortifications. Monluc ordered his engineer, Captain Toppiac, to demolish a number of houses and internal walls so that existing ramparts could be reinforced and several new forts built around the town's perimeter. Catholics whose homes had been knocked down during this programme were authorized to seize any house belonging to fugitive Protestants, while the few reformers that had remained in the town were forced to share their roof and food with garrison troops and construction workers.[56] The town was now prepared, and awaited the inevitable assault.

The planning and organizational measures implemented at Agen appear to have worked, as the integration of soldiery, militia and populace proved effective in staving off repeated assaults by Protestant forces over the following weeks. Further, Monluc's experience of urban resistance had ensured that Agen would survive without the main Catholic army being recalled: an important aspect, as it allowed La Mothe-Gondrin to continue

---

[54] Indeed, the pledge by Catholics of Agen to 'live and die' in the defence of the town became instantly celebrated, and was reported before the Bordeaux *parlement* within the week: BMB, ms 369, III, fo. 316.

[55] Labenazie, *Histoire de la ville d'Agen*, I, p. 268.

[56] ADLG, E Sup. Agen, EE 16 (16 December 1569).

protecting other Catholic communities across the Agenais. The fortitude of this defensive stand exemplified the progress made by Catholic activists across the region. It was a concerted and coordinated feat that would have seemed unimaginable to many in 1560. Then, organized militancy was a rarity, practised only by a few determined individuals. Over the following years, a coalition of the clergy and officials from the *jurade*, *présidial* and *sénéchaussée* had been formed that enabled Catholics to monopolize power at Agen and manipulate policy to oppose Protestant incursions. They were boosted by the support of the Agenais *états*, dominated at this time by the Catholic nobles and clergy who, as major landholders, were just as eager to halt Protestant attacks on their property. The *états* would prove an important buttress for the Catholic leadership at Agen, validating their political decisions and endorsing the diversion of regional finances into Catholic coffers.

The role of Monluc in these developments was, as elsewhere in the south-west, central to Catholic survival at Agen. It was Monluc who unified the clergy, nobility and magistrates in the confederation of 1563, and who inspired the new ethos of collective action to facilitate communal defence. Catholics of every social standing were roused to rise 'with teeth' to the challenge and to forge defensive cooperatives across the province. When opportunities for bipartisan cooperation presented themselves, Catholics rejected them out of hand. Such was the case with the introduction of *mi-partie* chambers within the *présidial* in 1563. These foundered within days of their introduction, as both faiths resorted to bias and favouritism to support their co-religionists rather than administer justice with impartiality. That the *mi-partie* experiment lasted at all was due largely to the indomitable spirit of Herman de Sevin, *juge-mage* and *président* of the *présidial*, whose defence of Protestant rights must have put Catholic militants in mind of Lagebâton's stubbornness within the Bordeaux *parlement*. Agen's survival in Catholic hands, then, was remarkable, especially given the intense onslaught by overwhelming Protestant forces, and the high concentration of reformed nobles and communities within the Agenais. So often the poor relation to the estimable citadels of Bordeaux and Toulouse, the town's contribution to the defence of Catholicism across the south-west, and its pivotal role in offering succour to its Catholic neighbours throughout the 1560s, should see it positioned firmly as a third and equal bastion of orthodoxy in the region. Such status is not reflected in the historiography of the religious wars to date.

A final point of interest relates to the role played by the de Nort family in this saga. The de Nort appeared to spawn a quasi-dynasty of Catholic activists at Agen during this period, headed by Martial de Nort, an old and trusted friend of Monluc, who held offices in the *jurade* and *présidial* courts throughout this period.[57] Martial's eldest son, Pierre, followed his father onto the *jurade*, while Antoine, his second son, served with distinction as an officer of the *sénéchaussée de l'Agenais*. Even the husband of Martial's eldest daughter also served on the *présidial*. While Martial and Antoine were often cited as members of Monluc's 'inner circle', Pierre became a trusted subordinate of the general's household staff, with all three serving in the Catholic coalition at Agen.[58] Protestant sources understandably vilified the de Nort for their zeal. Théodore de Bèze denounced Martial as 'a wicked man ... without faith or conscience ... a capital enemy of reformers', while Pierre was accused of committing numerous excesses against reformed communities at La Plume during 1561.[59] But there was nothing but praise from Protestant commentators for the black sheep of the de Nort family, Odet, Martial's third son. Odet had turned to the reformed church in 1558, preaching regularly at local *prêches* across the region. In 1560, he was appointed minister at the Protestant stronghold of La Rochelle, where he gained a reputation as a charismatic orator. His ability to rouse reformers to action brought condemnation from Catholics at Agen: Burie claimed that the unrest of January 1561 in the Agenais had been 'caused by the predications of Odet', while Tholin would assert that 'the *jurade* at Agen had its Brutus'.[60] Then, in April 1561, Antoine de Nort, Odet's brother, reported his sibling to the Bordeaux *parlement* as an iconoclast, involved in the sacking of several churches at Agen the previous month. Antoine concluded by requesting that action be taken to 'silence' such provocative activity.[61] This family split proved that even the most devout Catholic families could be divided along confessional lines during the Wars of Religion, an example that would be repeated many times across France during this time.

---

[57] Labrunie identified Martial de Nort as 'one of the most trusted of Monluc's councillors': Labrunie, 'Abrégé chronologique des antiquités d'Agen', p. 177.

[58] Labenazie, *Histoire de la ville d'Agen*, I, p. 275.

[59] See [Bèze], *Hist. eccl.*, I, pp. 874–7.

[60] Burie to Catherine de Medici (24 January 1561), *AHG*, 13, p. 151; Tholin, 'La ville d'Agen', XIV, p. 442.

[61] AMB, ms 767, fo. 366.

CHAPTER EIGHT

Confrontation and Insurrection at Toulouse

The third centre of Catholic militancy in the south-west was Toulouse. Situated on the western border of Languedoc, this fortified trading centre also sat on the banks of the river Garonne, its resident population of 50 000 swollen at various times by the arrival of merchants and traders from across Europe.[1] Governmental structures were dominated by eminent local families, staunchly provincial in their attitude. The civic corporation of Toulouse comprised eight elected city fathers, or *capitouls*, representing each of the town's eight *capitoulats*: Daurade, Saint-Étienne, Pont-Vieux, la Pierre, Dalbade, Saint-Pierre, Saint-Barthélemy and Saint-Sernin. Its jurisdiction over finance, justice, security and police derived from royal consent granted in the early thirteenth century, the only significant change being the creation of a parallel body, the *conseil de seize*, or *conseil de bourgeoisie*, in 1515, to deal with petty matters so as to relieve the growing administrative burden on the authorities.[2] The civic corporations of many towns in the south-west were perceived to be highly susceptible to religious innovation during the mid-sixteenth century, and the council at Toulouse was no exception. Sympathy for and affiliation with reform ideology came to mark the doctrinal persuasion of many of its *capitouls* during this time, so much so that, by 1560, Protestant representation within the administration began to concern Catholic leaders. Their fears were exacerbated by the rising number of reformed communities growing up in and around Toulouse, with the town's resident Protestant corpus estimated to have surpassed 9000 (18 per cent of the town's population) by 1562.[3]

Catholic influence in Toulouse centred on the *parlement*. Established in 1444, following a decree by Charles VII that a sovereign court be established within the château Narbonnais to ensure royal justice was upheld in this most distant outpost of France, the *parlement* of Toulouse began life as a *première chambre des enquêtes*. Between 1491

---

[1] For Toulouse population estimates, see Greengrass, 'The anatomy of a religious riot', p. 368, note 9.

[2] By 1650, the *conseil de seize* numbered over one hundred officials: Henri Ramet, *Le capitole et le parlement de Toulouse* (Toulouse, 1926), pp. 28–9.

[3] Schneider, *Public Life in Toulouse*, pp. 12–43.

and 1519, a *chambre criminelle*, or *tournelle*, was added, followed by a *chambre des requêtes* in 1543 and a *seconde chambre des enquêtes* in 1553.[4] By 1560, though, the rising number of cases dealing with 'religious offences' forced the creation of a new, temporary chamber at Toulouse, the *chambre extraordinaire*, which, at times, sat during vacations to clear the backlog of pending prosecutions.[5] As the *parlement* grew in size and prestige it began to encroach upon the jurisdiction of the town council, hearing appeals and intervening in the election of councillors.[6] Opportunities for contention between the two bodies thus increased steadily throughout the first half of the sixteenth century, only to multiply exponentially in the 1550s as the *capitouls* began to reveal their affiliation to the reform movement. This splintering of traditional orthodoxy placed council officials very much at odds with the largely Catholic *parlement*, who were by now attempting to censor pro-reform sentiment within the town, not least within its bureaucracy.

The remaining governmental bodies of Toulouse were split over these issues. Coming down firmly on the side of the Catholic *parlement* were the courts of the *sénéchaussée* and the *viguerie*, whose jurisdiction over policing and security offered Catholic magistrates additional influence within the region.[7] Taking a less zealous tone were the region's seven *présidiaux*: these new courts had been introduced in 1552 to augment the work of the *parlement* by dealing with criminal cases and civil litigation up to 2000 *livres*, though they lacked jurisdiction over appellate litigation. By favouring moderate over militant politics, though, the *présidiaux* found themselves at odds with Catholic hard-liners and, following the Protestant insurrection of 1562, they were forced to cede control of their chambers to the *parlement* until 1568.[8] The fourth body,

---

[4] Ramet, *Le capitole et le parlement de Toulouse*, p. 137. In 1549, the old château Narbonnais was dismantled to make way for a new *grand palais*, constructed under the guidance of Nicolas Bachelier.

[5] ADHG, B 53, fo. 969.

[6] By 1547, the *parlement* boasted four *présidents*, fifty-six *conseillers* (among them one George d'Armagnac, bishop of Rodez, soon to be cardinal and lieutenant of Toulouse), a *procureur-général* and two *avocats-généraux*. See Dubédat, *Histoire du parlement de Toulouse*, I, p. 324.

[7] The *viguerie* at Toulouse comprised the *viguier*, two *lieutenants*, several *conseillers*, a *procureur*, two *avocats du roi* and numerous *docteurs* and *greffiers*. See Ramet, *Le capitole et le parlement de Toulouse*, p. 120.

[8] Zeller, *Les institutions de la France*, pp. 175–7. The *présidial* at Toulouse was well staffed, consisting of a *juge-mage*, seven *conseillers*, a *lieutenant-principal* and *lieutenant-particulier*, a *juge-criminel* and his *lieutenants*, approximately thirty serving *avocats*, *procureurs* and *huissiers*, a *procureur du roy* an *avocat du roy'* and six *greffiers*. See Ramet, *Le capitole et le parlement de Toulouse*, p. 120.

the *états de Languedoc*, met so infrequently during the religious wars that its influence on events was minimal.[9]

Alongside these demographic and administrative similarities, Toulouse mirrored Bordeaux in other important ways: the infiltration of reform ideology into the region and its impact on communal relations. As at Bordeaux, it was through the University of Toulouse, another important seat of Humanist learning throughout the early sixteenth century, and the agitation of its *écoliers* that religious disturbances were first witnessed on the streets of Toulouse.[10] As early as 1534, the *parlement* was forced to ban all *écoliers* from carrying arms because of repeated clashes with local Catholic residents,[11] while the 1530s would witness the first burnings of students accused and convicted of heresy.[12] Throughout the 1540s, the *écoliers* were constantly in trouble with the *parlement*, most frequently for their involvement in running battles with Spanish residents of Toulouse.[13] On one occasion, in 1542, the scale of the fighting was such that the town guard were unable to restore the peace, and it was only when a band of local artisans joined the melee, aggrieved at their homes being damaged in the tumult, that the students were finally subdued. But pacification came at a cost. As well as a number of serious injuries, the *parlement* ordered several *écoliers* to be executed for inciting the riot, with many more exiled from the town. Two of the town gates had also been badly burned in the incident and needed replacing, while several nearby houses suffered extensive damage to their facades.[14]

The *écoliers* continued their defiance into the 1550s, despite more of their number being burned for rioting in 1555.[15] In the following year measures were implemented to provide greater protection for students: the creation of 'nations' within the university, with the *écoliers* organized in distinct bands, and captains appointed to coordinate defence and oversee discipline.[16] These quasi-military cadres mirrored developments at the *collège de Guyenne*, and

---

[9] For the limitations upon the influence of the *états* of Languedoc during the religious wars, see Zeller, *Les institutions de la France*, pp. 57–70.

[10] Davies, *Languedoc and its Gouverneur,* p. 28; Philippe Wolff, *Histoire de Toulouse* (Toulouse, 1974), pp. 264–9.

[11] *Arrêt du parlement* (27 February 1534), AMT, AA 17, no. 55.

[12] Dubédat, *Histoire du parlement de Toulouse*, I, p. 174.

[13] See, for example, *Arrêt du parlement* (14 May 1540), AMT, AA 18, no. 35; ADHG, B 37, fo. 458ᵛ (31 May 1544).

[14] Dubédat, *Histoire du parlement de Toulouse*, I, pp. 192–3. For similar confrontations between *écoliers* and Catholics at Avignon, see Venard, *Réforme Protestante*, pp. 438–41.

[15] AMT, BB 269, fo. 74.

[16] For the organization of *nations* at the University of Toulouse, and an overview of student life there, see John Charles Dawson, *Toulouse in the Renaissance* (New York, 1966), pp. 95–140; Wolff, *Histoire de Toulouse*, pp. 266–7.

elicited a similarly harsh response from the Toulouse *parlement*, who ordered they be disbanded with immediate effect.[17] The court also instructed all hoteliers and innkeepers to refrain from accommodating student gatherings, and urged the clergy to check their churches for illicit assemblies each night.[18] But these initiatives met with only limited success, as throughout 1560 armed bands of *écoliers* were reported roaming the streets of Toulouse with impunity, disrupting Catholic ceremonials and damaging property.[19]

The spread of evangelical fervour across western Languedoc left Catholics bewildered. Yet the *écoliers* and itinerant preachers would not have complete licence, as Catholic individuals and small groups soon began to confront the reformers at every opportunity. As at Bordeaux, it was those members of the community whose day-to-day activities brought them into contact with the reformers who were at the vanguard of the Catholic reaction, most notably the clergy and *confrères*, whose services and processions came under frequent attack, and the *basoche*, the actors and musicians who provided accompaniment for Catholic ceremonial across the city. But whereas at Bordeaux it was the symbiotic relationship between the Confraternity of Saint-Yves and the *basoche* that fired Catholic activists against the town's *écoliers*, at Toulouse there was a subtle difference: there was no overt interaction between *confrères* and *basoche* within the town. This was due to the fact that at Toulouse the *basoche* were independent of the corporation of *avocats*, having been established as a feature of town life long before the birth of the confraternity. They had their own institutions and traditions, quite separate from the confraternal environment, and while they were still the sole performers at the festivities surrounding Saint-Yves ceremonials at Toulouse, they were far from being the subsidiary group.[20]

---

[17] AMT, AA 17, no. 210.

[18] AMT, AA 17, no. 210.

[19] For the unrest of 4 May 1560, see AMT, CC 1705, fo. 22. For the unrest during the Toulouse *jour des jeux floral* in 1560, see AMT, BB 11, fo. 182ᵛ. For the illegal assembly of *écoliers* at a *prêche* on rue des Vigoreux on 10 March 1560, see Lafaille, *Annales de la ville de Toulouse*, II, p. 207.

[20] As stated above, it was traditional that the *basoche* of French towns provided the music, performances and even the cakes and hats of flowers for those attending the festivities surrounding Saint-Yves. This tradition was adhered to at Toulouse. See ADHG, E 1013, pièce 1. For an informative history of the corporations of *avocats* and *procureurs* within the *parlement* of Toulouse, see André Viala, *Le parlement de Toulouse et l'administration royale laïque, 1420–1525 environ* (Albi, 1953), pp. 301–57. For informative histories of the *basoche* at Toulouse, see G. Boyer, 'La basoche Toulousaine au quinzième siècle, d'après les archives du parlement', *Mémoires de la société archéologique du midi de la France*, 18 (1932), pp. 64–71; Abbé Cau-Durban, 'Statuts de la basoche du sénéchal de Toulouse', *Mémoires de la société archéologique du midi de la France*, XVI (1908), pp. 166–84; René Glangeaud, *La basoche de Toulouse* (Toulouse, 1912); E. Vaïsse-Cibiel, 'Notes rétrospectives sur la basoche Toulousaine', *Mémoires de l'académie impériale des sciences, inscriptions et belles-lettres de Toulouse*, 6 (1868), pp. 221–43.

There was another important distinction between the Bordeaux and Toulouse *basochiens*. At Toulouse, there were two distinct corporations of players: the *basoche du palais*, represented only by procurers, clerks and secretaries of the *parlement*, and the *basoche de la sénéchaussée et de la viguerie*, composed mainly of lesser and apprentice clerks.[21] While both groups could trace their roots to the registration of the *parlement* in 1444, their customs and devotions had developed in quite varied ways.[22] The *basoche du palais* were based within the *parlement* chapel, dedicated to the Holy Trinity, while the *basoche de la sénéchaussée* held Saint John the Evangelist as their patron, taking mass at the collegial church of Notre Dame in the Carmelite convent.[23] But while the *basoche du palais* were permitted to elect an honorific *roi* to represent the corporation before the *parlement*, the *basoche de la sénéchaussée* were refused this right, having to content themselves with a titular *sénéchal* who, while able to speak on behalf of his members before the court, lacked the privileges associated with the office of *roi de la basoche*.[24] G. Boyer has suggested that the *basoche du palais*, which had a high concentration of 'bonne bourgeoisie' and rising nobility among their corpus, actively perpetuated this disparity to maintain a separation between themselves and the lower ranking officials from the *sénéchaussée* and *viguerie*.[25]

In one respect, however, the Bordeaux and Toulouse *basochiens* were very similar: their overexuberance and unruly behaviour were rarely forcibly reprimanded by the Catholic *parlement*. There appear to be two explanations for this temperate approach. Firstly, many of the magistrates at Toulouse had started out as *basochiens* during their youth, and so identified with and were lenient towards such exuberance.[26] Secondly, it became clear from early on that it would be the *basoche* who would champion the cause of orthodoxy against the evangelicals on the streets of Toulouse, and they therefore required a degree of support from the Catholic magistrates.

---

[21] Cau-Durban, 'Statuts de la basoche', p. 168. Paris had four such corporations: *la basoche du palais*, *la basoche du châtelet*, *la basoche de la chambre des comptes* (also known as *l'empire de Galilée*) and *les enfants sans-souci* (also known as *les Sots*): Harvey, *Theatre of the Basoche*, p. 17.

[22] The *basoche du palais*, in fact, claimed an unbroken lineage back to King Dagobert. See Boyer, 'La basoche Toulousaine', p. 64.

[23] The *basoche du palais* celebrated their feast day on Trinity Day, at the end of Easter, while the *basoche de la sénéchaussée* celebrated on 25 November, the feast of Sainte-Cathérine. See Glangeaud, *La basoche de Toulouse*, p. 5.

[24] Dubédat, *Histoire du parlement de Toulouse*, I, p. 311.

[25] Boyer, 'La basoche Toulousaine', p. 64.

[26] For examples of *basochien* unruliness being treated leniently by the court in the early sixteenth century, see ADHG, B 20, fo. 73 (8 February 1524); AMT, FF 609, II (*Arrêt du parlement*, 28 January 1537). See also Glangeaud, *La basoche de Toulouse*, p. 4; Dubédat, *Histoire du parlement de Toulouse*, I, p. 314.

The *basochien* counter-offensive at Toulouse thus deviated little from the course of events at Bordeaux: songs and performance were saturated with Catholic doctrine and polemic; student-organized proceedings were interrupted and evangelicals attacked on the streets; and Protestant misdemeanours and crimes were reported to the authorities so as to support calls for more stringent anti-reform legislation. Yet in another important way the two were quite different. The *basoche* at Bordeaux drew on the religiosity of their senior colleagues in the Confraternity of Saint-Yves for statements of dogma and polemic. At Toulouse, however, the two groups drew from their own confraternal base: the *basoche de la sénéchaussée* had established their confraternity, dedicated to the Holy Trinity, in November 1516;[27] while the *basoche du palais* followed suit somewhat later, being granted permission by the royal council to establish their own brotherhood in 1560, having previously frequented the Church of Our Lady of Nazareth, the native church of the Confraternity of Saint-Yves.[28] For Vaïsse-Cibiel, the switch by the *basoche du palais* from sharing the Nazareth church to the creation of a dedicated confraternity chapel revealed the extent to which penitential fervour and reverence for Catholic tradition had come to dominate the responses of Toulousains to the increasing threat posed by the reform movement in the south-west, and especially the troublesome *écoliers* and evangelists.[29]

The wisdom in supporting the *basoche* was brought home to Jean de Mansencal, the *premier président* of the *parlement*, in 1561, when over four hundred *écoliers* from the university gathered outside his house to demand a specific place of worship within Toulouse.[30] Further provocation followed, with *écoliers* and *basochiens* clashing regularly across Toulouse, despite a series of decrees aimed at restricting the movement of the students and demanding the disarming of all such groups.[31] Matters became so

---

[27] See ADHG, B 20, fo. 110. See also Cau-Durban, 'Statuts de la basoche', p. 167.

[28] The *basoche du palais* had a private decorated chapel within the Church of Our Lady of Nazareth. This church of the Confraternity of Saint-Yves still stands, just inside the *Porte de Montgaillard*, bearing the inscription of a clerk of the *basoche* on its wall: 'Sanctus Yves erat Brito, Advocatus et non latro, Res miranda populo': Dubédat, *Histoire du parlement de Toulouse*, I, p. 263. The *avocats* of the *confrérie de Saint-Yves* were still using the church of Nazareth for their ceremonials in 1760. See N. Ricard, *Panégyrique de Saint-Yves, Patron de MM. les Avocats (prononcé dans l'église de Nazareth)* (Toulouse, 1764).

[29] Vaïsse-Cibiel, 'Notes rétrospectives sur la basoche Toulousaine', p. 227.

[30] *HGL*, 11, p. 333.

[31] At the *Pré des Études*, in July 1563, hundreds of students gathered to interrupt a *basochien* performance before launching a violent assault against the few assembled members of the town guard. See Lafaille, *Annales de la ville de Toulouse*, II, p. 259. Such activity continued intermittently throughout the decade, with further reproving *arrêts* issued in 1565 and 1568, and numerous students were brought before the courts for assembling under 'nations', electing captains, carrying weapons and various other illegal activities. See *Arrêt du parlement* (1565), ADHG, B 58, fos 461–2; *Arrêt du parlement* (18 January 1568), AMT, AA 18, no. 173.

unruly, in fact, that in late 1562 the governor of Toulouse, George, Cardinal d'Armagnac, informed the crown that even the town's villains were now dressing in scholastic robes as a disguise while breaking the law so as to take advantage of the poor reputation of the *écoliers*.[32] Throughout these confrontations, the Toulouse guard struggled to maintain order, often having to request assistance from various bodies to disperse the larger crowds.[33] Here, the authorities clearly suffered in comparison with the Catholic administration at Bordeaux from the absence of an energized confraternal militia that could augment the guard in times of trouble.

In order to address this problem, the *capitouls* moved to create a new policing body within Toulouse to ensure security and maintain the peace. Control over policing measures and deployment of the guard had customarily been the remit of the civic corporation and, throughout the 1540s, the size of the guard at Toulouse remained constant at seventy men, commanded by a captain, two lieutenants and eight sergeants, all lodged in permanent accommodation near the town's prison.[34] Now, though, a new subsidiary force of one hundred men was raised, to be placed under the jurisdiction of the guard captain, but to be selected by the town's *dizainiers*, who would also accompany the guard in its daily duties, to avoid charges of bias and sectarianism.[35] By late 1561, however, the rising scale of the unrest meant that even this measure was proving ineffective in quashing violent episodes within the town, forcing the *capitouls* to raise and dispatch everlarger ad hoc patrols containing mostly non-commissioned citizens.[36] The Catholic *parlementaires* took issue with these developments. They complained to the crown that the *capitouls* were coopting a disproportionate number of Protestant citizens into the guard who, in turn, were allowing greater numbers of their co-religionists through the town gates.[37] The magistrates alleged that the crown's *arrêts*, which aimed to prevent illicit preaching, armed assemblies and the distribution of seditious propaganda, were being compromised by these activities, and requested that the *capitouls* vet more carefully those deployed to guard the town.[38]

---

[32] AMT, BB 269, fo. 89ᵛ.

[33] Lafaille, *Annales de la ville de Toulouse*, II, p. 208.

[34] AMT, CC 1705, fos. 16; 26. Lamouzèle stated that this was organized along the model adopted by the royal army, in that the *capitouls* selected the guard captain but trusted in his judgement to elect suitable subordinates and capable soldiers: Edmond Lamouzèle, *Essai sur l'organisation et les fonctions de la compagnie du guet et de la garde bourgeoise de Toulouse au XVIIe et au XVIIIe siècle* (Tulle, 1906), p. 14.

[35] *Délibérations du conseil* (26 September 1560), AMT, BB 11, fo. 199ᵛ.

[36] AMT, BB 11, fo. 224ᵛ; CC 1708, fo. 31; CC 1699, fo. 462.

[37] AMT, AA 18, no. 80.

[38] Specifically the two *arrêts* of 15 January 1561, ADHG, B 54, I, fo. 72, and 2 May 1561, AMT, AA 18, no. 71.

In an attempt to calm the situation, the crown appointed a local Catholic noble, Antoine de Lomagne, the *sieur* de Terride, as military governor of Toulouse on 1 September 1561. His remit was twofold: to act as mediator in the dispute between *parlement* and *capitouls* over policing and security, and to bolster royal authority by ensuring that the crown dictates were implemented fully. By October, Terride had garrisoned his entire force within the walls of Toulouse and removed authority over the guard from the corporation until further notice.[39] The *capitouls*, however, were outraged at such an affront to their traditional prerogatives and asserted that the town's charter not only placed control of the guard in their hands, but precluded the appointment of a town governor, or the garrisoning of royal troops, without the consent of the city council.[40] They were also unhappy about the appointment of such a staunch Catholic to the governorship: Terride had been an active supporter of the Catholic party at Bordeaux and had served as a captain under Monluc since 1560. Protestant grandees at court baulked at such a résumé and, in December 1561, the crown was forced to bow to pressure and recall Terride. If Terride's appointment had proved contentious, the tenure of his replacement, the *comte* de Crussol, would be an unmitigated disaster. Not only was the count's promotion opposed vehemently by Catholics at Toulouse, who found such a controversial candidate unpalatable as town governor and refused to cooperate with his councillors, but Crussol soon defected from royal office to assume the role of military protector for Protestants in Languedoc.[41]

The controversy over Terride and Crussol's tenure only served to heighten confessional tensions at Toulouse. Matters were not helped by the inflammatory rhetoric emanating from Calvinist ministers and psalm-chanting students on the one hand, and Catholic preachers and the activists of the *basoche* on the other. It was during this turbulence that a syndicate of Catholic clergy, judges and lawyers was alleged to have been active at Toulouse.[42] Little is known of the conduct of this militant presence, however, until the appointment of two Catholic *présidents* of the *parlement*, Latomy and du Tournoir, to its leadership in March 1562.[43]

---

[39] ADHG, B 54, II, fos 760–61, 802.

[40] AMT, AA 18, no. 76.

[41] Dubédat, *Histoire du parlement de Toulouse*, I, p. 371; Lafaille, *Annales de la ville de Toulouse*, II, p. 210.

[42] Greengrass, 'The anatomy of a religious riot', pp. 370–71.

[43] Unfortunately, there is a paucity of surviving archival material to enable a more detailed survey of the syndicate in late 1561. Whereas, at Bordeaux, the political and financial machinations of its syndicate left a brief yet discernible trail within the *registres du parlement*, similar records are not available at Toulouse, destroyed perhaps by defeated Leaguers in the 1580s and 90s, keen to erase any references to their past misdemeanours.

Then, numerous councillors, advocates, procurers and captains are seen enlisting and pledging to join in the extirpation of 'all those of the new religion'.[44] For the *Histoire ecclésiastique*, the duke of Guise was behind this oath, as a letter was delivered to 'the Catholic council at Toulouse' from the duke's Paris *hôtel* ordering the *parlement* henceforth to treat all reformers as traitors, as the king had revoked the edict of January.[45] This of course was a falsehood, and the letter appears apocryphal, but the episode serves to reveal the intensity of the struggle between the faiths at this moment, and the urgency of Catholic leaders to take and hold the moral high ground in the contest.

The formation of the syndicate revealed the rising militancy that was characteristic of sectarian relations in Toulouse during early 1562. For Denis Crouzet, this manifestation of Catholic angst was fuelled by anger at the concessions granted to the reformed church by January edict, and by its exclusion of the *parlement* from jurisdiction over the sites of reformed worship. The establishment of a reformed consistory in Toulouse in late January 1562 did little to alleviate Catholic anxiety.[46] In an attempt to defuse these tensions, the *parlement* and *capitouls*, now overtly alienated along confessional lines, agreed to hold a summit meeting to debate recent developments.[47] The *capitouls* opened the disputation, held on 3 February 1562, by expressing concern at the continuing infringement on policing and security by the *parlement*. The magistrates countered by arguing that the growing number of illegal *prêches* and armed assemblies held by reformers required a greater policing effort to maintain the peace. When the *capitouls* began their counter-argument, a number of militant Catholics rose and walked out of the meeting, stating that they were unwilling to debate with 'known heretics'. As they left, they presented the chairman with a remonstrance detailing Catholic grievances against the Protestant community of Toulouse and damning the complicity of the *capitouls*. The fact that the remonstrance was already prepared and signed – it had been drawn up at a secret meeting of

---

Philippe Tamizey de Larroque has examined those materials that survive and, while he found little evidence to confirm the structure or activities of the Toulouse syndicate in its initial phase, he did accept that it 'existed on paper in late 1561'. See Tamizey de Larroque, 'Lettres inédites du Cardinal d'Armagnac', p. 26.

[44] Greengrass, 'The anatomy of a religious riot', pp. 370–77; see also [Bèze], *Hist. eccl.*, I, p. 911.

[45] [Bèze], *Hist. eccl.*, I, pp. 824–5, 911.

[46] Crouzet, *Les guerriers de Dieu*, I, pp. 380–81. In fact, Crouzet saw the syndicate as a milestone in the evolution of Catholic activism at Toulouse, the first step in a progression through ever-increasing levels of militant Catholicism that would culminate in the hegemony of the *Sainte Union* after 1584.

[47] For details of the debate, see ADHG, B 55, fo. 178.

Catholic militants four days earlier – suggested that this bipartisan endeavour had been doomed from the start.[48]

Needless to say the *capitouls* and moderate officials condemned this deception and blamed Catholic radicalism for the current state of confessional relations across the region. This argument foundered somewhat two days later, though, when a report was presented before the *parlement* stating that several *capitouls* and much of the town guard had recently been sighted attending an illegal *prêche* in a suburb of Toulouse. This not only confirmed the militants' suspicions, but it begged an important question for Catholics: could the *capitouls* be trusted to preside over the contentious issue of validating sites of reformed worship – jurisdiction had only recently been taken out of the hands of the *parlement*s and given to local councils by the edict of January 1562 – if they and their families were regular attenders of these assemblies?[49]

Sectarian tensions were now at breaking point. In April 1562, the crown's carefully nurtured policy of conciliation and coexistence shattered at Toulouse. The first critical event occurred on 2 April, with the attempted appropriation of a corpse from a reformed burial service by a Catholic congregation, who wanted the body interred within the local Catholic cemetery. The confrontation soon became violent, with the town guard needed to separate the worshippers and restore order. The situation escalated during the evening, however, as several Protestants attempted to seize the Town Hall to express their grievances against Catholic intimidation. The authorities were only able to effect a truce by offering both communities significant military concessions: perhaps not the best solution for long-term stability, but for the current volatile situation it was effective. As a result, Protestants were now allowed to maintain a 'security force' of two hundred guards, though they were to remain unarmed, while Catholics were permitted a similar number, to be commanded by four professional captains.[50] Unfortunately, these concessions failed to secure détente, as the four Catholic captains were unwilling to take orders from the *capitouls*, and refused to allow their men to assist in council-sponsored searches of Catholic houses for hidden weapons.[51]

By May 1562, the whole country was in the grip of sectarian conflict. At Toulouse, further contestation flared between the faiths at the decision by the *sénéchal* and *parlement* to convoke the *ban-et-arrière ban* to secure the town against the threat of insurrection. As they had with Terride's

[48] 'Remonstrances faites aux capitouls sur les exces commis par les Protestants' (31 January 1562), ADHG, B 55, fo. 174.

[49] AMT, BB 269, fo. 81 (4 February 1562).

[50] Greengrass, 'The anatomy of a religious riot', pp. 373–4.

[51] [Bèze], *Hist. eccl.*, III, p. 8.

garrison troops, the *capitouls* objected vehemently to the presence of the *ban* within the town, citing clauses within the civic charter that prevented armed soldiers gathering within Toulouse without their consent. The *parlement*, though, ignored these protests and, on 10 May, over two hundred armed Catholic nobles entered the town.[52] But despite this ominous Catholic presence, and the continuing machinations of the syndicate, it would be the Protestants who seized the initiative at Toulouse. In the early hours of 13 May 1562, reformers erected barricades at strategic points in the town, overran the *maison de ville*, broke into the town arsenal and distributed arms and munitions to their supporters.[53] The rebels were on the verge of gaining control of one of the major citadels of the south-west of France, a coup that would enhance Protestant military potential in the region enormously.

The Catholic response says much about its capacity to rally and organize various sections of society to a common objective. The *parlement*'s first reaction was to send for the leading Catholic captains of the region: Monluc, Terride, Negrepelisse and Bellegarde. While Monluc and Bellegarde moved to intercept a Protestant relief army travelling south, Terride and Negrepelisse arrived at Toulouse the following day and deployed their troops.[54] Requests for help had also been dispatched to neighbouring Catholic nobles, and within twenty-four hours Toulouse brimmed with armed elite retinues.[55] The Catholic counter-offensive was now directed from the *parlement* building by the *premier président*, Mansencal, and *présidents* Latomy and de Paulo. According to Georges Bosquet and the *Histoire ecclésiastique*, this committee established a number of ad hoc commissions to collect finances, to oversee the distribution of arms and artillery, and to interrogate suspects.[56] The town guard was also reorganized to make it more effective. Firstly, the main body was divided into smaller sections to allow each unit to be deployed more rapidly, and to concentrate on more specific areas of the town. Sixty additional Catholics were then levied to boost these numbers, with experienced

[52]   AMT, BB 104, fo. 530.

[53]   ADHG, B 55, fos 414^v–15; AMT, GG 824, fos 22–7. For details of the insurrection at Toulouse in May 1562, see Emile Connac, 'Troubles de mai 1562 à Toulouse', *Annales du Midi*, 3 (1891), pp. 310–39; Davies, 'Persecution and Protestantism', pp. 31–51; Greengrass, 'The anatomy of a religious riot', pp. 367–91.

[54]   BN nouv. acq. français, 6001, fos 136–7. Ironically, Terride and Negrepelisse had been ordered by the crown to secure Toulouse only five days earlier, but could not travel to the town in time to prevent the insurrection.

[55]   Lafaille, *Annales de la ville de Toulouse*, II, pp. 226–8.

[56]   Again, the *Histoire ecclésiastique* attributes this response to the Catholic syndicate, [Bèze], *Hist. eccl.*, III, pp. 20–40. Bosquet also alludes to this Catholic collective, but does not give it a formal title. See AMT, GG 1022 (15 May 1562).

military veterans appointed as captains and sergeants to command each sector of the town, thereby replacing the civilian officers who had led the guard in peacetime. Precise routes were devised for the patrols, with passwords required for each checkpoint and barricade, and all Catholics of the town were required to wear a white cross, sewn onto their garments to indicate their confession. Finally, strict regulations were drawn up by the committee to govern the conduct and discipline of the guard, with disobedience punishable by death.[57]

The syndicate played a vital role here too. Unlike the situation at Bordeaux, where Lange's association comprised lesser officials of the *parlement*, the Toulouse corpus was a more heterogeneous entity, including members of the clergy, merchants and bourgeoisie, as well as lawyers, judges, *confrères* and *basochiens*.[58] Many of these men had been active in the street fighting of the previous months, with some no doubt veterans of the confrontations with the *écoliers* of the preceding decades. Having such experienced militants manning the barricades and rousing the citizenry to action would prove invaluable during the skirmishes, and the combination of sound organization, astute guard deployment, intervention from local noble retinues and popular activism from syndicate and citizens turned the tide in favour of the Catholic forces. On 19 May, the Catholic leadership felt confident that the battle was won, and began cleansing the town's administration, summarily dismissing those Protestant *capitouls* and magistrates who had not yet fled the town, and filling the vacant offices with trusted Catholics.[59] This policy had an immediate benefit. Before the insurrection, any sizeable deployment of Catholic troops and militia on the streets of Toulouse elicited determined complaints from the *capitouls*, who were rarely backward in citing their ubiquitous civic charter to support their claims. Now, though, with much of the civic corporation peopled by staunch Catholics, protestations against such deployment fell away.[60] As Ramet observed, by August 1562

[57] For these developments, see AMT, EE 26 (May 1562). See also AMT, AA 14, no. 4.

[58] Greengrass, 'The anatomy of a religious riot', pp. 380–81.

[59] The *parlement* appointed Guillaume La Laine, bourgeois, Jehan de Borderia, *avocat*, Pierre Madron le jeune, François de Saint-Felix, *docteur*, Ramon Alies, *avocat*, Etienne de Rabestans, *seigneur* de Colomiers, Gaston du Pin, *bourgeois* and Laurent de Puybisque, *seigneur* de la Landelle. Their oath of office was sworn the same day, 19 May, before the *premier président* Jehan de Masencal and *présidents* Antoine de Paulo, Jehan Daffis, Nicolas Latomy and Michel Dufaur: AMT, AA 18, no. 88.

[60] ADHG, B 55, fo. 569. It should be noted, however, that, as soon as the ousted consuls were reinstated to office by royal decree, in November 1562, they demanded that all Catholic troops vacate the town immediately, and that the privileges of the civic corporation be respected once more in full.

the *parlement* had redefined the town council as a tool of the Catholic party, rather than the irritant it had tended to be in former years.[61]

Recrimination and retribution now followed. In June, the *capitoul*, Mandinelli, became the first consul to be condemned for his part in the unrest; his goods were confiscated and sold off to contribute towards the repair of the town.[62] Further purges ensued, with seven more *capitouls* condemned in absentia, their effigies hung in the Place Saint-George before a vociferous Catholic crowd. Each was banished from Toulouse in perpetuity, fined 100 000 *livres* and excluded from the nobility, a punishment also visited on their immediate family members.[63] As a warning, the court ordered that their sentences be read out each 17 May to remind the citizens of Toulouse of the ever-present threat posed by Protestantism to society.[64] Such was the new mood of fanaticism at this time that even moderate Catholics came under suspicion, the most prominent being the *président*, Dufaur, who was accused of aiding and abetting the insurrectionists. In fact Dufaur was only saved from the ignominy of arrest and prosecution by the personal intervention of Monluc, who vouched for his long-time friend's orthodoxy.[65]

The Catholic victory against the rebellion of May 1562 owed much to the willingness of the nobility, magistrates, bourgeoisie and minor officials of Toulouse to unite in defence of the town. The experience and fervour of activists such as the *basoche* and the syndicate also helped, ensuring that Catholic tactics were carried out effectively and forcefully, and with the full support of the Catholic community. In the weeks following the insurrection, two individuals were singled out by the *parlement* for their professionalism and swiftness of action during the crisis. The first was Bellegarde, the *sénéchal*, whose staunch resistance at the town gates against overwhelming Protestant forces was awarded formal recognition by the magistrates, so as to 'stimulate the zeal of the defenders of the true Catholic church in future battles'.[66] The second commendation

---

[61] Ramet, *Le capitole et le parlement de Toulouse*, p. 29.

[62] AMT, AA 18, no. 89. The sale of Mandinelli's property raised 1000 *livres*.

[63] AMT, AA 14, no. 1.

[64] AMT, AA 18, no. 96.

[65] Dubédat, *Histoire du parlement de Toulouse*, I, p. 398. Dufaur had served as a *juge au présidial* at Toulouse (1531–35), *juge-mage* at Toulouse (1535–47), *président du parlement* at Toulouse (1557–72) and was appointed *conseiller au grand'conseil* in May 1556. See [Monluc], *Commentaries, 1521–1576*, p. 1249, note 3. For accusations and subsequent enquiry into the role of Dufaur in the insurrection of May 1562, see AMT, GG 826 (17 May 1562).

[66] The *parlement* suggested that the crown should grant Bellegarde a number of ecclesiastical benefices in recognition of his services: *Parlement* of Toulouse to Charles IX (18 July 1562), ADHG, B 1906, fo. 75ᵛ; *Parlement* of Toulouse to Pius IV (13 November 1562), ADHG, B 1906, fo. 84.

was offered to Monluc and his captains for their tireless work in routing the Protestant forces outside the town. Raymond de Pavie, baron de Fourquevaux, may have overstated the Gascon general's personal intervention when he noted that 'without the help of Monluc, Toulouse would have been lost'.[67] But his was certainly not a lone voice, as many militant contemporaries lauded the role played by Monluc and his forces here.

Catholics at Toulouse, then, had survived a most stern test. Moreover they achieved a degree of supremacy by the summer of 1562 that far exceeded the political situation of their compatriots at Bordeaux, who were still fighting against the intransigence of Lagebâton and the moderate party within the *parlement* as much as they were at war with Protestant armies on the battlefield. The Catholics of Toulouse would now use their success as a springboard for more confident action, with three significant episodes of militancy emerging in subsequent years: an oath-bound noble league, founded in March 1563; a coalition administration that would govern the region during the crises of 1567 and 1568; and a crusade of September 1568, financed by the *parlement*, sanctioned by the papacy and nurtured within the town. Although diverse in nature and ambition, these three phenomena would reveal a maturation of Catholic militancy over the decade, to the extent that, by 1570, Toulouse would be established as an unassailable Catholic stronghold of the south-west.

---

[67] Fourquevaux to Saint-Sulpice (17 June 1562); Cabié, *Guerres de religion dans le sud-ouest*, pp. 4–5.

CHAPTER NINE

Militant Ascendancy at Toulouse

In the aftermath of the failed Protestant coup of 1562, Catholics at Toulouse moved to secure the town against a repeat occurrence. The *parlement* and town council were purged of reform sympathizers, the guard was reinforced and Catholic nobles patrolled the hinterland. In September 1562, one of the heroes of the defence, George, Cardinal d'Armagnac, received promotion to the office of *lieutenant du roi* at Toulouse, augmenting Catholic hegemony within the town.[1] But if Toulouse was now firmly in Catholic hands, large areas of western Languedoc were falling to the armies of Duras and Crussol, two of the most able Protestant captains of the period. When the reformers won a series of stunning victories at Montauban, Pamiers and Castres, Toulouse was left more isolated than ever. In October 1562, Armagnac, who now assumed a more prominent role in Catholic leadership at Toulouse, dispatched an urgent appeal for reinforcements to the crown, noting that the town was making preparations for an imminent assault.[2] But, rather than send troops, the royal council advised the cardinal that it would be implementing a truce in an attempt to bring both sides to the bargaining table. To show good faith, the crown had published an amnesty, with immediate effect, granting a pardon to all prisoners held since the start of the troubles.

Catholics met this decision with disbelief, and no little trepidation, as the jails of Toulouse were crowded with captured Protestant captains and their defeated soldiers. Freeing so many fighting men while the town was still surrounded by Duras's forces seemed suicidal, and the *parlement* refused to ratify the amnesty. It dispatched a *conseiller* of the court, François de la Garde, to report Catholic disenchantment at the crown's policy, and to ask to be exempted from the amnesty. But the king refused, reaffirming the edict on 9 November 1562, and ordering the Toulouse *parlement* to open the gates to its cells.[3] Matters worsened in December when intelligence revealed that Duras and Crussol intended to 'hijack' the

---

[1] AMT, AA 18, no. 103 (1 September 1562); ADHG, B 55, fo. 512. George, Cardinal d'Armagnac (born 1500), bishop of Rodez (1529), bishop of Vabre (1536), bishop of Lescar (1555), cardinal of Toulouse (1544), archbishop of Toulouse (17 August 1562). See Abbé Cayre, *Histoire des évêques et archevêques de Toulouse* (Toulouse, 1873), pp. 329–31.

[2] Cardinal d'Armagnac to Catherine de Medici (14 October 1562), AMB, ms 299, fos 127–9.

[3] Dubédat, *Histoire du parlement de Toulouse*, I, p. 401.

états of Languedoc, due to open later that month at Carcassonne, to extort yet more concessions on behalf of the reformers. A secret assembly was convened to decide the Catholic response. Present were the region's leading militants: Armagnac; cardinal Lorenzo Strozzi, bishop of Albi and king's lieutenant in the Albigeois; *présidents* Jean Daffis and Antoine de Paulo; numerous magistrates of the court; and leading representatives of the Catholic nobility including Monluc, Terride, Negrepelisse, Joyeuse and Forquevaux.[4] It was agreed that Monluc should move his troops from Agen to guard Toulouse and its environs for the duration of the *états* in case Protestant forces attempted to assail the town while all eyes were on Carcassonne.[5] In his *Commentaires*, Monluc boasts that he 'did not need to be asked twice' to take on this duty,[6] though in reality he must have been slightly concerned as the centre of his military jurisdiction lay in Guyenne, not Languedoc, which was the seat of his long-time antagonist, the Constable of France, Anne de Montmorency.

This pre-emptive move appeared to work, as Duras declined confrontation with Monluc's forces. Angered by the threat of Protestant intimidation, the *états* promulgated a radical agenda. After venting their fury at the crown's recent bias towards the reformers, the delegates passed a motion calling for the raising of 300 000 *livres* to fund the reclamation of Catholic lands lost during the fighting. The sum would be accumulated through three initiatives: the sale of sequestered Protestant goods and property, a tax on non-Catholic citizens of Toulouse and fines against those failing to attend mass at Easter. To facilitate the latter, registers of all those attending Easter mass across Languedoc were to be compiled, with Armagnac and Joyeuse appointed to bank the accumulated funds.[7] The momentum had shifted back to the Catholic powers at Toulouse, and Armagnac used this breathing space for consolidation. Monluc was persuaded to remain at Toulouse for the time being and help coordinate Catholic military policy, while *présidents* Daffis and de Paulo orchestrated Catholic reorganization of authority within the *parlement* and among the *capitouls*. In December 1562, the two were competing against each other for the vacant office of *premier président* of the court, after the

---

[4] Monluc to Catherine de Medici (10 December 1562), BN ms français, 15 877, fo. 446; [Monluc], *Commentaires et lettres*, IV, pp. 182–5.

[5] The mayor of Bordeaux, Antoine de Noailles, wrote that Monluc had been summoned to Toulouse by Armagnac to 'keep an eye on the intrigues of Crussol while the *états de Languedoc* are held at Carcassonne', Antoine de Noailles to Catherine de Medici (7 December 1562), *AHG*, 17, p. 284.

[6] [Monluc], *Commentaires, 1521–1576*, p. 576.

[7] For the text of the deliberations of the *états de Languedoc* (Carcassonne, 11–27 December 1562), see ADHG, C 2281, fos 113–56. See also Armagnac to Charles IX (22 December 1562), BN ms français, 15 877, fo. 468.

death of the incumbent, Jean de Mansencal. Daffis gained most votes and duly assumed the premiership.[8] Meanwhile, in another close ballot, Bellegarde was re-elected to the office of *sénéchal*, defeating Jacques de Peyrusse, *sieur* de Merville, the brother of the Bordeaux governor, d'Escars. While both were proven Catholic hard-liners, Bellegarde's extra political and military experience was preferred by the Catholic leadership, and his valiant service during the recent coup must have gained a few extra votes.[9] In a letter to Catherine de Medici, Monluc related how such initiatives were helping to forge close bonds between the Catholic leadership at Toulouse, a unity that would, in his opinion, 'greatly enhance the prospect for security across the region'.[10]

As if to reinforce this accord, Armagnac and Monluc made great show of rewarding two of their most trusted captains, Negrepelisse and Forquevaux, presenting each in February 1563 with *l'ordre du roi* at a lavish ceremony in the cathedral of Saint-Étienne at Toulouse. The service was attended by numerous Catholic dignitaries from across the region, including the exiled bishops of Castres and of Tarbes, who performed the ceremonial mass.[11] Then, later that same month, Armagnac ordered the *président des enquêtes*, Jean Barthélemy, to set aside 500 *livres* from court funds towards the building of a Jesuit *collège* at Toulouse.[12] The re-establishing of Jesuit influence in Toulouse had long been a priority for the cardinal, who had already permitted a number of Jesuit refugees from Pamiers to reside in the old Augustinian monastery on rue Saint-Jérome after 1561.[13] In September 1566, Armagnac's designs would come to fruition, with the founding of a Jesuit *collège* 'for the instruction of the young' at the *hôtel de Bernuy*, on rue Gambetta, financed from the *parlement*'s coffers.[14] To head this establishment, Armagnac secured the services of Edmond Auger, the leading Jesuit theologian of the region,[15]

---

[8] ADHG, B 55, fo. 575ᵛ.

[9] 14 January 1563. ADHG, B 1906, fo. 83ᵛ.

[10] Monluc to Catherine de Medici (28 December 1562), BN ms français, 15 877, fos 473–4.

[11] AMT, BB 269, fo. 89ᵛ.

[12] ADHG, B 56, fo. 178.

[13] ADHG, B 58, fo. 79. For the history of the Jesuits in Toulouse, see Jules Chalande, 'Les établissements des Jésuites à Toulouse au XVIe et XVIIe siècle', *Journal de Toulouse*, 29 (August 1926), pp. 1–35; Lafaille, *Annales de la ville de Toulouse*, I, pp. 278–80; P. Delattre, *L'établissement de Jésuites en France* (5 vols, Engheim, 1949–57), IV, p. 1274; Émile Picot, *Les Italiens en France au seizième siècle* (Rome, 1995); E. Piaget, *Histoire de l'établissement des Jesuites en France (1540–1640)* (Leiden, 1893).

[14] AMT, BB 173, fo. 51; ADHG, B 1907, fo. 69ᵛ.

[15] See 'Contrat passé entre le syndic de la ville et M. Edmond Auger, principal de la religion et congrégation des Jesuites en la province d'Aquitaine, pour l'établissement d'un collège à Toulouse, destiné à l'instruction de la jeunesse' (6 September 1566), AMT, AA 14, no. 113.

and although Auger would leave Toulouse in March 1569 to join Lange and Roffignac at Bordeaux, the court would report in 1571 that the Jesuit presence within the town was 'vibrant'.[16] It was also some time during January 1563 that Armagnac and Monluc held further talks over the state of affairs in Languedoc. Little is known about this 'secret' meeting, but over the following weeks Catholic military activity at Toulouse was noticeably more intense.[17] The *parlement* voted to set aside 500 *livres* per month to maintain Monluc within the town, while Strozzi and Forquevaux were each charged with procuring large quantities of cannon balls and gunpowder from Marseille and Narbonne, respectively.[18] Monluc now split his time between his two administrative centres, re-organizing his forces under Terride at Toulouse before ensuring his Catholic garrisons across the Agenais were provided with one month's pay in advance so as to allow him and his captains to concentrate on affairs in western Languedoc.[19] It was during one of these return trips, in early February, that Monluc oversaw the creation of the Catholic confederation at Agen.[20]

At Toulouse, meanwhile, Catholics set about re-emphasizing their authority within the town. On 3 February 1563, the *parlement* requested and was granted permission from the crown to confiscate all goods and property from those reformers found guilty of causing unrest.[21] Soon afterwards spies were deployed to watch the houses and track the movement of suspect Protestants, so as to report any suspicious activities to the court.[22] But the Catholic powers were not entirely unopposed here, as many of the *capitouls* dismissed from power the previous year had since been reinstated to office by crown dictate. They now set about making life difficult for their opponents. Their first act of defiance came in response to Armagnac's restructuring of the guard. The lieutenant had wanted to deploy six Catholic captains, each with a corps of one hundred armed men, to patrol the streets night and day with immediate effect, only for the *capitouls* to stall over their consent for several

---

[16] AMT, BB 173, fo. 111. It is interesting to note that, when the Jesuits were once more expelled from France in 1594, following the accession of Henry IV, their companies at Toulouse and Tournon were the only two to be allowed to remain.

[17] For these meetings, see *HGL*, 5, p. 249.

[18] AMT, BB 269, fo. 89ᵛ; *Commentaires*, p. 576.

[19] *Ordonnances de Monluc* (4–6 March 1563), [Monluc], *Commentaires et lettres*, IV, pp. 199–201, 201–2.

[20] *Ordonnance de Monluc* (4 February 1563), [Monluc], *Commentaires et lettres*, IV, pp. 190–95.

[21] Catherine de Medici to *parlement* of Toulouse (3 February 1563), AMT, AA 44, no. 22; Charles IX to *parlement* of Toulouse (3 February 1563), AMT, AA 44, no. 23.

[22] AMT, BB 107, fos 178–80.

weeks.[23] In early March, the *parlement* lost patience with the council and sent Catholic troops to remove the keys to the gates from the town hall and hand them over to the cardinal's captains.[24]

Throughout this time, rumours had begun to circulate alleging that Armagnac and Monluc were in the process of creating a military league of Catholic nobles, similar to that established recently at Agen, under the auspices of the *parlement* at Toulouse. It seems that intelligence of such a 'plot' emanated from two sources: testimony given before the Bordeaux *parlement*, on 9 February, by a certain captain Peyrot;[25] and a report presented before the Spanish ambassador in Madrid that same week by a gentleman named La Rivoire.[26] It would appear, however, that Catholic commanders may have been toying with their Protestant rivals, leaking the rumours in the hope of tempting their opponents into premature responses, as Peyrot was none other than Monluc's Agenais captain, while La Rivoire was a personal secretary to Armagnac. Myth became reality on 2 March 1563 as the new militant association was formally unveiled at a ceremony within the town's cathedral, attended by the usual suspects: Armagnac, Strozzi, Daffis, de Paulo, Monluc, Terride, Negrepelisse and Bellegarde, along with most of the town's officials and leading bourgeoisie, and many Catholic nobles from the surrounding countryside.[27]

The statutes of the Toulouse league were more mature than those of its predecessor at Agen, not only laying out Catholic plans to counter Protestantism but outlining expected standards of social behaviour and religious observance of adherents.[28] They also stipulated that all Catholics sign up to and support the association without delay and exception: anyone who contravened the directives was to be fined heavily. As such, copies of the league's ordinance were then printed and distributed to all the towns of the *ressort*, where they were to be proclaimed by town criers and displayed for all to see. This appears to have been a deliberate attempt by the Catholic hierarchy to legitimize its confederation by employing protocols usually reserved for the publication of royal edicts.

---

[23] AMT, BB 269, fo. 89.

[24] AMT, BB 107, fo. 296.

[25] Ruble, *Jeanne d'Albret*, p. 347, note 1.

[26] La Rivoire to Saint-Sulpice (14 February 1563), Cabié, *Guerres de religion dans le sud-ouest*, p. 23.

[27] Courteault, *Blaise de Monluc, Historien*, p. 472.

[28] 'Traite d'association et ligue de ceux de Toulouse pour la deffense de la religion Catholique', AMT, AA 18, no. 110. For secondary material relating to the Toulouse league, its oath and the pledge to take up arms to defend Catholic religion wherever necessary, see [Bèze], *Hist. eccl.*, III, pp. 60–65; *HGL*, 5, p. 249; Lafaille, *Annales de la ville de Toulouse*, II, pp. 62, 254; Lecler, 'Aux origines de la Ligue', p. 196.

Of course, the text was replete with the usual deferential formulations, professing that the association had been formed 'at the king's pleasure'. Such phrases were intended to protect Catholics from charges of subversion, although, in reality, the leaguers had no intention to attend to the wishes of the crown.

Just as at Agen, Bordeaux and Cadillac, Catholic aspirations at Toulouse were foiled by the arrival of the peace of Amboise, which banned all such associations from the towns and countryside of France.[29] Although the edict was not fully ratified by the *parlement* until the arrival of Henry de Montmorency-Damville, the new governor of Languedoc, on 21 July 1563, the Catholic leadership at Toulouse dissolved their league with immediate effect.[30] Reaction to this setback was mixed. Armagnac spared little time in warning Catherine de Medici of the dangers that her concessions had imposed on the fragile nature of affairs in Languedoc: 'we are in great danger from the seditious now ... and now that our adversaries hold the countryside, the populace is taking up arms once more and fighting one another, with little I can do to prevent this. The people are shouting that I should act, that this peace has created a black cloud under which their throats will be cut, and I fear our enemies will come to take the town once more'.[31] Monluc, on the other hand, was more reserved, noting in his *Commentaires* that 'the king commanded me to observe fully the peace edicts, which I had always done ... so I departed Toulouse ... war would not be started under my government'.[32] So, while the edict was debated at Toulouse, Monluc withdrew to his home at Estillac and busied his troops with affairs at Agen. If the general had decided to curb his militant tendencies and toe the royal line at this moment, the same cannot be said for Armagnac and the *parlementaires* at Toulouse who, despite ratifying the Amboise edict within a month of its arrival, refused to distribute it or to display it on open view anywhere across the province, claiming that it was so unpopular it would provoke the Catholic populace into civil disobedience.[33] This was in stark contrast, then, to the fanfare that had greeted the distribution and posting of the league's ordinances the previous month.

---

[29] The edict of Amboise was dispatched to Toulouse on 19 March 1563, carried by the *seigneur* de Caylus. It arrived on 8 April, and was provisionally registered by the *parlement* the following week, on 15 April. AMT, AA 14, no. 19.

[30] ADHG, B 56, fo. 472ᵛ.

[31] Cardinal d'Armagnac to Catherine de Medici (13 April 1563), AMB, ms 299, fos 116–19.

[32] [Monluc], *Commentaires, 1521–1576*, p. 589.

[33] Cardinal d'Armagnac to Catherine de Medici (16 April 1563), AMB, ms 299, fos 119–22.

Unlike its sister associations at Agen and Cadillac, the Toulouse league has received a fair amount of historiographical analysis over recent years. Ruble speculated that it was born as much out of Catholic disenchantment at crown policy as out of distaste for Protestantism, and he saw the exasperated militant delegates at the *états* of Languedoc in December 1562 as its architects. For Ruble, the *états* and the secret conference between Monluc and Armagnac were the forums in which the template for the association – and the league at Agen for that matter – was conceived. This would explain why the two bodies were so similar in structure and intent.[34] If this is correct, then perhaps the mobilization of troops and armaments under Monluc, Strozzi and Negrepelisse in January and February 1563 was also part of this design, a scheme to create an independent Catholic army able to be deployed in the interests of the leaguers across the south-west. De Lamar Jensen, on the other hand, pointed out that the text of the *traite d'association* of the Toulouse league encouraged participation from a broad spectrum of the community, and so should not be seen entirely as a tool of the Catholic elite.[35] For Jensen, the involvement of the middle and lower orders, even if they were ultimately directed by the elites, was an important characteristic of the early militant bodies across the south-west, not just at Toulouse. The participation of the *basoche* and the syndicate in the defence of Catholicism at Toulouse tends to bear out this theory. Here, street performances by minor and apprentice officials of the court were able to energize the wider community, while the syndicate assumed a more menacing tone once formal conflict was under way after 1562. In both instances, the activism of popular and bourgeois elements served to assist the Catholic leadership in instigating organized responses to Protestant threats and to augment the defence of Catholicism in the town. The terms of the ordinance itself also tend to support this supposition: 'it is useful and expedient to demand that confederation and association will be made between the ecclesiastical estate, the nobility and the commune of the third estate, and the habitants of the towns, dioceses, *sénéchaussées, vigueries et juridictions* of the *ressort* of the *parlement* of Toulouse'.[36]

In his study of the later *Sainte Union*, Mark Greengrass accepted that a broad spectrum of society was involved in part in the activities of the league at Toulouse, but stressed that contributors were strictly governed by the rigid infrastructure imposed by the governing elite of the sovereign court: 'individuals from the *parlement* played a leading role in the organ-

---

[34] [Monluc], *Commentaires et lettres*, IV, p. 190 note 1; *HGL*, 5, p. 249.

[35] See Jensen, *Diplomacy and Dogmatism*, p. 39.

[36] AMT, AA 18, no. 110.

isation, and the *ressort* of the *parlement* was regularly used to delineate their region. The *parlement* legalised them and encouraged neighbouring towns and nobles to join movements, which it saw as self-defensive organisms to supplement the efforts of local governors and seneschals'.[37] Denis Crouzet placed far more emphasis on the penitential ethos driving the Toulouse league. For Crouzet, Armagnac's *association* was an amalgam of sorts, possessing both an elite head and a more inclusive body, with magistrates, nobles, clergy, bourgeoisie and citizens all active in their own way, each empowered to fulfil their respective, if disparate, goals. Yet contemporary understanding of these goals was far from cohesive: some wanted the association to defend their traditions and prerogatives; others wanted it to protect their space and property; while others desired that it should inflict violence upon, or bring to justice, heretics and villains. To Crouzet, the league was strong, yet malleable, able to cater for various interested groups while unifying Catholics under a single banner.[38]

A noticeable omission from these studies is any discussion of the potential of the league to secure Catholic hegemony at Toulouse. This is puzzling considering the tangible revisions that were made to the town's taxation and militia-levying structures by the Catholic leadership at this time, and especially the controversial punitive measures taken against local Protestant communities to finance the Catholic war effort. Such legislative authority was certainly not available to the activists at Agen and Bordeaux or to Catholic nobles at Cadillac in 1563. And, despite its termination in late April, the spirit of such endeavour can be seen to have persisted in subsequent policy decisions taken by the Catholic hierarchy. On 10 May 1563, for example, the *parlement* ordered all serving officials to profess their faith publicly before Armagnac in the town's cathedral and to swear 'to live and die in the observation of the constitutions of the Holy Mother Roman Catholic Church'.[39] Those that refused were duly ostracized from government. Dubédat saw this as evidence that the Catholic hierarchy intended to consolidate their domination of political and military affairs at Toulouse despite the setback of the peace edict, with this oath-swearing ceremony reinforcing the sense of community and cooperative spirit that had been engendered during

---

[37] Mark Greengrass, 'The *Sainte Union* in the provinces: The case of Toulouse', *SCJ*, 14, 4, (1983), pp. 471–2.

[38] Crouzet, *Les guerriers de Dieu*, I, pp. 380–86. Again, Crouzet saw this association as a precursor to later crusading ideology at Toulouse, its *raison d'être* no longer simply the defence of the Catholic faith and the curtailment of Protestant injustices, but the reinvigoration of the Catholic Church across France.

[39] ADHG, B 56, fos 285–96ᵛ (10 May 1563).

recent months.[40] The crown, however, was concerned at such discrimination and dispatched two *maîtres des requêtes* from Paris to force Armagnac and Daffis to refrain from excluding non-Catholics from office. But the leaders at Toulouse were not prepared to allow Protestants who had participated in the coup of May 1562 to serve within the town's government, and chose to frustrate the *maîtres des requêtes* at every turn, much as their Bordeaux counterparts had done at the arrival of royal commissioners. Their means of doing so was ingenious. Daffis ordered that the procedure for appellants claiming wrongful dismissal from office as a result of the 'profession of faith' be changed. Instead of receiving a single hearing before an appeal panel and judge, each appellant would now be interrogated before a special committee of magistrates. This committee would review the evidence and determine a decision, but maintained licence to transfer any contentious cases to Paris for arbitration. This was a perfect means of procrastination, for if the initial hearing was time-consuming in itself, the dispatching of trial material to Paris and the return of the crown's verdict was an extremely lengthy process. Further, once the court had received the crown's judgement, it had the option of restarting the proceedings from scratch, effectively initiating a retrial. Catholic lawyers made such good use of this tactic that on average each appeal by disgruntled reformers took over six months to resolve.[41]

Another aspect of the commissioners' work to be frustrated by Armagnac and Daffis was the restitution of Protestant goods confiscated over the past year. In late May 1562, the *maîtres des requêtes* complained that their investigations were being hampered by Catholic magistrates who now refused to countenance any appeal that concerned articles or property that had 'changed in their nature or usage since confiscation'.[42] Further, they noted that the facility to allow the families of deceased Protestants to reclaim inherited offices was also being incorrectly administered, as Catholic magistrates were demanding that indisputable first-hand testimony be presented before lawyers for validation before the case could proceed to court. In most instances, finding such testimony was difficult enough; now, Protestant appellants had also to convince Catholic officers of its validity. And, as Lafaille noted sardonically, even

---

[40] Attending were Armagnac, Daffis, de Paulo, Latomy, Barthélemy, Reynier, Boyer, de Molinier, du Solier, d'Alzon, Hébrard, du Tournoer, Coignard, Forest, Fabry, Papus, Bonald, de Lauselergie, d'Aussonne, d'Arjac, Boisson, de Gargas, Bruet, de Guilhemette, d'Ouvrier, de Nupces, de Murel, Ambes, de Montfort, Richard, de Prohenques, du Luc, de Lagarde, Rudelle, d'Anticamareta, d'Hautpoul, Benoit, Vezian, de la Chassaigne, de Salluste, Rangouse, de Sabatier, Burnet, Masencal, Hellet, Durand, la Mamye, Laissac and Lacroix. See Dubédat, *Histoire du parlement de Toulouse*, I, p. 409.

[41] See, for example, ADHG, B 56, fos 347^v, 472^v.

[42] AMT, AA 16, no. 104.

when victims were fortunate enough to have some part of their body of wealth restored, in many cases 'the head was missing'.[43] The *maîtres des requêtes* had two additional indictments of Catholic insensitivity to conciliatory politics to report. The first concerned the grand procession that took place on the streets of Toulouse on 17 May 1563 to mark the one-year anniversary of the defeat of the Protestant coup.[44] The *maîtres des requêtes* relayed detailed descriptions of this event to the king, revealing how Catholics from all strata of the population of Toulouse life – nobles, magistrates, bourgeoisie and artisans – were present. The royal court responded by deeming this ceremony too provocative, given the current political climate, and issued an *arrêt* banning the procession from being staged again.[45] The commissioners also took exception to the fact that the Toulouse authorities had allowed the *basoche* militia to resume its role within the town guard.[46] Again, Catholics were found guilty of disregarding the terms of the Amboise edict and ordered to remove such 'popular elements' from street patrols.[47]

An interesting episode rounded off this period of confessional tension at Toulouse. In October 1563, Damville made his *grand entrée* into the town, his first as governor of Languedoc, escorted by Monluc, Armagnac, Strozzi, Terride and over four hundred Catholic nobles.[48] The *entrée* was pure Catholic theatre: a guard of honour comprising members of the *basoche* and confraternities of Toulouse, in full regalia, met the governor and his entourage at the city gate before accompanying him on a procession through the streets to the *parlement* palace. There the assembled magistrates, bourgeoisie and members of the syndicate welcomed the governor with a lavish reception, followed by a solemn mass at the cathedral.[49] To many, the splendid paraphernalia of the event, and the sheer number of assembled Catholic dignitaries and citizens, served to

---

[43] Lafaille, *Annales de la ville de Toulouse*, II, p. 256.

[44] ADHG, B 56, fo. 307ᵛ.

[45] The Catholics of Toulouse appealed against this decision, but the crown's verdict was upheld in May 1564; AMT, AA 14, no. 41. Attempts were made to revive the procession by the Catholic leadership of Toulouse in May 1569, in order to reinvigorate Catholic morale at the renewal of war. See ADHG, B 63, fo. 224. But it would only be under the auspices of the militant Leaguers in May 1589 that the procession was formally reinstated within the town.

[46] ADHG, B 56, fos 383, 554, 584ᵛ–5.

[47] Charles IX to *parlement* of Toulouse (14 July 1563), AMT, AA 14, no. 11.

[48] Monluc to Charles IX (8 October 1563), [Monluc], *Commentaries et lettres*, IV, p. 278.

[49] For full details of Damville's arrival at Toulouse in October 1563, see Franklin Charles Palm, *Politics and Religion in Sixteenth-Century France: A Study of the Career of Henry of Montmorency-Damville, Uncrowned King of the South* (Gloucester, MA, 1927), pp. 50–52; Lafaille, *Annales de la ville de Toulouse*, II, p. 256.

confirm the triumph of Catholicism at Toulouse. As Joan Davies pointed out, the arrival of yet another 'extreme Catholic' to champion the defence of orthodoxy in the south-west seemed to secure Catholic hegemony at Toulouse and its environs for the immediate future.[50] But Damville's tenure would not, as many had hoped, see anti-Protestant militancy promoted across the region. Instead, the governor employed an unequivocal approach to the administration of his province, a policy grounded in explicit adherence to the royal edicts in order to secure stability as a matter of urgency.[51] This was a big disappointment to Catholics, who had expected a degree of leniency, if not complete partiality, from their co-religionist. It was a setback that, when combined with the recent withdrawal of Monluc to Agen, and the news that Armagnac was being considered for the office of governor and legate to the papal enclave of Avignon, left Catholic foundations less solid than the militants would have liked.[52] The period between 1564 and 1567 therefore saw both faiths dabble with détente in an attempt to consolidate their power bases and define their roles within the new political structure.

In September 1567, however, the renewal of hostilities across France shattered the armistice, sending Catholic authorities across the south-west scurrying to re-establish their militant infrastructures. Monluc, who was now splitting time between the region's Catholic centres, urged the Toulouse *parlement* to look to the security of the town, warning that the current threat of insurrection was 'equally as grave as during the last war'.[53] He ordered Terride to organize military preparations at Toulouse, advising that eight Catholic captains, each with a minimum retinue of fifty soldiers, should be deployed to secure the town's districts.[54] Catholic magistrates and *capitouls* took their place in the guard once more, while members of the clergy were ordered to remain in their churches, and women in their homes, in order to prevent fires breaking out, which would draw off much-needed manpower.[55] The *parlement*, meanwhile,

---

[50] Joan Davies asserted that at this point Damville was widely regarded as an 'extreme Catholic', with his reputation as a chameleon in religious matters only being applicable to his attitude during the 1570s: Davies, *Languedoc and its Governor*, pp. 50–51.

[51] Damville's *ordonnance* of 18 October 1563, for example, required that Protestants and Catholics adhere to the letter of the edict of Amboise in equal measure: AMT, AA 14, no. 15.

[52] Armagnac was appointed *gouverneur d'Avignon* in November 1565 and papal legate to the enclave in May 1566. See Venard, *Réforme Protestante*, pp. 491–2. Armagnac would be raised to *vicaire-général* at Avignon on 30 March 1568. See ADHG, B 62, fo. 131.

[53] Monluc to Charles IX (31 September 1567), AMT, AA 48, no. 15.

[54] AMT, BB 269, fo. 93. In December 1567, Monluc ordered that the soldiers be lodged in Protestant houses, and that Protestant goods be confiscated to fund the war effort: AMT, AA 14, no. 125.

[55] AMT, AA 14, no. 135.

ordered the Catholic nobles of the region to assemble their retinues and to 'take up arms and cut to pieces all those who opposed the king',[56] while the crown notified the court that it should 'close for all business other than for war'.[57] With Damville occupied in eastern Languedoc, Bellegarde, the *sénéchal* of Toulouse, now assumed military control of the town, allowing Monluc and Terride to coordinate extramural defences.[58] And with Armagnac now ensconced in the papal court at Avignon, Daffis assumed a more prominent role in Catholic organization. Both men were kept busy during the winter of 1568, with the *sénéchal* overseeing the removal of suspect *capitouls* from office and their replacement by suitable Catholic candidates,[59] while Daffis ordered an increasingly paranoid *parlement* to ban all dances and public games within the town and to outlaw the wearing of masks, false beards and wigs, and clothes that offered a disguise.[60] Dubédat suggested that this was not simply a police measure, but an act of expiation and a sign of the penitential fervour that subsumed the mind-set of militant Catholics.[61]

A brief lull in the conflict between March and August 1568 saw an intensifying rather than a lessening of Catholic zeal at Toulouse. Bellegarde continued to remodel the guard, cutting the new captaincies to four but appointing two magistrates to accompany each on their duties, a further attempt to convince the population that only cooperative defence would secure the town.[62] Then, on 5 May 1568, the *parlement* once more demanded that all magistrates swear to 'live as Catholics according to the constitutions of the Roman Catholic church', with those that refused summarily expelled.[63] The following month the *capitouls*, once the epitome of moderate government in Toulouse, conceded that desperate measures were required and followed suit, granting Catholics of the *sénéchaussée* permission to 'cut to pieces' any Protestant caught attending illegal gatherings.[64] When the inhabitants of Toulouse submitted a remonstrance to the crown expressing their desire to 'remain under the authority of the One True Catholic church, to the exclusion of all other faiths',

---

[56] AMT, AA 48, no. 16.

[57] Charles IX to Bordeaux *parlement* (7 October 1567), AMT, AA 14, no. 120.

[58] AMT, AA 18, no. 191; ADHG, B 62, fo. 9ᵛ.

[59] 21 November 1567, ADHG, B 62, fo. 3.

[60] The edict was validated in January 1568. See AMT, AA 18, no. 194. It was then reconfirmed on 19 February 1569. See AMT, AA 18, no. 228.

[61] Dubédat, *Histoire du parlement de Toulouse*, I, p. 432.

[62] AMT, AA 15, no. 5; Dubédat, *Histoire du parlement de Toulouse*, I, p. 432.

[63] ADHG, B 62, fo. 145ᵛ.

[64] AMT, BB 173, fo. 65. The *parlement* confirmed these moves, granting Catholics permission to sound the *tocsin* at the first sign of trouble, and to employ any level of force deemed appropriate in the face of Protestant violence. See ADHG, C 3498, fo. 49.

all strata of Toulouse society had openly professed their commitment to the Catholic cause.[65]

When war returned to the region in late August 1568, Toulouse Catholics were quick to give their opinion as to why the conflict was so interminable: 'it is impossible to live in peace with diversity of religion … there is only schism, division and contradiction in the kingdom, and all natural forces and kinships are broken and violated'.[66] This well-practised mantra struck at the heart of the crown's ideology over toleration, and must have been a bitter pill for the royal council to swallow, especially as it now depended on the numerous Catholic factions across France to support the royal army against Condé and the ever-increasing Protestant forces. At Toulouse, the Catholic authorities had moved to a heightened state of alert, their experience of planning and organization of recent years standing them in good stead. Punitive legislation was now more prevalent than ever. In September 1568, further purges of high and low offices were made, while extensive sequestration orders were implemented against Protestants and new taxes and fines for misdemeanours introduced.[67] In fact, such was the increase in litigation caused by these impositions that, on 18 September, Daffis was forced to extend the current session of the *parlement* into the vacation, and increase the number of *conseillers* serving in the chambers, simply to allow all cases to be dealt with effectively.[68]

While these responses were by now tried and tested mechanisms with which to subjugate Protestants, and indeed were proving the staple of Catholic policy across the region, a new and quite remarkable innovation was taking shape at Toulouse: a crusade. Simply to mention *la croisade* in this corner of western Languedoc was to evoke centuries-old traditions of extirpating heresy. With many among the Catholic authorities now fearing that continued Protestant military successes would leave Toulouse isolated, perhaps susceptible to a siege, the decision to create a late sixteenth-century version of such a renowned penitent–militant body in

---

[65] 'Remonstrance fait par les magistrats et habitans de Toulouse contre ceux de la nouvelle religion' (3 July 1568), AMT, GG 825.

[66] AMT, BB 12 (27 August 1568).

[67] For a full list of officials removed from office during this purge, see 'Remonstrances présentées au Roi par les délégués de la ville de Toulouse, avec les réponses de Sa Majesté', AMT, BB12 (28 August 1568). For a roll of tax levied against Protestants of Toulouse in 1568, see AMT, GG 825 (1568). For lists of goods seized from seventy-one suspects in Toulouse, and the profits of the sale of these items, see ADHG, B 63, fos 172–99. For confiscation of private wheat supplies, see AMT, AA 15, no. 25. For deliberations of the *parlement* of Toulouse concerning confiscations of Protestant property during this period, see 'Affaires de Michel Dufaur', AMT, GG 826 (1568, 1569).

[68] ADHG, B 62, fos 423–4.

order to energize the Catholic defenders seemed a logical, if slightly desperate, act. The identity of those who actually took this decision, however, is less than clear. The transcripts of court sessions make no reference to the call for the crusade being made by any authoritative figure within the town council or *parlement*. But they do include reference to a sermon against heresy, delivered before the court in early September 1568 by an *avocat*, Jean de Cardonne, in which the Catholic leadership of Toulouse was urged to revive its sacred league of 1563 in the fight against Protestantism.[69]

Cardonne's sermon can be seen as representative of the heightening of penitential fervour in Toulouse during this period, driven by the revival of militant confraternities across the region, and the influx to the town of mendicant preachers such as the Jacobin friar, Melchior Flavin, the Jesuit, Jean Palatier, and Catholic theologians such as Cérès and Laleine.[70] Catholic domination of the *parlement* at this time was such that, unlike what happened in 1562, few restrictions were placed on these speakers. They were thus allowed to preach with impunity from the cathedral, with their content as radical and as confrontational as required. The *parlement* reflected the penitential fervour that was gripping the town, modifying its *arrêts* to curtail dances, masques, public games and unauthorized music within the town.[71] But it was Cardonne's sermon that appeared to be the catalyst for subsequent events, as the *avocat*'s plea that the 1563 league be re-established so that Catholics could combine to eradicate heresy at Toulouse somehow found its way to Rome. There, it was interpreted quite differently by the papacy. Instead of supporting moves to recreate the earlier association, papal emissaries confirmed on 12 September that the Holy See had consented to a Catholic crusade being launched from Toulouse.[72] In fact, two crusades were validated by the Vatican, affirming both a 'crusade against heretics' and a 'crusade against reformers', with papal bulls issued to confirm each.[73] Thus, over the following weeks,

---

[69] Dubédat, *Histoire du parlement de Toulouse*, I, p. 434.

[70] As a further example of the close-knit Catholic network being created at Toulouse, Laleine would soon be promoted to the office of the Inquisition at Toulouse, serving under cardinal Armagnac. See Dubédat, *Histoire du parlement de Toulouse*, I, pp. 432–3.

[71] For problems of civil disturbances during 'la ville en fête' in sixteenth-century France, see Chevalier, *Les bonnes villes de France*, pp. 263–85.

[72] *Preuve* 31, *HGL*, 9, pp. 534–5.

[73] Both were registered before the Toulouse *parlement* on 12 September 1568. For the papal bull confirming 'la ligue et croisade faite à Toulouse contre les hérétiques', see *Preuve* 31, *HGL*, 9, pp. 535–36. For the papal bull confirming 'la croisade faite à Toulouse contre ceux de la nouvelle religion', see *Preuve* 32, *HGL*, 9, pp. 536–7. The 'Publication de la croisade faite à Toulouse contre ceux de la nouvelle religion' (12 September 1568) is also presented in 'Preuves de l'histoire de Languedoc', *HGL*, 12, pp. 885–6.

large numbers of Catholics began making towards the cathedral of Saint-Étienne in Toulouse to profess their faith and attend mass for the crusade, with men of fighting age urged to sign up and be allocated to a company so as to serve as crusaders.[74]

If historians have distanced themselves from the Catholic leagues of the 1560s, they have overlooked the crusade. The reason for this neglect may lie in the fact that, despite sizeable financial investment and the patronage of numerous elites, the crusade never managed to do much crusading at all. The enterprise began positively enough, with the *parlement* validating the letters establishing the crusade and appointing a *capitoul*, d'Hispanie, a dependable Catholic, to oversee the levy of troops.[75] Its initial source of funding was to be voluntary contributions from the Catholic nobility and clergy of Toulouse, but this soon proved inadequate. But with *parlement* unwilling to contribute directly (this was to be an entirely autonomous operation, making no demands on crown revenue) d'Hispanie was forced to seek permission for a one-off 'crusader tax' on the population of Toulouse. This proved most successful, with records revealing that over 60 000 *livres* were raised in October 1568 alone, although a mere 6000 *livres* came from Catholic coffers, with the bulk of the tax burden falling on the town's Protestant community.[76]

The *parlement* did contribute indirectly to crusading philosophy, nevertheless, by proposing that all Catholics distinguish themselves during these turbulent times by wearing a white cross on their garments and painting a white cross on their doors.[77] Whether this was intended to mimic crusader tradition or was merely coincidental is hard to ascertain, but it would not be the first, or last, time that identifying marks would be used to distinguish confessional allegiance during the religious wars. At Agen, for example, Monluc frequently ordered Catholics to differentiate themselves within the community by displaying a white cross, as did the Bordeaux *parlement* during the insurrection of 1562. Members of Monluc's confraternity at Limoges were also required to sport similar identifying symbols,[78] while the leaders of towns witnessing provincial massacres in response to the Saint Bartholomew's day episode in Paris in 1572 similarly urged the Catholic populace to wear white crosses on their

---

[74] The *croisade* was solemnized under the device: 'Eamus nos moriamur cum Christo', *HGL*, 9, p. 48.

[75] AMT, BB 12, fo. 195.

[76] AMT, BB 12, (October 1568).

[77] *HGL*, 9, p. 48.

[78] For the wearing of white crosses by the *Confrérie de la Sainte-Croix* at Limoges, see Cassan, *Le temps des guerres de religion*, p. 238; Jean-Marie Constant, *La Ligue* (Paris, 1996), p. 57.

garments so as to distinguish them from the intended victims of the slaughter.[79] This penitential symbolism was most widely used by the Catholic League after 1584, however, where such sartorial statements were not saved solely for times of crisis, but, as Mark Greengrass demonstrated, were regularly worn as a means of identifying confessional affiliations and loyalties within the community.[80]

While Protestants found these practices both divisive and ominous, they were not averse to employing variants on the theme themselves. On several occasions during December 1562 and February 1563, Catholic notables awoke to find that their doors had been daubed with white marks, often resembling significant portentous symbols such as the gallows, portcullis and cross.[81] As several of these doors belonged to eminent Catholics such as Roffignac, Lachassaigne, Fauguerolles, Sanssac and numerous *conseillers* of the court, the *parlement* ordered the *sieur* de Candalle to investigate. He concluded that the marks were a precursor to an attack, and advised the occupants to arm themselves in readiness and the court to step up patrols of the guard in these streets.[82] In fact this phenomenon must have been fairly common across the south-west of France during the 1560s, for when Charles IX wrote to Damville in August 1564 to enquire about the state of the peace in Languedoc, he warned the governor that there could not be stability within the province until all such sectarian graffiti was removed or painted over.[83]

At Toulouse, the raising of the crusading army made steady progress. In December 1568, d'Hispanie informed the *parlement* that the *grand-prieur* of Toulouse, Pierre de Beaullac-Tresbons, *sieur* de Fronton, had assumed command of the *compagnie de la croisade*.[84] The appointment of Fronton would prove most astute. The office of *grand-prieur* at Toulouse was steeped in crusader mythology, and had been filled continuously since its inception in the twelfth century to oversee the operations of the Knights Hospitaller.[85]

---

[79] See Luc Racaut's chapter on Catholic violence during the 1572 Saint Bartholomew riots, 'The problem of violence during the French Wars of Religion', in Luc Racaut, *Hatred in Print. Catholic Propaganda and Protestant Identity during the French Wars of Religion* (Aldershot, 2002), pp. 23–37.

[80] Greengrass, 'The Sainte Union in the Provinces', p. 472.

[81] December 1562, AMB, ms 771, fo. 116; 19 February 1563, AMB, ms 771, fo. 463.

[82] AMB, ms 771, fo. 138.

[83] AMT, AA 14, no. 51.

[84] AMT, BB 12, fo. 195ᵛ.

[85] M.A. du Bourg listed the holders of the office of *grand-prieur* de Toulouse during this period: Claude de Gruel de la Bourehl, 1552–55; Pierre de Beaullac-Tresbons, 1555–69; Balthazar des Comtes de Vintimille, 1570–75; Mathurin de Lescur-Romegas, Prieure d'Irlande, 1575–81; Antoine-Scipion de Joyeuse, 1581–89: M.A. du Bourg, *Histoire du grand-prieur de Toulouse* (Toulouse, 1883), p. 25.

Linking this new crusade to such an historic ancestry would connect the fight against Protestantism with this time-honoured folklore. But there was another motivating factor here for Catholics. The *grand-prieur* was a major landowner in the town of Fronton, located midway between Toulouse and Montauban. It had been an important Catholic stronghold throughout the 1560s, its solid fortifications and notorious *donjon des Hospitaliers* which housed a large Catholic garrison making the town difficult to assail. On 17 October 1567, however, the Protestant *vicomtes* de Paulin, Montclar and Caumont, together with the *comte* de Bruniquel, had laid siege to the town with an army approaching 7000-strong, and had at length broken its defences. When Fronton asked the crown for succour, his request was refused as Damville had insufficient forces to challenge Paulin's men.[86] The *grand-prieur* would have to recover the town himself, then, and he had been nurturing such designs for over sixteen months. His appointment as head of the Toulouse crusade, therefore, could also be seen as a symbol of Catholic intention to redress inequities and regain lost land, as well as to triumph over Protestantism.

The progress of the crusade continued steadily into 1569. In January, the clergy of Toulouse agreed to pay 1000 *livres* towards the acquisition of further supplies for the troops,[87] while in the following month a consignment of fresh gunpowder was delivered to the *tour Saint-Jean* for distribution among the *compagnie*.[88] The fluid military situation across the province left Catholic resources elsewhere stretched to breaking point. When Bellegarde's forces became trapped at Mazère, in the *comté* of Foix, by a large Protestant army under the *vicomte* d'Arpajon, the *parlement* had little option other than to deploy the underprepared *compagnie* as relief.[89] The crusaders were armed and dispatched on 15 April 1569, reaching Bellegarde ten days later. The *capitouls* put the best gloss possible on this premature posting: 'the *compagnie* has set forth to extirpate the enemies of the true faith ... for the good of the land'.[90] But the mission was not to be the glorious campaign of Catholic hopes, as Montgommery had reached Mazère first and relieved d'Arpajon's troops. Bellegarde's retreating forces, even augmented by the crusaders, were no match for the combined Protestant forces and were defeated outside Foix. The crusade of Toulouse thus disappeared from the archives at this point, presumably routed in the battle. It would make one final contribution to

---

[86] Bourg, *Histoire du grand-prieur de Toulouse*, p. 272.

[87] AMT, BB 12, fo. 196.

[88] AMT, BB 12, fo. 213[v].

[89] D'Hispanie to Toulouse *grand conseil* (15 April 1569), AMT, BB 12, fo. 229[v]. See also *HGL*, 9, p. 32.

[90] *Capitouls* of Toulouse to Armagnac (25 April 1569), AMT, BB 173, fo. 121.

the saga, though: it was a single shot from a musketeer of the *compagnie de la croisade* that ended the life and career of the *vicomte* d'Arpajon.[91]

So, given the premature demise of the *compagnie*, would it be justified to see the crusade as having any relevance to affairs at Toulouse during the period? The answer would have to be yes, for to dismiss such an innovation out of hand would be to fail to acknowledge its impact on contemporaries. After all, this was a Catholic organization that was sanctioned by the papacy, promulgated through the *parlement*, supported by magistrates and *capitouls*, and financed by various bodies including the local clergy. Two historians concur with this assessment. For Denis Crouzet, the crusade was not an act of desperation by Toulouse Catholics. It was another manifestation of the prevailing penitential sentiment of the period, a direct result of the 'angoisse eschatalogique' that crippled French society during the second half of the sixteenth century. It was thus a 'holy army of the faithful', an expression of Toulouse's staunch Catholicism and the ultimate demonstration of Catholic militancy.[92] Crouzet's notion is engaging, but it should also be noted that the *compagnie* was as much a political as it was a penitential entity, a tool of the magistrates as much as a talisman of the church. Robert Harding affirmed this duality by revealing that the *parlement's* counterparts at Bordeaux offered financial assistance to assist in the maintaining of the crusade, keen no doubt to encourage the establishment of additional military forces in the region, but also to welcome any vehicle that captured the imagination of the region's Catholic communities and energized them into defending orthodoxy with zeal and fervour.[93]

The endeavours of Catholic militants at Toulouse during the 1560s were thus varied, but ultimately successful in securing the town and its environs as a centre of orthodoxy in the south-west. Initial communal activism had given the citizens and administrators some experience of confronting Protestantism before the outbreak of war, but the Catholic hierarchy were still caught off-guard by the coup of May 1562, and came close to losing the town to the reformers. Concerted action from the local nobility and well-coordinated counter-offensives from within the town itself by combined forces of militia, magistrates and local elite retinues saved the day. Immediately, a backlash was launched that would see the determined repression of Protestants, a policy that would become common practice among Catholic juntas over the decade. Despite renewed violence after 1567, Toulouse remained firmly in Catholic hands throughout the period, and although the crusade of 1568/69 ultimately

---

[91]   AMT, BB 173, fo. 121^v.
[92]   Crouzet, *Les guerriers de Dieu*, I, pp. 386–96.
[93]   Harding, *Anatomy of a Power Elite*, pp. 63–4.

failed, it symbolized the changing psychological state of the townsfolk of Toulouse: Catholics were no longer prepared to sit and wait to be assailed; they were now prepared to seize the initiative and take the fight to subversive forces within, and without, society.

CHAPTER TEN

Rebellion and Wider Catholic Activism: Béarn and Navarre

One feature that marked Catholic militancy in the south-west during the 1560s was the interconnectedness of activism across regional and national borders. Such cooperative spirit was exemplified by the desire of Catholic powers such as Spain and the papacy to oust from government the Calvinist queen of Navarre, Jeanne d'Albret; by the associations of Guyenne and western Languedoc to offer succour to the Catholic rebels; and by all Catholic parties to re-establish orthodoxy within these independent territories. The Spanish king, Philip II, was especially perturbed that Calvinist enclaves existed so close to his northern borders. His initial attempt to overturn Jeanne's legislative proselytizing of Béarn and Navarre had failed when Antoine de Bourbon, the king of Navarre, died in November 1562. The Spanish ambassador, Chantonnay, had enticed Antoine into joining the Catholic Triumvirate in the hope he might be able to steer his queen away from her path of reform. This had been a pipedream, of course, as Jeanne's faith would prove more resolute than many contemporaries imagined.[1] At Navarre's death, then, Philip changed direction and moved large numbers of troops onto his northern borders to intimidate Jeanne. Meanwhile, his emissaries heaped further pressure on the government at Pau by reminding Jeanne that the political dispute over the southern territories of Navarre, which Spain had lost to the Bourbons in 1517, had not yet been settled satisfactorily.[2] Madrid was joined in this offensive by the papacy, which had long viewed the queen of Navarre as little more than a heretic who had too long escaped censorship. For Rome, the spread of Calvinism across Béarn and Navarre had proved disastrous, with many clergymen chased from their parishes and numerous churchgoers assaulted. The indignation felt by Spain and the papacy at the ineffectiveness of the French crown in this matter is evident in a letter from Chantonnay to François Vargas, the Spanish ambassador to Rome, in late 1561: 'now that times of peace are gone ... and we head towards general ruin ... the only remedy possible, independent of a general council, is your majesty. If the queen mother of France refuses our offer to protect the Catholic faith in this kingdom ... you are disposed to

---

[1] [De Thou], *Histoire universelle*, IV, pp. 124–26; Ruble, *Antoine de Bourbon*, III, pp. 225–27, 255–58.

[2] For the conquest of Navarre in 1517, see Bryson, *Jeanne d'Albret*, pp. 50–53.

use all force necessary [and] to form a league to regain authority'.[3] For Chantonnay, the Spanish king was the sole champion of Catholic recovery in the region, and the establishing of a formal league was a necessary engine in any attempt to neutralize the threat posed by Jeanne d'Albret.

But Catholic claims that the French crown was impassive to events in Béarn and Navarre were not strictly true. In late 1562, Catherine de Medici had attempted to reassert royal prerogatives over the Albret lands of Foix and Armagnac by transferring military jurisdiction back into the hands of Monluc and the regional *sénéchaux*, and had sent stern warnings to Jeanne's bishops that unless they returned to the Catholic fold they would forfeit office.[4] Yet neither policy had had much impact, and direct intervention by the French crown in Béarn and Navarre remained negligible throughout 1562. Opposition to Jeanne's reforms, therefore, was left to Catholic groups within the towns of the region. This was first evident in July 1563, at the decision by Jeanne to begin the purging of Catholic paraphernalia from the cathedrals and churches of the region. At Navarrenx, Pau, Monein and Nay, for example, members of the clergy and armed citizens united to resist attempts to strip their churches, while, at Lescar, Catholics focused their rage against the town's Calvinist bishop, Louis d'Albret, the queen's uncle, who was seen as the architect of reform and the driving force behind the programme of cleansing.[5] When the government at Pau ordered the deployment of two thousand armed soldiers to protect the officials removing Catholic vestiges, the confrontations became more violent, with episodes often deteriorating into running battles or iconoclastic riots.[6] For disgruntled Catholics there was but one remaining outlet for legitimate dissent: the *états de Béarn*. In August 1563, the *états* met to formulate their grievances against the crown's provocative policy. Led by Antoine de Montesquiou, *sieur* de Sainte-Colomme, a respected Catholic and a former key adviser at Jeanne's court, a remonstrance was presented before the royal council at Pau on behalf of all Catholics of Béarn and

---

[3] Chantonnay to Vargas (7 November 1561), Weiss, *Papiers d'état du Cardinal de Granvelle*, VI, pp. 399–401. For further correspondence over this matter, see also Vargas to Philip II (30 September 1561), ibid., VI, pp. 342–68; Vargas to Philip II (3 October 1561), ibid., VI, pp. 369–96; Vargas to Philip II (7 November 1561), ibid., VI, pp. 401–8; Vargas to Philip II (15 November 1561), ibid., VI, pp. 413–18; Vargas to Philip II (22 February 1562), ibid., VI, pp. 511–27.

[4] See, for example, 'Les articles accordés par monseigneur de Monluc, lieutenant pour le Roy en son pays et duché de Guyenne, aux manans et habitans de la ville de Lectore et estrangiers' (2 October, 1562), [Monluc], *Commentaires et lettres*, IV, pp. 162–7; Dubarat, *Documents et bibliographie sur la réforme en Béarn*, pp. 24–7.

[5] Ritter, 'Jeanne d'Albret', p. 65; Dartigue-Peyrou, *Jeanne d'Albret et le Béarn*, p. 43.

[6] Ritter, 'Jeanne d'Albret', pp. 65–6.

Navarre.[7] However, the *procureur-général* of Béarn rejected the appeal on the grounds that it 'opposed the will of her majesty'. Soon after, Jeanne rebuked the *états* for their impertinence and terminated the assembly, ordering Saint-Colomme to retire to his lands in disgrace.[8] Catholics of the region were now utterly disenfranchised.

In one respect, the defeat of the *états* made the subsequent outburst of sectarian violence at Oloron somewhat inevitable. Still aggrieved at the restrictions imposed on their practice of their faith, Catholics at Oloron were incensed when Protestant officials returned in December 1563 to complete the removal of statues from the cathedral of Sainte-Marie. Led by Abbadie, a senior canon of the cathedral, a group of dissidents erected barricades to prevent Jeanne's men from gaining access to the grounds. When news of this stalemate spread, Abbadie was joined by Charles, *comte* de Luxe, the leader of Catholic resistance in Basse-Navarre, who had rallied a number of troops to support his co-religionists at Oloron.[9] But, in another respect, this was a quite unexpected turn of events. Situated only 18 kilometres south-west of Jeanne's capital of Pau, Oloron had been one of the initial hotbeds of reform activity in Béarn, and the site of numerous *prêches* during the 1550s.[10] It was also the seat of the renowned Calvinist bishop, Gerard Roussel, and so its conversion to a 'godly centre' of reform ideology had seemed to be an inevitability. Catholic defiance, then, must have come as a shock to the government of the region. The sense of personal affront felt by Jeanne d'Albret at this rebellion was apparent in that she led the military backlash herself.[11] With Saint-Colomme sidelined and Catholic forces not yet gathered in concerted numbers, the royal army quickly recaptured the town. Oloron's resistance, however, had given the Béarnais government food for thought and, remarkably, Jeanne decided to re-evaluate the policy of purging Catholic churches as a result. In February 1564, the crown went further,

---

[7] The Sainte-Colomme family were key players in Catholic militancy in Béarn and Navarre during this period. Antoine de Montesquiou, *sieur* de Sainte-Colomme et d'Aydie-en-Béarn, was the head of the family. His son, Jacques II de Sainte-Colomme, *seigneur* de Escoarrabaque, was involved with the Catholic league at Oloron in 1568, while his two sons, Jacques III de Sainte-Colomme, *abbé* de Sauvelade, and Tristan de Sainte-Colomme were prominent in Terride's invasion of Béarn in 1569. A fifth family member, Antoine's brother, Bernard de Sainte-Colomme, is less conspicuous, but also held authority within the region. See Jaurgain, 'Les capitaines châtelains de Mauléon', pp. 310–15.

[8] See *Preuve* 62, Salefranque, 'Histoire de l'hérésie de Béarn', XLIV, p. 199.

[9] For details of the Oloron rebellion in 1563, see Dartigue-Peyrou, *Jeanne d'Albret et le Béarn*, p. 80.

[10] Greengrass, 'The Calvinist experiment in Béarn', p. 123. Dartigue-Peyrou states that, of all the d'Albret lands, Oloron was the first to witness significant levels of radical Protestantism before 1555: Dartigue-Peyrou, *La vicomté de Béarn*, pp. 478–80.

[11] See Jaurgain, 'Les capitaines châtelains de Mauléon', p. 313.

publishing a *simultaneum*, a declaration of liberty of conscience for all subjects that effectively offered tacit toleration of Catholicism across Béarn and Navarre.[12] However, the *simultaneum* faltered over the requirement that the two faiths share the use of religious sites such as churches and burial grounds, as neither Catholic nor Calvinist welcomed concessions over sacred space. It soon became apparent, therefore, that this attempt at conciliation was a dead end, and both crown and rebels steeled themselves for renewed confrontation.

Throughout these events, the papacy had done little to support the Catholic rebels, preferring to back Spanish intrigues rather than intervene directly. In September 1563, though, it decided to deploy the Inquisition against the queen of Navarre and her Protestant officers. The Inquisition had already proved fairly successful in confronting rising numbers of heresy accusations in France during the early 1550s, despite reservations from Gallican magistrates, working alongside the *chambres ardentes* of the regional *parlements*. The cardinal of Lorraine had been instrumental in this initiative, taking charge of the nomination of prelates who would lead the investigations within the provinces. Significantly, Lorraine had appointed cardinal Armagnac as Inquisitor General for the south-west in 1557, extending his jurisdictional remit to include the territories of Béarn, Navarre, Foix and Albret soon thereafter.[13] The papal Inquisition was far from an anachronism at this time. The Inquisitor General possessed two potent weapons: the visitation and the papal *monitoire*. Inquisitorial visitations were infrequent, but effective during the 1560s, with the Inquisitor able to enter any town in southern France to accuse or arrest a heresy suspect, regardless of rank.[14] In early 1564, Armagnac employed this prerogative to seize two merchants who had fled to Roussillon to evade warrants for arrest on charges of heresy.[15] While the capture and trial proved a success, contention arose when it was revealed that Armagnac had enlisted Spanish infantry, drawn from a nearby border garrison, to effect the arrest. The courts at Pau and at Paris were outraged, as Roussillon lay within Jeanne d'Albret's jurisdiction, but Philip II was more than happy to support Armagnac's actions.

---

[12] Ruble, *Jeanne d'Albret et la guerre civile*, I, p. 69; Roelker, *Queen of Navarre*, p. 267.

[13] Dubarat, *Documents et bibliographie sur la réforme en Béarn*, p. 57. For the reintroduction of the Inquisition into France in the 1550s, see Venard, *Réforme Protestante*, pp. 329–39; Sutherland's chapter, 'Was there an Inquisition in Reformation France?', in her *Princes, Politics and Religion*, pp. 13–29.

[14] The commission allowed the Inquisitor to 'act without respect to nation, quality, or person … privileged to chastise those guilty of heresy'. See Freer, *The Life of Jeanne d'Albret*, p. 244.

[15] Freer, *The Life of Jeanne d'Albret*, p. 244.

The benefit of being able to call on military support from Spain would prove a tremendous asset for the Inquisition in the south-west, as a French ambassador to the Council of Trent noted in 1562: 'Spanish military aggression now provides the backbone to Armagnac's inquisitorial dealings.'[16] This was an especially troubling development for Protestant communities of the region, who were already forced to live under the shadow cast by the various Catholic associations. And where visitations failed, the Inquisitor had recourse to the papal *monitoire*, a summons that ordered the accused to appear in person before the papal court in Rome, usually within a given time period, to answer specific charges.[17] It was just such a sanction that Armagnac employed against Jeanne d'Albret and Louis d'Albret in September 1563, giving both six months to appear before Pius IV in Rome or suffer excommunication, at which point their lands would be deemed forfeit and given over to the 'first despoiler' as a further penalty.[18]

The *monitoire* had immediate and significant ramifications. The *parlements* at Bordeaux and Toulouse issued decrees stating that as the queen was in the process of being excommunicated, her sovereign rights to Béarn and Navarre were invalidated, and her principalities should be returned to her *suzerain-paramount*, the king of France. As a consequence, Jeanne's abolition of Catholicism in Béarn and Navarre was also declared illegal, with the sovereign courts ordering all recent legislation advocating reform within these territories to be rescinded.[19] For the French crown, however, the *monitoire* was another instance of papal interference in the government of France; only recently, the Inquisition had investigated alleged heretical tendencies among several French bishops, much to the annoyance of Catherine de Medici. And although the regent had complained to Rome over this violation of agreed Gallican liberties of the French clergy, little reassurance had been forthcoming from the Holy See.[20] The French crown was thus more vociferous when

---

[16]   Saint-Sulpice to Lanssac (July 1562); Cabié, *Ambassade en Espagne de Jean Ébrard*, p. 28.

[17]   Robin Briggs has shown that a version of this *monitoire* had been used by the French church during the early sixteenth century to force witnesses to testify on pain of excommunication: Robin Briggs, *Communities of Belief. Cultural and Social Tensions in Early Modern France* (Oxford, 1995), p. 190.

[18]   See [Condé], *Mémoires de Condé*, IV, p. 594; Freer, *The Life of Jeanne d'Albret*, pp. 211–15. For the full Latin version of the papal *monitoire* against Jeanne d'Albret (28 September 1563), see Dubarat, *Documents et bibliographie sur la réforme en Béarn*, pp. 27–38.

[19]   Roelker, *Queen of Navarre*, pp. 220–25.

[20]   This programme would continue into 1566, and would only be concluded when Pius V issued the papal bull of 11 December that condemned six French bishops for heresy: Jean de Gelais, bishop of Uzès; Antoine Caracciolo, bishop of Troyes; Charles Guillart, bishop of Chartres; Jean de Monluc, bishop of Valence; Louis d'Albret, bishop of Lescars, and Claude Régin, bishop of Oloron. See Roelker, *Queen of Navarre*, p. 240.

protesting against the declaration that Jeanne's lands be open to the 'first despoiler', which at this juncture seemed likely to be the troops of Philip of Spain. French legists argued that Rome had no power to cede her lands to a third party, as the queen of Navarre was technically still answerable to her suzerain lord, the king of France. Charles IX thus declared the *monitoire* invalid and, in a stern letter to Saint-Sulpice, the French ambassador in Rome, he reiterated that France would no longer accept papal interference in or close to its territories.[21] To conclude the matter, both the *conseil privé* and the *parlement de Paris* ordered the *parlements* at Bordeaux and Toulouse to annul the 'first despoiler' decrees with immediate effect.[22]

By the summer of 1564, however, rumours abounded that the Catholic powers of Europe were planning a collective military incursion against Jeanne d'Albret, to arrest her and bring her to justice. Pierre Olhagaray claimed that the scheme originated in correspondence between Philip II and Pius IV, and dictated that Armagnac, Monluc, d'Aspremont, d'Escars and the *vicomte* d'Orthe, governor of Bayonne, move their forces into Navarre from Guyenne and Languedoc, driving Jeanne and her entourage from the security of Pau into the arms of an invading Spanish army, which would assemble at Barcelona under the pretence of manoeuvring to expel a nearby Moorish community.[23] Significantly, Freer claimed that, once captured, the queen would be delivered to the Inquisition in Spain, not to Armagnac, no doubt to serve as a bargaining chip for Madrid in its relations with the papacy.[24] It is difficult to discern the precise nature of this plot. Dubarat intimated that a formal league was established between the Catholics of Guyenne, Spain and the papacy to facilitate the capture of the queen, with d'Orthe, Départ, the governor of the château Hâ at Bordeaux, and Dominge, a Béarnais captain, coordinating the military wing of this organization.[25] D'Aubigné, on the other hand, believed this

---

[21] Charles IX to Saint-Sulpice (30 November 1563), in Cabié, *Ambassade en Espagne de Jean Ébrard*, pp. 186–7. See also Olhagaray, *Histoire des comptes de Foix*, p. 554.

[22] Dubarat, *Documents et bibliographie sur la réforme en Béarn*, pp. 38–43.

[23] Olhagaray, *Histoire des comptes de Foix*, p. 559.

[24] See Freer, *The Life of Jeanne d'Albret*, pp. 230–40. Two independent inquisitorial systems existed in southern Europe at this time: the papal Inquisition, as discussed, and the Spanish Inquisition, which thrived as a tool to subdue heresy across the Iberian peninsula. Philip II had removed the Spanish Inquisition from papal control in the late 1550s, assuming leadership of its many sections, validating all appointments and determining its activities thereafter. See Henry Kamen, *The Spanish Inquisition. An Historical Revision* (London, 1997). Forneron has shown that Philip rejected any interference from Rome in the running of his Inquisition, and was especially dismissive of attempts to censor its activities through the issuing of papal bulls. See Henri Forneron, *Histoire de Philippe II*, I, pp. 187–8.

[25] Dubarat, *Documents et bibliographie sur la réforme en Béarn*, p. 79.

to have been a Jesuit plot, an assertion rejected out of hand by Mirasson, who stated that the whole episode was nothing more than an artifice: Catholic propaganda concocted to intimidate Jeanne and force her to reintroduce Catholicism within her lands.[26] Monluc was cagey about these events in his *Commentaires*, hinting at the existence of a Catholic alliance against the queen of Navarre, but distancing himself from any involvement.[27]

Despite the extensive Catholic powers arrayed against her, the queen of Navarre pushed on with her reform programme. In May 1566, the uneasy truce of the previous two years came to an end as Catholic activity was once more censured across Béarn and Navarre.[28] The clergy of Béarn were exasperated at this, and formally opposed the publication of the patent.[29] They were further aggrieved the following month, when the Synod of Nay voted to renew the suppression of idolatry, and to intro-duce a Calvinist, puritan code of morals for the population of Jeanne d'Albret's territories.[30] At Oloron, Catholic outrage manifested itself in the formation of a league in 1567, headed by Gabriel de Béarn, *sieur* de Gerdrest, and supported by leading local dignitaries such as Jacques de Saint-Colomme, *seigneur* de Escoarrabaque, the former town governor, Jean de Bordenave, baron de Monein, François de Béarn, *sieur* de Bonasse, Henri de Navailles, *sieur* de Peyre, his son-in-law Guy de Biran, *sieur* de Gohas, Jean, *sieur* d'Armendaritz, and two *avocats* of the civil courts at Pau, Guillaume Tasta and Jean de Supersantis. The principal canons of the cathedrals of Oloron and Lescar promised to finance this league, while Charles, *comte* de Luxe, offered the services of his Basse-Navarrais troops once more.[31] This was a major coup for the Catholic party at Oloron. As the brother of the murdered noble, Tristan de Moneins, slain during the Gabelle riots at Bordeaux in 1548, Luxe was an important political and military figure in the region. He also had strong links to the Catholic associations of the south-west, having served under Monluc in the campaigns of 1562–64, and having been identified as one

---

[26] D'Aubigné, *Histoire universelle*, II, p. 295; P. Mirasson, *Histoire des troubles du Béarn, au sujet de la religion, dans le XVIIe siècle* (Paris, 1768), p. 480.

[27] [Monluc], *Commentaires, 1521–1576*, p. 586.

[28] 'Extraits des ordonnances de Registres du Parlement de Navarre' (1566), Salefranque, 'Histoire de l'hérésie de Béarn', XLIV, p. 193.

[29] Those writing in opposition included Martin de Lacu, *avocat et procureur* to the bishop of Lescar (*Preuve* 57); Pierre Arbusio, *avocat et procureur* to the bishop of Oloron (*Preuve* 58); Bernard de Sorberio, *avocat et procureur* to the cathedral chapter at Lescar (*Preuve* 59); Martin de Luger and Jean de Supersantis, *avocats et procureurs* to the cathedral chapter at Oloron (*Preuve* 60), Salefranque, 'Histoire de l'hérésie de Béarn', XLIV, p. 196.

[30] Roelker, *Queen of Navarre*, p. 268.

[31] Dartigue-Peyrou, *Jeanne d'Albret*, p. 80.

of the Catholic cartel accused of attempting to 'sell' Guyenne to Spain in 1564.[32] His son, Valentin de Domezain, baron de Moneins, was also present here, another distinguished Catholic leaguer who had served with distinction under Monluc, and who had been active in the rebellion at Oloron in 1563.[33]

The leaguers were to receive a further boost with the defection of two of Jeanne d'Albret's key advisors: Armand de Gontaut, *seigneur* d'Audaux, the *sénéchal* of Béarn, and Claude Régin, bishop of Oloron. Audaux had masterminded the military successes of Jeanne's forces against the Catholic forces in 1563, and had been appointed *lieutenant-général* of the kingdom during the queen's visit to the French court in 1564. His desertion was thus a major coup for the rebels. Régin's contribution to Jeanne's successes, meanwhile, had lain in the religious field, most notably the implementation of Calvinist reform doctrine across Béarn and Navarre. The precise reason for their defection is not evident, although the alienation of elite prerogatives to nominate benefices may have been a contributing factor to their dissatisfaction.[34] What is clear, though, is that the leaguers could claim a good deal more legitimacy for their cause now that Jeanne's chief ministers were supportive. The significance of these developments was not lost on the Béarnais government, who tried to reconcile with their former advisers almost immediately. In November 1567, Jean d'Etchart, the *procureur-général* of Béarn, was dispatched to Oloron to lure Audaux back to court, but failed. He then sought to separate Luxe and Domezain from the leaguers by feigning an assault into Basse-Navarre, only to find that Luxe had guarded his homeland well by establishing paramilitary groups composed of nobles, townsfolk and farmers of the valleys. The misdirection failed, as had the government's strategy.[35]

If Jeanne's manoeuvrings were beginning to stall, Catholic activity was proving more fruitful. The presence of Luxe, Audaux, Régin and Gerdrest at Oloron meant that Catholic forces could be moved from a defensive to an offensive footing, with coalitions of nobles, clergy and officers of the courts boosting their numbers.[36] The capture of Jeanne d'Albret and the revocation of reform legislation seemed attainable goals once more, and

---

[32] Ritter, 'Jeanne d'Albret', p. 82.

[33] The Luxe/Moneins family had strong bonds with many of the great Catholic families of the region, including marriage ties with the houses of Saint-Colomme and Terride. See [Monluc], *Commentaires, 1521–1576*, p. 944, note.

[34] For the defection of Régin and Audaux, see Roelker, *Queen of Navarre*, pp. 279–80.

[35] Bordenave, *Histoire de Béarn et Navarre*, p. 145. See also 'Manifeste des gentilshommes de la Basse-Navarre et du peuple, qui ont pris les armes pour la défense de la réligion catholique', in Communay, 'Les Huguenots dans le Béarn et la Navarre', pp. 129–39.

[36] Olhagaray, *Histoire des comptes de Foix*, p. 565.

the leaguers set about consolidating towards this aim. Domezain was dispatched to meet Monluc at Agen to request reinforcements from Guyenne, while a similar petition for aid was sent to Madrid.[37] Escoarrabaque, meanwhile, journeyed to Paris to seek consent from the French crown for the league at Oloron,[38] while in January 1568, Navailles attempted to convince d'Albret to defect by forwarding a series of letters which relayed news of various Catholic victories under Anjou and Guise.[39] At Pau, Jeanne d'Albret was becoming increasingly perturbed by Monluc's role in affairs, and complained to the Bordeaux *parlement* that his interference was compromising her ability to defend her borders.[40] Monluc countered by stating that he was merely patrolling his own territory and, in any case, it was illegal for the queen of Navarre to mass troops in Foix and Albret, as only the king's lieutenant had authority to levy such soldiers. In this, Monluc was supported by the new *premier président* of the *parlement*, Christophe de Roffignac, Monluc's long-time Catholic associate, who dismissed Jeanne's claim. The French crown, however, was less than happy with the *parlement*'s response, expressing concern more at the build-up of Spanish troops on the southern borders of Béarn than at the queen's activities, and rebuked Roffignac for his interference.[41]

But the league was about to be betrayed before it could press home its advantage. In early March 1568, a Catholic noble, Jean de Belzunce, *seigneur* de Monein, informed one of Jeanne's spies that the forces at Oloron intended to march towards Pau within the week.[42] At nearby Ossau, Armand de Saint-Geniès, baron d'Audaux, another Catholic noble still loyal to Jeanne, rallied the queen's forces and moved to cut off the rebels' path.[43] The Catholic army was thus encircled by royal troops and forced to surrender. Its leaders were spared execution, though, when Charles IX intervened, ordering Bertrand de Salignac, *seigneur* de La Mothe-Fénelon, to negotiate a truce between the two parties. In a public show of reconciliation, many of the leaguers, including Luxe, Audaux, Domezain, Sainte-Colomme, Antin and Gabriel de Béarn, were awarded the highest honour possible, the *collier de l'ordre de Navarre*, in return

---

[37] Jaurgain, 'Les capitaines châtelains de Mauléon', II, p. 265.

[38] Olhagaray, *Histoire des comptes de Foix*, p. 566.

[39] Navailles to Louis d'Albret, bishop of Lescar (15 January 1568); *Preuves*, 79–80; Salefranque, 'Histoire de l'hérésie de Béarn', XLV, pp. 32–4.

[40] Jeanne d'Albret to Bordeaux *parlement* (February 1568), BN ms français, 22 373, fo. 308.

[41] Charles IX to Roffignac (25 February 1568), BN ms français, 22 373, fo. 373.

[42] Olhagaray wrote of Monein's betrayal of his fellow Catholics: 'Ce fut un eschec et mat au dessein de ces ligues': Olhagaray, *Histoire des comptes de Foix*, p. 566.

[43] Salefranque, 'Histoire de l'hérésie de Béarn', XLV, p. 59.

for a commitment to respect Jeanne's authority.[44] This mollification of the Catholic nobles would rankle with Protestant commentators for decades after the event, many seeing it as little more than the 'buying off' of rebels and traitors. Olhagaray, a Basse-Navarrais himself, was especially outraged by the award made to Charles de Luxe, whom he saw as the arch-enemy of many reformed communities of the lower Pyrenees.[45] Indeed, it soon became apparent that Jeanne's olive branch had failed to secure the loyalty of any of the leaguers and, with the resumption of sectarian conflict across France in September 1568, the rebels reneged on their pledge and returned to reconstitute their forces within Béarn and Navarre.

With such an escalation of affairs, the queen with her advisors fled to the security of La Rochelle on 6 September 1568.[46] This was an astute decision, as Jeanne managed to evade capture by the converging armies of Monluc, Sainte-Colomme and Fontenilles by a single day.[47] But her absence left the government of Béarn and Navarre in turmoil, and many of its territories rose in defiance of the queen's recent legislation. The *comté* of Foix was immediately garrisoned by Spanish troops, who claimed to be supporting the fledgling Catholic rebellion there. This move perturbed the French crown which, on 18 October, ordered the *parlements* of Bordeaux and Toulouse to issue edicts authorizing the seizure by royal troops of all lands, castles and towns of Béarn, Foix, Navarre, Armagnac and Bigorre before Spain could consolidate its forces there.[48] The crown also ordered the *parlements* to promote Charles de Luxe to the office of *lieutenant pour le roi de France*, to assume authority over Jeanne's government in the name of the French king.[49] Moves were

---

[44] Olhagaray, *Histoire des comptes de Foix*, p. 585.

[45] Olhagaray, *Histoire des comptes de Foix*, p. 574. Luxe later received numerous rewards for his services to the French crown during the 1560s: an outright gift of 20 000 *livres*, an annual pension of 800 *livres*, the *vicomté* of Soule and *l'ordre royale de Saint-Michael*. See Roelker, *Queen of Navarre*, p. 287.

[46] Bryson, *Jeanne d'Albret*, p. 189.

[47] Courteault, *Blaise de Monluc, Historien*, p. 513.

[48] Olhagaray, *Histoire des comptes de Foix*, pp. 578–80. On 19 November 1568, the Toulouse *parlement* ordered a *conseiller*, Pierre Ferrandier, to begin seizing lands belonging to Jeanne d'Albret in the *comtés* of Rodez and Rouergue: *HGL*, 9, p. 48. Freer has transcribed a letter from Charles IX to the Toulouse *parlement* (18 October 1568), which reveals the political intrigues of the crown in claiming to be merely 'looking after' Jeanne's territories until her return: 'We have found no remedy better calculated to obviate the evil designs of those who would do the said queen disservice, than to take possession of her territories': Freer, *The Life of Jeanne d'Albret*, pp. 299–300.

[49] 'Lettres du roi de France au parlement de Toulouse, portant commission à Charles de Luxe de se saisir des terres de la Reine de Navarre' (18 October 1568), in Jaurgain, 'Les capitaines châtelains de Mauléon', II, pp. 310–11.

then put in place to make this campaign self-financing. On 2 November 1568, the Bordeaux *parlement* ordered the seizure of all Jeanne's properties, goods and supplies in Guyenne to pay for troops and supplies.[50] Two weeks later, on 15 November 1568, the *parlement* at Toulouse claimed jurisdiction over Béarn, and dispatched a number of officials to Pau to take over its administration. But it soon became apparent that Monluc, in consultation with Roffignac at Bordeaux, had formulated a similar claim over this realm, on the basis that, as Jeanne had fled as a traitor, her lands were now forfeit and open to any legitimate party. The dispute was referred to the French crown which ordered that, for the moment, Luxe should remain in control of these lands.[51]

In December 1568, the Bordeaux *parlement* dispatched *conseillers* Belcier and Malbrun to act as advisors to Luxe, promising the new leader the full support of the administration and the Catholics of Guyenne.[52] From his headquarters at Oloron, Luxe promoted his former league compatriots, Domezain, Sainte-Colomme, Bonasse and Guy de Gohas to serve on a temporary council. He also opened communications with Monluc, who was at that time leading a company of Catholic nobles from Guyenne – including Leberon, Savignac, Caumont and Lauzun – against the Protestant *vicomte*, Piles, whose forces had besieged several Catholic Béarnais towns.[53] Luxe then attempted to lure Jeanne's key advisor, Louis d'Albret, to the Catholic side, dispatching Régin to tempt the bishop away from his queen by arguing that Luxe's commission had already seen the re-establishment of order across the troubled lands. But Louis d'Albret could not be persuaded.[54]

Despite this flurry of activity, by February 1569 much of Béarn and Navarre still remained outside the control of Luxe and French royal authority. Charles IX was forced to raise the stakes, instructing the *parlements* and Catholic generals of the south-west to prepare for a full-scale invasion. On 4 March, Roffignac assured Luxe that 'justice would soon be done in the lands of Jeanne d'Albret, but under the name and authority of the king'.[55] But the choice of commander to lead the royal army into Béarn and Navarre would prove controversial. Monluc had seemed the obvious candidate, but the duke of Anjou, the crown's *lieutenant-général* and overall military

---

[50] ADG, 1B 314, *Arrêt du parlement* (2 November 1568), fo. 2.

[51] Bordenave, *Histoire de Béarn et Navarre*, p. 166.

[52] *AHG*, 13, p. 253.

[53] O'Reilly, *Histoire complète de Bordeaux*, II, p. 249.

[54] Bishop of Oloron to bishop of Lescar (24 November 1568), *Preuve* 94, Salefranque, 'Histoire de l'hérésie de Béarn', XLV, p. 69. Louis d'Albret was such a pivotal figure in events that the Catholic party tried again in April 1569 to tempt him to their cause: *Preuve* 106, Salefranque, 'Histoire de l'hérésie de Béarn', XLV, p. 111.

[55] ADG, 1B 319, *Arrêt du parlement* (4 March 1569), fo. 42.

commander in the south-west at the time, chose to appoint Terride instead, claiming that Monluc was required to defend Guyenne from the Protestant *vicomtes*.[56] Monluc naturally suspected the hand of his rival, Damville, in this 'sleight'.[57] Yet Monluc would not be cut out of the loop entirely. Serving as *commissaire des vivres* in Terride's army was the Béarnais captain, Jean de Fleurdelis, *sieur* de Lannevielle et de Gallos.[58] This was an astute appointment, for Fleurdelis was a proven organizer of men and a successful commander in the field. He was also well known to the Catholic parties of the south-west, having served under Charles de Luxe and commanded three companies of Basque *gens de pied* during the Catholic rebellions in Basse-Navarre between 1564 and 1567, and so was familiar with the geographical and political pitfalls facing the army as it moved into Béarn.[59] But this would prove a valuable appointment for Monluc too, for Fleurdelis was a trusted adjutant of the Gascon general, having served as *commissaire de guerres* in Monluc's forces in Guyenne between 1561 and 1564, and as *commissaire ordinaire* under Negrepelisse in the Agenais during 1568.[60] Throughout the campaign, therefore, Monluc was kept in touch with proceedings through communiqués from his loyal captain, so much so in fact that when Valentin de Domezain and Bernard de Saint-Colomme were later questioned in Paris about the invasion, both attested that 'the captain Fleurdelis ... seemed to have been employed as much by Monluc as by the *sieur* de Terride'.[61]

Terride's army entered Béarn on 28 March 1569, and was soon joined by the forces of Luxe and the Béarnais captains Sainte-Colomme, Bonasse, Escoarrabaque, Gerdrest, Domezain, Eschaux, Armendaritz and many others.[62] Their first test came at Orthez, where combined action from French and Béarnais troops won the day. Terride now sought

[56] 'Commission de Monsieur d'Anjou frère du Roy, à monsieur de Terride, pour saisir le pays de Béarn', in Olhagaray, *Histoire des comptes de Foix*, pp. 585–8.

[57] For Courteault's analysis of the hostility between Monluc and Damville in 1569, see Courteault, *Blaise de Monluc, Historien*, pp. 534–53.

[58] Communay, 'Les Huguenots dans le Béarn et la Navarre', pp. 127, note 1, 131.

[59] BN ms français, 25 803, fos 314–16.

[60] For Fleurdelis' service as *commissaire de guerres* under Monluc, see Muster Rolls of Blaise de Monluc (7 December 1562), BN ms français, 25 800, fo. 58. For his appointment as captain under Monluc, see Charles IX to Monluc (May 1563), BN nouv. acq. français, 6001, fos 7–8; Lestrade, 'Les Huguenots en Comminges. Documents inédits', II', pp. 40–41. For his service under Negrepelisse in 1568, see BN nouv. acq. français, 8627, fo. 63. Fleurdelis had also been charged with delivering the controversial edict of Amboise to the Toulouse *parlement* in April 1563. See Courteault, *Un cadet de Gascogne*, p. 200.

[61] BN pièce orig. vol. 1010, dossier 23 011, Domesain no. 2. It was from Fleurdelis that Monluc learned of Terride's defeat at Orthez in 1569. See Courteault, *Blaise de Monluc, Historien*, p. 548.

[62] *Preuve* 106, Salefranque, 'Histoire de l'hérésie de Béarn', XLV, p. 111.

to establish an interim military administration capable of augmenting Luxe's shadow government, recently set up at Pau. To ensure that the Béarnais and Navarrais nobility saw this as legitimate, the *états* of Béarn were called and duly validated this policy.[63] The second step was to delegate offices in the new administration. Terride's appointments have been viewed by Protestant commentators as little more than a rewards system for those Catholic militants active in the rebellions and leagues of recent years: Audaux was reappointed *sénéchal* of Béarn; Navailles received the governorship of Pau; Escoarrabaque was reinstated as governor of Oloron; Sainte-Colomme was given command of Terride's *gens de pied* (with du Tilh made his chief adjutant); Régin became Terride's *commissaire des finances*; Bordenave the *président du conseil militaire*; Luger was charged with enforcing legislation; while the *avocat*, Jean de Supersantis, who had served under Terride as a delegate of the Catholics of Béarn to the Toulouse *parlement* during 1563, was made *procureur-général* of the royal army.[64] Such was the magnitude of the administrative changes made by Terride in April 1569 that, when Jeanne d'Albret returned to power in September, it required three specific *ordonnances* to remove the rebels and reinstate her legitimate government officials.[65]

The next major test for Terride's army came at the end of May, as his forces prepared for the assault on the fortified defences of Navarrenx. Terride was joined in this operation by his former leaguer from Toulouse, Negrepelisse, and by most of the Béarnais nobility. It soon became apparent, though, that the Catholic attacks were being easily blunted. Amid recriminations over Terride's incompetence, Charles IX ordered Monluc to send reinforcements from Comminges. Monluc's captain, the baron de Fontenilhes, was dispatched to facilitate this, but, by late July, despite numerous meetings with the councillors and nobles of Comminges, no reinforcements were forthcoming and only small quantities of wheat and munitions had been sent.[66] Such inactivity infuriated Monluc, who was already embroiled in a heated debate with Damville over the course of the campaign. Monluc had long sought permission from Damville, now

---

[63] Present at the *états de Béarn* in May 1569 were Jean de Cassanave, *abbé* of de la Reule, representing the clergy of Navarre; Gerdrest, Audaux, Sainte-Collome, Bonnasse and Seridos, appearing for the nobility; Jeannot de Gramont, a *jurat* at Morlaas, Raimond de Nabera, de Laruns and Peyrouton de Pauyadie, from Ossau, and Bernard de Medalon and Arnaud de Croharé, from Nay, representing the third estate: Dubarat, *Documents et bibliographie sur la réforme en Béarn*, p. 107; Olhagaray, *Histoire des comptes de Foix*, pp. 593–6.

[64] Dartigue-Peyrou, *Jeanne d'Albret et le Béarn*, p. 121. See also *Preuve* 112, Salefranque, 'Histoire de l'hérésie de Béarn', XLV, p. 142. For promotion of Jean de Supersantis, see AMT, BB 172, fos 147, 165.

[65] *Preuve* 119, Salefranque, 'Histoire de l'hérésie de Béarn', XLV, pp. 149–50.

[66] Lestrade, *Les Huguenots en Comminges. Documents inédits*, I, p. 69.

notional commander of the royal army in the south-west, to lead his forces into Béarn to relieve Terride, but had been denied at each request. Damville argued that a second Catholic force at Navarrenx was too great a gamble, especially given the potential instability that Monluc's absence from Guyenne would pose to the security of the region as a whole.[67] Monluc was outraged at Damville's reticence and commenced a propaganda blitz, presumably to avoid recrimination should the royal forces be defeated. On 9 August 1569, he met several Catholic captains to express his concern at Damville's intransigence,[68] before dispatching a series of letters to Terride, Luxe and various Catholic leaders, each copied to Damville, spelling out his desire to help but noting that the restrictions on his movement meant that his hands were tied. One missive in particular captured Monluc's frustration, a letter dated 14 August 1569, in which he informed Henry de Navailles, governor of Pau, that, while the conflict raged in Béarn, he and Bellegarde, the *sénéchal* of Toulouse, were forced to sit and 'play with their fingernails'.[69] Ironically, the following day Terride's beleaguered army succumbed to the inevitable and surrendered before Navarrenx to the *comte* de Montgommery. Terride, Gerdrest and Gohas managed to escape the field, only to be recaptured at Orthez three days later. The rest of the Catholic nobility were taken prisoner, including Sainte-Colomme, Escoarrabaque, Bordenave, du Tihl and many of the leaguers from Oloron and Lescar.[70] On 21 August, Terride, Gerdrest and Gohas were transferred back to Navarrenx where they, along with captains Candau, Salies and Pordéac, were stabbed to death for having taken flight.[71]

The defeat of the rebellion allowed Jeanne d'Albret to return to Navarre in September 1569. A list of Catholic rebels was drawn up with orders that their lands and wealth be confiscated and a warrant issued for their arrest.[72] As a result, the Catholic coalition melted away. Some, like Luxe, Domezain, Peyre and Bonasse fled to Basse-Navarre to rejoin

---

[67]   *HGL*, 9, p. 56.

[68]   [Monluc], *Commentaires, 1521–1576*, pp. 691–2.

[69]   Bordenave, *Histoire de Béarn et Navarre*, p. 265.

[70]   Other Catholic nobles captured at the siege of Navarrenx were Francis, *sieur* de Méritaing; Bertrand de Béarn, dit le capitaine Salies; Henric, *sieur* d'Abidos; Joanot, *sieur* d'Abère; Jacques de Lassalle, *sieur* de Candau; Domecq de St-Abit, Jean de Suus; Jean de Puy, *soliciteur*; Jacques de Vispalier, *controlleur* de Navarrenx; Forticq de Lasalle, and Frère Jean de Navarrenx. See *Preuve* 118, Salefranque, 'Histoire de l'hérésie de Béarn', XLV, p. 149.

[71]   Jaurgain, 'Les capitaines châtelains de Mauléon', pp. 317–18.

[72]   See 'Ordonnance de Jeanne d'Albret sur la justice, les rebelles, les ecclésiatiques et la confiscation des biens' (29 September 1569), *Preuve* 130, Salefranque, 'Histoire de l'hérésie de Béarn', XLV, pp. 176–9; 'Ordonnance de Montgommery, confisquant les biens ecclésiastiques' (2 October 1569), *Preuve* 129, ibid., XLV, pp. 175–6; 'Ordre de confisquer les biens de certains personnages' (5 November 1570), *Preuve* 134, ibid., XLV, p. 185.

Catholic forces there. Others, such as Escoarrabaque, d'Idron and Tristan de Sainte-Colomme, continued to fight against Montgommery's forces, each of them to fall at the siege of Tarbes in 1570.[73] De la Torte, one of the chiefs of the Catholic league at Lescar, was later captured and hanged for his part in the rebellion,[74] while only Audaux and Supersantis reconciled with Jeanne, both returning to serve in her government.[75] The following years saw only intermittent contact between these Catholic allies of the south-west. In November 1569, the continuing, though sporadic, violence along the Guyenne– Béarn/Navarre border saw the French diplomat, Lanssac, urge the king to send a great noble to unite the disparate factions in Guyenne.[76] Charles declined to act, content to leave Monluc and Damville to smooth over their dispute and administer royal authority throughout the region. Then, in July 1570, Monluc and his captains held council with Luxe, Moneins and Bernard de Saint-Colomme at Rabestens, near Tarbes, to discuss the possibility of a joint assault on Jeanne d'Albret. Luxe proposed that, should Monluc assist in their struggles against the queen of Navarre, he could count on a large Catholic force from Basse-Navarre.[77] But with Luxe now a resident in Paris, a fixture of the royal court, Monluc hesitated at such an offer. He knew that Luxe had become embroiled in a legal battle with Jeanne d'Albret, which precluded his return to head an army of Basse-Navarrais, and so doubted his commitment to this endeavour. Consequently the plan was aborted, and Monluc returned to his 'official' duties as *lieutenant du roi*. Whether or not Luxe ever intended to retake the field, he continued to work tirelessly for the Catholic cause in the south-west from Paris. In August 1571, he secured a stay of execution from Catherine de Medici for those Catholics held prisoner for their part in the rebellions of the 1560s, claiming that they were merely following directives of the French *parlements* in 'securing' Jeanne's lands in her absence.[78] Then, in September 1571, the queen of Navarre offered Luxe a compromise, urging him to return to his lands as a loyal subject to oversee the rebuilding of the government

[73] Dubarat, *Histoire de Béarn*, pp. 282, 303; Olhagaray, *Histoire des comptes de Foix*, p. 625.

[74] Bordenave, *Histoire de Béarn et Navarre*, p. 281.

[75] See 'Entérinement des lettres de grâce de Jean de Supersantis' (23 June 1571), *Preuve* 143, Salefranque, 'Histoire de l'hérésie de Béarn', XLV, pp. 191–2. Audaux later became a favourite of Jeanne's heir, Henri de Navarre, receiving the governorship of Béarn from him in 1584.

[76] Lanssac to Charles IX (21 November 1569), *AHG*, 10, p. 346.

[77] Monluc to Catherine de Medici (9 July 1570), [Monluc], *Commentaires, 1521–1576*, pp. 770, 1378, note. Monluc's captains at the meeting were Gondrin, Saint-Orens and d'Orthe.

[78] Luxe to Catherine de Medici, (August 1571); Roelker, *Queen of Navarre*, p. 287.

there.[79] Luxe declined, preferring the relative safety of the capital to recriminations in his homeland.

It has been shown that the sphere of influence of Catholic activists of the south-west reached far wider than the defence of orthodoxy at Bordeaux, Agen and Toulouse. The success of Monluc, Armagnac, Terride, Negrepelisse, Candalle, Bellegarde and the Basse-Navarrais forces of Charles de Luxe in supporting the Catholic rebels of Béarn and Navarre exposed the extent and interconnectedness of Catholic militant networks and affiliations across the region, and their desire to intervene and support fellow co-religionists in the fight against the inexorable advance of the reformed church. Such reciprocal affiliation has rarely been assessed by historians, with the leagues formed by the Béarnais rebels usually viewed as isolated entities, unconnected to activism within Guyenne and Languedoc. Military and financial support from Spain and the papacy also proved beneficial to the militants' cause, although these external powers were rarely attempting to save Catholicism in France: Madrid sought to secure its northern borders and regain former territories; Rome sought, through the Inquisition, to re-establish a presence within France that had been severely limited by the overtly prohibitive Gallican sensibilities of consecutive sixteenth-century monarchs. Yet, while each of these disparate Catholic bodies had quite distinct motives, when united against the reform movement they became a potent force, offering a lifeline for the supporters of orthodoxy in the south-west.

---

[79] Jeanne d'Albret to Luxe (29 August 1571, 11 September 1571, 25 September 1571); Rochambeau, *Lettres d'Antoine de Bourbon et de Jehanne d'Albret*, pp. 323–7.

CHAPTER ELEVEN

Conclusion

This study has shown that urban centres were pivotal to sectarian fortunes in the south-west during the 1550s and 1560s. Catholics were able to maintain authority within the region only because militants secured control of Bordeaux, Agen and Toulouse; had these bastions succumbed to Protestant assault, the surrounding Catholic communities would have fallen inexorably as a consequence. Conversely, the failure of the reform movement to capture these key citadels proved a fatal weakness in its struggle for hegemony over the region. Not only were Protestant forces denied dominant strategic platforms from which to orchestrate their campaigns, but Catholic resistance gained sufficient time for the defenders to regroup and plan counter-offensives of their own.[1] The numerous activists of the south-west deserve most of the credit for this resurgence. At Bordeaux, Catholic militants defied intense Protestant sorties and the best efforts of moderates to censor their activities to achieve political and military parity by 1563. The ensuing stalemate allowed uncompromising figures such as Roffignac and Montferrand to assume greater authority within local government structures, and to begin implementing policies that would consolidate and then expand Catholic power, so that by the late 1560s radical consensus was pre-eminent within the town. At Agen, it was the urban patricians who staved off initial Protestant aggression through adept political manoeuvring and the astute use of coalition committees to secure control of administrative functions. These juntas then marshalled the local nobility and harnessed an eager citizenry to the Catholic cause, urged on by the rhetoric of Monluc, who accentuated the sense of siege mentality felt by many so as to rouse the populace to participate in the unified defence of their town. At Toulouse, Catholics were sparked into action following the attempted coup of May 1562. Committees were formed to coordinate defiance, and the local nobility, magistrates and populace engaged in integrated resistance, much like that at Agen. Once the town was secured, however, the Catholic leadership determined that absolute power over governmental procedure was essential to prevent a repeat of the insurrection. The conciliatory agendas advocated by the crown were thus rejected in favour of repressive policies which sought to restrict, censure and penalize the

---

[1] David Bryson also stated that the Protestant failure to take Bordeaux in 1562 weakened their position in Guyenne. See Bryson, *Queen Jeanne*, pp. 147, 311–14.

Protestant minority of Toulouse, with the proceeds from the fines and sequestrations served against the reform movement used to finance the war effort.

The multifaceted nature of Catholic militancy was fundamental to these successes. From the syndicates, leagues and confederations through to the coalition councils, confraternities and crusading ideals, leading activists proved themselves potent forces within provincial affairs. Prominent were the military captains of the region. These men – among them the *sieurs* de Candalle, d'Escars, Terride, Tilladet and Negrepelisse – were an elite corpus, born and bred locally, keen to defend their homes and protect personal privileges as much as to secure Catholicism. Many served in Monluc's royal forces across the south-west, though all offered independent support to local urban councils in time of crisis and, on occasion, collaborated with neighbouring elites to establish local confederations intent on extirpating Protestantism from their community. Of equivalent social stature, and of equal importance to the course of Catholic activism, were the magistrates of the sovereign courts at Bordeaux and Toulouse. The *parlements*, long riven by contention, faced new tensions in the 1550s. The infiltration of reform ideology into the court chambers challenged established traditions and threatened the supremacy of orthodoxy as the guiding principle behind provincial government. Catholic magistrates became exasperated at the equivocal nature of royal legislation which seemed to them to condone the legitimization of Protestant religious, political and military prerogatives, while seeming to malign Catholic actions. Militant *présidents* and *conseillers* such as Roffignac, Malvin, Baulon and Daffis led the Catholic rejoinder to the relentless drive by the crown to enforce conciliatory legislation, sanctioning combative confrontations with reformers and acting as patrons for local activists rather than bowing to demands for accommodation and toleration. The agendas set by these men would provide the blueprint for Catholic wartime administration in the region for years to come. Working alongside these notables were the civic councillors, lesser officials and members of the clergy. These men, among them Lange, Montferrand and Melon at Bordeaux, Lalande and de Nort at Agen, and Bellegarde at Toulouse, managed the coalition juntas so as to usurp and dominate the institutional bodies of the region during the conflict. Their control over political, military and fiscal matters became so complete that by 1570 each had secured an iron grip on their Protestant minorities, and had set about major reorganization of the town guard and fortification of their urban defences. The success of these various determined individuals in underpinning the defence of orthodoxy lends support to the controversial assertion of John Bossy, that the persistence of French Catholicism through the crises of the Reformation was 'largely the result of the voluntary association of French Catholics',[2] at least where the south-west is concerned.

It is important to note, however, that 'grass roots' activism also played an important role in bolstering Catholicism across the region, as embodied in the bitter conflict between *basochiens* and the emerging evangelical movement on the streets of Bordeaux and Toulouse throughout the 1540s and 1550s. The participation of such 'popular' elements challenges three established maxims: firstly, it shows that Catholic militancy was not the prerogative only of elite Leaguers after 1584, as has traditionally been assumed; secondly, it reveals that spontaneous sectarian activism was not a phenomenon solely of the war years, but that it had been a feature of the urban landscape from the early 1540s; thirdly, it attests that Catholic renewal in Guyenne and western Languedoc had commenced long before the Council of Trent published its agenda for reform in the 1560s, and suggests that Catholic revival in the south-west predated the influence of Trent and proceeded largely independently of it. Whether such 'lowly sorts' were enfranchised by their communal activism is difficult to determine. For example, while the *basoche*, as apprentices and trainee clerks, would normally have been excluded from sanctioned activism against Protestant groups, it is possible to detect a degree of benevolence from social superiors during the confessional disturbances at Bordeaux and Toulouse, eager to offer patronage and protection in return for securing the services of elements capable of boosting the local militia force as required. Such reciprocal engagements reveal that power politics and confessional zeal went hand in hand in these fraught times. That the traditions and totems of orthodox religiosity were under direct threat is evident in many aspects of Catholic behaviour during the period: in the prevalence of penitential fervour in the polemic; in the ubiquitous use of sacred oaths and pledges to confirm membership of the leagues and associations; in the resurgence of confraternal activism and the prominence of the local clergy in the political sphere; and in the establishment of that most zealous of penitential militia forces at Toulouse: the crusade.

These findings, and especially the rivalries between competing bands of religious enthusiasts on the streets of the south-west, find resonance in Philip Benedict's study of pre-war Rouen,[3] and in Ann Ramsey's examination of mid-century, low-level corporate activism at Paris, where 'attitudes towards these mixed religious, trade and political associations are a key to understanding the socially complex strands of Catholic militancy

---

[2] Bossy, 'Leagues and associations', p. 171.
[3] Benedict, *Rouen during the Wars of Religion*, Chapters 1–4.

that emerge from the 1540s onwards'.[4] There are noticeable differences, however, between northern and southern exemplars. At Rouen, the proximity of the town to the royal court meant that factional rivalry played a sizeable role in the disturbances, whereas the geographical distance of Bordeaux, Agen and Toulouse from court struggles meant that sectarian incidents here were more likely to be genuine religious affairs than echoes of distant political or noble controversies. At Paris, the distinction was more to do with the extent and cooperative nature of Catholic activism: the corporations and confraternities of the capital tended to be confined within *quartiers*, their affiliates concerned strictly with local causes, whereas the militant bodies of the south-west performed on a much larger stage, ranging over multiple administrative districts, their leadership serving jointly on numerous sister corporations, their manpower and resources often pooled to better protect the area. That these distances and diversities did not limit Catholic potential, or lessen the cohesiveness of Catholic militancy in the south-west, was due to the strong and multifarious bonds linking military commanders and senior officials. Here, simple ad hoc arrangements and 'loops of association'[5] allowed militants to maintain communications and forge cohesive yet flexible unions as necessary, without being restricted by the more prescriptive ties of clientage adopted by elite families and their lieutenants elsewhere in France. Again, the absence of grandee and governor influence in the region played its part in facilitating such adaptable relations. As a result, the capacity for organization and fund raising of the militants of the south-west was advanced and very much local, and, despite the fact that many of their cooperatives fell foul of crown dictate, the affiliations and *amitiés* that were established remained long after the associations had being dismantled, to govern connections and interactions between activists for years to come.

Overarching these bodies was the enigmatic Gascon captain, Blaise de Monluc. Monluc provided leadership for many of the militant factions, directing Catholic forces and determining policy as required. His experience in defending urban centres against a belligerent enemy proved crucial, with Bordeaux, Agen and Toulouse all benefiting from his

---

[4] Ramsey, *Liturgy, Politics, and Salvation*, pp. 21–2. See, especially, Parts 1 and 2.

[5] The term 'loops of association' is used by the English social historian, Stephen Hipkin, to describe expedient relations between small groups who had a common, if short-term, political focus in their opposition to enclosure in seventeenth-century England: Stephen Hipkin, '"Sitting on his Penny Rent": Conflict and Right of Common in Faversham Blean, 1595–1610', *Rural History* 11, 1 (2000), p. 23. An important study of civic and collective identity and association within the urban setting in England during the sixteenth and seventeenth centuries is found in Jonathan Barry and Christopher Brooks, *The Middling Sort of People. Culture, Society and Politics in England, 1550–1800* (London, 1994), pp. 84–9.

personal management of resistance during the 1560s. The strategy to secure each centre was based on four maxims developed by Monluc during his military operations in the Italian Wars, and epitomized in his coordinated rearguard action against overwhelming odds at Siena in 1555: seize governmental authority, remove suspicious elements, legislate to repress the resident minority and energize the populace.[6] Monluc also added a degree of legitimacy to Catholic endeavours through his title as *lieutenant du roi* in Guyenne, although Protestants would contend that he bowed to radical tendencies too often, to the detriment of impartial observance of royal authority in the region. This dual role as activist and royal servant is a reminder of the complicated situation faced by many Catholics during this period, controversies inherent in the offices held by high-ranking militants who also served as *lieutenants, gouverneurs, sénéchaux* and *prévôts*. Similar contention faced Catholic magistrates of the *parlements* at Bordeaux and Toulouse. Many felt betrayed at the crown's inactivity over continuing violence against Catholic communities and bewildered as each royal edict seemed to make further concessions to reformers rather than address Catholic grievances. The numerous amnesties that released Protestant prisoners from captivity were especially galling to these magistrates, so much so that Parker and Schneider have suggested that several deemed it their duty to appoint themselves 'defenders of royal authority' in order to rescue crown policy from the mire.[7]

More exasperating still was the crown's decision in 1563 to require the provincial judiciary of France to execute its policy of religious toleration. Many militants of the south-west were thus cast as enforcers of conciliatory dictates that amongst other things charged them with dismantling Catholic associations and censuring unlawful Catholic assemblies or face prosecution and loss of office for defying royal authority. If Nicola Sutherland has described these edicts as 'curious, contradictory, self-defeating and provisional',[8] it would be interesting to note the tone and colour of the language used by Roffignac, Lange, Lalande et al., at this development. Resistance to Catholic designs came from local government as well as from the royal court, though, in the shape of moderates such as Jacques-Benoît de Lagebâton, the *premier président* at Bordeaux. These

---

[6] For Monluc's actions at the siege of Siena in 1555, see [Monluc], *Commentaires, 1521–1576*, pp. 280–358; Evans, *Blaise de Monluc*, pp. 194–365; Roy, *Blaise de Monluc*, pp. 132–78.

[7] David Parker, *The Making of French Absolutism* (London, 1983), p. 37; Schneider, *Public Life in Toulouse*, p. 96.

[8] Nicola M. Sutherland, *The Huguenot Struggle for Recognition* (New Haven, 1980), p. 128.

men derided partisan politics and strove to secure and maintain peace through adherence to crown directives, despite being outnumbered by hostile Catholic officials. But although Lagebâton managed to curb Catholic militancy at Bordeaux through the early 1560s, and his counterpart at Agen, Herman de Sevin, succeeded in implementing *mi-partie* chambers across the Agenais in 1563, both were forced to flee the region as extremist juntas under Montferrand and Lalande gained control of the town councils. For Mark Greengrass, the sectarian conflict was thus shaped 'by rights as well as by rites', with jurisdictional prerogatives and loyalties to office conflicting with confessional tendencies.[9] Contemporaries were just as aware of these tensions, with the baron de Biron, a leading Bordelais noble, warning the Bordeaux *parlementaires* to refrain from becoming embroiled in disputes over religion at the expense of performing their principal duties, but to adhere strictly to the letter of their commission,[10] while Burie cautioned royal officials at Bordeaux and Toulouse similarly that a sovereign court should not be a tool to be wielded by zealots in opposition to royal authority, but a mediator of peace between the king and his people.[11]

Similar contradictions over obligations existed for the Catholic military captains of the south-west. Here, the crown's ambiguous management of its forces served to complicate matters. Robert Harding has shown that Catherine de Medici allowed her generals considerable liberty to interpret and execute the law during the early phase of the wars.[12] The *lieutenants* and *sénéchaux* were thus left to their own devices more than the crown would have preferred, and were rarely restrained by their absentee governors. The ramifications were significant, as the deployment of troops and levying of urban militia often fell to military officers who had committed themselves to the Catholic cause. As a result, there was no coherent royal strategy for the region, and as crown resources were limited and the exchequer invariably tardy or negligent in meeting financial obligations, the captains were obliged to rally their personal retinues and those of their neighbours to pacify the countryside on numerous occasions. As the majority of these men were Catholic, and serving under Monluc, Protestant disenchantment at the neutrality of crown forces was understandably high. One option open to the crown was to hire in troops from foreign powers – a necessity, in fact, during the first war, as the royal forces garrisoned in Guyenne were minimal. This

9 Greengrass, 'The anatomy of a religious riot', p. 390.
10 Biron to Burie (30 October 1560), [Biron], *Letters and Documents*, I, pp. 6–7.
11 Jean de Métivier, *Chronique du parlement de Bordeaux* (2 vols, Bordeaux, 1886), II, pp. 288–9.
12 Harding, *Anatomy of a Power Elite*, p. 52.

meant that Monluc and his captains were able to deploy several companies of Spanish troops at many of the early skirmishes in the south-west, much to the dismay of Protestant communities. Rumours of collusion with Madrid and Rome spread at such collaboration, fuelled by increasing sums contributed from Spain and the vocal support offered by the papacy to the Catholic associations. The integral nature of the Catholic war effort in the south-west soon became apparent in the union of these forces to assist the Catholic rebellions at Oloron, Lescar and Basse-Navarre, and to overthrow the Calvinist government of Jeanne d'Albret. The diversity and degree of Catholic activism was now apparent. The sphere of influence of the militants was shown to be extensive, certainly not confined to one arena or a single association, while the disparate social strata were seen to be working in unison: the magistrates formulated policy, the lesser officials and councillors implemented legislation, the armed nobility enforced these dictates and the popular elements confronted Protestants on the streets. It was this homogeneity and interconnectedness that secured the survival of Catholicism in the south-west between 1540 and 1570: first enabling the defence of the towns, then the consolidation of power, then the formulation of a counter-offensive. This phenomenon is only just beginning to be understood and explored by historians.

Map of South-West France, c. 1560

Select Bibliography

Manuscript sources

Agen

Archives départementales de Lot-et-Garonne
E Supplément Agen, 422 (La Plume BB2, 1563–64).
E Supplément Agen, 2630 (Francescas BB1, 1550–82).
E Supplément Agen, 2386 (Casteljaloux BB1, 1561–77).
E Supplément Agen, 2429 (Casteljaloux EE1, 1562).
E Supplément Agen, 2981 (Sos BB1, 1500–1720).
E Supplément Agen, AA: 43.
E Supplément Agen, BB: 30–31, 60, 86.
E Supplément Agen, CC: 52, 57, 61–2, 65–7, 70, 302, 306.
E Supplément Agen, EE: 16, 56.
E Supplément Agen, FF: 13, 31–33, 199, 212.
E Supplément Agen, GG: 196, 201–2.

Bordeaux

Archives départementales de la Gironde
1B: 124–359.
6E: 63.
H: 2378, 2380, 2512.
G: 35, 39–45, 287, 479.

Archives municipales de Bordeaux
AA: 19.
BB: 11–12, 153, 165, 192, 196.
CC: 4–5, 1099, 1100a, 1102, 1102b.
DD: 3g, 3h.
EE: 1–3, 6–11, 14, 34–5.
FF: 5a, 14.
GG: 928–30, 937.
Manuscrits: 213, 222, 297, 299, 371, 421, 502/1,2, 592, 601/5, 666, 753, 763–77.

Bibliothèques municipales de Bordeaux
H: 8613.

Manuscrits: 367, 369 ii, 369 iii, 370, 383, 712, 8, ii, 728, 738, 828 v, 1003, 1497 iii.

Paris

Bibliothèque nationale
Dupuy: 588.
Fonds italienne: 1721.
Manuscrits français: 3159, 3185–6, 3189, 3197, 3210, 3217, 3242, 3362, 3960, 5011, 6911, 6948, 10 752, 15 547–8, 15 558, 15 591, 15 596, 15 871–82, 20 461–2, 22 369, 22 372–3, 25 800–803.
Nouvelle acquisitions françaises: 6001, 6013, 8625–9, 20 052–3, 20 598–9.
Pièces originales: 1010.

Toulouse

Archives municipales de Toulouse
AA: 6, 14–21, 44, 48, 53.
BB: 11–12, 62, 101–8, 152, 172–6 ii, 223, 269.
CC: 256, 259, 354, 356–7, 616, 1939–40.
EE: 4, 11–12, 26, 45–6, 87.
FF: 191–6, 373, 609, 620–21.
GG: 824–8, 1022.

Archives départementales de la Haute-Garonne
1G: 370, 488.
B: 20, 37, 50, 52–64, 1906–7, 3440–44.
C: 2281–2, 3498.
E: 1013.

Printed primary sources

Aubigné, Théodore Agrippa d', *Histoire universelle* (10 vols, ed. A. de Ruble, Paris, 1886–1909).
Aubigné, Théodore Agrippa d', *Les tragiques* (2 vols, ed. F. Lestingant, Paris, 1995).
Bèze, Théodore de, *Correspondance de Théodore de Bèze* (26 vols, ed. H. Aubert, Geneva, 1960–2002).
Bèze, Théodore de, *Histoire ecclésiastique des églises réformées au royaume de France* (3 vols, ed. G. Baum and E. Cunitz, Nieuwkoop, 1974).

Biron, Armand de Gontaut, baron de, 'Correspondance inédite du maréchal Armand de Gontaut-Biron', *Archives historiques du département de la Gironde*, 14 (1873), pp. 1–271.

Biron, Armand de Gontaut, baron de, *The Letters and Documents of Armand de Gontaut, Baron de Biron, Marshall of France (1524–1592)* (2 vols, ed. S. Ehrman and J. Thompson, Berkeley, 1936).

Boëtie, Estienne de la, *Mémoire sur la pacification des troubles* (ed. M. Smith, Geneva, 1983).

Brantôme, *Oeuvres complètes de Pierre de Bourdeille, seigneur de Brantôme* (11 vols, ed. L. Lalanne, Paris, 1864–82).

Cabié, Edmond, *Ambassade en Espagne de Jean Ébrard, seigneur de St. Sulpice de 1562 à 1565* (Albi, 1903).

Cabié, Edmond, *Guerres de religion dans le sud-ouest de la France et principalement dans le Quercy, d'après les papiers des seigneurs de Saint-Sulpice de 1561 à 1590. Documents transcrits, classés et annotés* (Paris, 1906).

Castelnau, Michel de, *Les mémoires de Messire Michel de Castelnau, seigneur de Mauvissiere et de Concressaut, ausquelles sont traictées les choses plus remarquables qu'il a veues et negotiées en France, Angleterre, et Escosse, soubs les rois François II et Charles IX, tant en temps de paix qu'en temps de guerre* (Paris, 1671).

Charles IX, *Lettres de Charles IX à M. de Fourquevaux, ambassadeur en Espagne (1565–1572)* (ed. C. Douais, Paris, 1897).

Condé, *Mémoires de Condé, ou recueil pour servir à l'histoire de France, contenant ce qui s'est passé du plus mémorable dans le Royaume* (6 vols, London, Paris, 1743).

Darnal, Jean, *Chronique Bordelois. Supplément* (Bordeaux, 1619).

Dast le Vacher de Boisville, J.N., *Inventaire sommaire des registres de la jurade de Bordeaux, 1520 à 1783 (Archives municipales de Bordeaux, 6–13)* (Bordeaux, 1947).

Este, Hippolyte d', *Négociations ou lettres d'affaires ecclésiastiques et politiques escrites au Pape Pie IV et au cardinal Borromée par Hippolyte d'Este, Cardinal de Ferrara, légat en France au commencement des guerres civiles* (Paris, 1658).

Fourquevaux, Raymond de Rouer, sieur de, *Dépêches de M. de Fourquevaux, ambassadeur du roi Charles IX en Espagne (1565–1572)* (3 vols, ed. C. Douais, Paris, 1896–1904).

Gaches, Jacques, *Mémoires sur les guerres de religion à Castres et dans le Languedoc (1555–1610)* (Geneva, 1970).

Granvelle, Antoine Perrenot, cardinal de, *Papiers d'état du cardinal de Granvelle, d'après les manuscrits de la bibliothèque de Besançon* (9 vols, ed. C. Weiss, Paris, 1841–52).

Haton, Claude, *Mémoires de Claude Haton (1553–1582)* (2 vols, Paris, 2001).

Lafaille, Germain de, *Annales de la ville de Toulouse* (2 vols, Toulouse, 1687, 1701).

L'Estoile, Pierre de, *Mémoires et journaux de Pierre de l'Estoile. Nouvelle collection; mémoires pour servir à l'histoire de France* (ed. Michaud and Poujoulat, Paris, 1837).

L'Hôpital, Michel de, *Oeuvres complètes de Michel de l'Hospital, chancelier de France* (5 vols, ed. P.J.S. Duféy, Geneva, 1968).

Lorraine, Cardinal Charles de, *Lettres du cardinal Charles de Lorraine (1525–1574)* (Geneva, 1998).

Lurbe, Gabriel de, *Chronique Bordeloise* (Bordeaux, 1594).

Medici, Catherine de, *Lettres de Catherine de Médici* (10 vols, ed. H. de la Ferrière and G. Baguenault de Puchesse, Paris, 1880–1909).

Métivier, Jean de, *Chronique du parlement de Bordeaux* (2 vols, Bordeaux, 1886).

Monluc, Blaise de, *Blaise de Monluc, Commentaires 1521–1576* (ed. Paul Courteault and J. Giono, Paris, 1964).

Monluc, Blaise de, *Commentaires et lettres de Blaise de Monluc, maréchal de France* (5 vols, ed. A. de Ruble, Paris, 1864–72).

Monluc, Blaise de, *Lettres de monsieur Blaise de Monluc, chevalier de l'ordre, cappitaine de cinquante homes d'armes de ses ordonnances: escriptes au Roy touchant le gouvernement de la Guyenne, avec la response de la Majesté audit sieur de Monluc* (Lyon, 1571).

Olhagaray, Pierre, *Histoire des comptes de Foix, Béarn, et Navarre, diligemment recueillie tant des precedens historiens, que des archives desdites maisons* (Paris, 1629).

Pasquier, Étienne, *Lettres historiques pour les années 1556–1594* (Geneva, 1966).

Philip II, *Correspondance de Philippe II sur les affaires des Pays-Bas (1558–1577)* (6 vols, ed. L.P. Gachard, Brussels, 1848–79).

Ræmond, Florimond de, *L'histoire de la naissance, progrez et decadence de l'hérésie de ce siècle* (2 vols, Paris, 1610).

Rochambeau, Marquis de, *Lettres d'Antoine de Bourbon et de Jehanne d'Albret* (Paris, 1877).

Salefranque, Pierre de, 'Histoire de l'hérésie de Béarn. Manuscrit de Pierre de Salefranque, conseiller du roi, secrétaire du parlement de Navarre', in *Bulletin de la société des sciences, lettres et arts de Pau*, IIe Série, XLIII–XLVI (ed. Abbé Dubarat, Pau, 1920–23).

Thou, Jacques-Auguste de, *Histoire universelle, depuis 1543 jusqu'en 1607* (16 vols, London, 1734 and Basle, 1742).

Secondary sources

Andrieu, Jules, *Histoire de l'Agenais* (2 vols, Agen, 1893).

Anquetil, Louis Pierre, *L'esprit de la Ligue, ou histoire politique des troubles de France pendant les XVIe et XVIIe siècles* (2 vols, Paris, 1818).

Arnaud, *Histoire des Protestants du Vivarais et du Velay, pays de Languedoc* (Toulouse, 1888).

Ascoli, P.M., 'French provincial cities and the Catholic League', *Occasional Papers of the American Society for Reformation Research*, 1 (1977), pp. 15–37.

Baguenault de Puchess, Gustave, 'La politique de Philippe II dans les affaires de France: 1559–1598', *Revue des questions historiques*, 25 (1879), pp. 5–66.

Barrère, Abbé Joseph, *Histoire religieuse et monumentale du diocèse d'Agen, depuis les temps les plus reculés jusqu'à nos jours* (2 vols, Agen, 1855–6).

Barry, Jonathan and Christopher Brooks, *The Middling Sort of People. Culture, Society and Politics in England, 1550–1800* (London, 1994).

Baudouin, A., 'Les *'mea culpa'* de Blaise de Montluc', *Mémoires de l'académie des sciences, inscriptions et belles-lettres de Toulouse*, vol. I, (Toulouse, 1901), pp. 21–30.

Bellecombe, A. de, *Aide-mémoire pour servir a l'histoire de l'Agenais* (Auch, 1899).

Benedict, Philip (ed.), *Cities and Social Change in Early Modern France* (London, 1989).

Benedict, Philip, *Rouen during the Wars of Religion* (Cambridge, 1981).

Benedict, Philip, 'The Saint Bartholomew's massacres in the provinces', *HJ*, 21 (1978), pp. 205–25.

Benedict, Philip, *'Un roi, une loi, deux fois*: Parameters for the History of Catholic–Reformed Co-Existence in France, 1555–1685', in Ole Peter Grell and Bob Scribner (eds), *Tolerance and Intolerance in the European Reformation* (Cambridge, 1996).

Birnstiel, Eckart, 'Les chambres mi-parties: les cadres institutionnels d'une juridiction spéciale', in Jacques Poumarède and Jack Thomas (eds), *Les parlements de Province. Pouvoirs, justice et société du XVe au XVIIIe siècle* (Toulouse, 1996), pp. 121–38.

Bordenave, Nicolas de, *Histoire de Béarn et Navarre* (ed. P. Raymond, Paris, 1873).

Borderie, Louis Arthur de la, *Monuments originaux de l'histoire de Saint Yves* (Saint-Brieux, 1887).

Boscheron-Desportes, C.B.F., *Histoire du parlement de Bordeaux depuis sa création jusqu'à sa suppression (1451–1790)* (2 vols, Bordeaux, 1877).

Bossy, John, 'Leagues and associations in sixteenth-century French Catholicism', *Studies in Church History*, 23 (1986), pp. 171–89.

Bossy, John, 'The Counter-Reformation and the people of Catholic Europe', *P&P*, 47 (1970), pp. 51–70.

Bourg, M.A. du, *Histoire du grand-prieuré de Toulouse* (Toulouse, 1883).

Bourgeon, G., *La réforme à Nérac. Les origines (1530–1560)* (Toulouse, 1880).

Bourgeon, Jean-Louis, *Charles IX devant la Saint-Barthélemy* (Geneva, 1995).

Boutrouche, Robert (ed.), *Bordeaux de 1453 à 1715* (Bordeaux, 1966).

Boyer, G., 'La basoche Toulousaine au quinzième siècle, d'après les archives du parlement', *Mémoires de la société archéologique du Midi de la France*, 18 (1932), pp. 64–71.

Briggs, Robin, *Communities of Belief. Cultural and Social tensions in Early Modern France* (Oxford, 1995).

Brives-Cazes, M., *Notices historiques sur la bazoche de Bordeaux du XVe au XVIIIe siècle* (Toulouse, s.d.).

Bryson, David, *Queen Jeanne and the Promised Land. Dynasty, Homeland and Religion and Violence in Sixteenth-Century France* (Brill, 1999).

Carroll, Stuart, *Noble Power during the French Wars of Religion. The Guise Affinity and the Catholic Cause in Normandy* (Cambridge, 1998).

Carroll, Stuart, 'The Guise affinity and popular protest during the Wars of Religion', *FH*, 9 (1995), pp. 125–51.

Cassan, Michel, *Le temps des guerres de religion. Le cas du Limousin (vers 1530–vers 1630)* (Paris, 1996).

Catalogne, Roland de, 'Monluc et la réforme à Toulouse', *Archistra*, 42–3 (October–December 1979), pp. 67–88.

Cau-Durban, Abbé, *Histoire des évêques et archevêques de Toulouse* (Toulouse, 1873).

Cau-Durban, Abbé, 'Statuts de la basoche du sénéchal de Toulouse', *Mémoires de la société archéologique du Midi de la France*, 16 (1908), pp. 166–84.

Chalande, Jules, 'Les établissements des Jésuites à Toulouse au XVIe et XVIIe siècle', *Journal de Toulouse*, 29 (August 1926), pp. 1–35.

Champion, Pierre Honoré, *Charles IX, la France et le contrôle de l'Espagne* (2 vols, Paris, 1939).

Chavanon, Christian, *Béatification professionnelle de Saint Yves* (Bordeaux, 1936).

Chevalier, Bernard, *Les bonnes villes de France du XIVe au XVIe siècle* (Paris, 1982).

Christin, Olivier, 'From repression to pacification: French royal policy in the face of Protestantism', in Philip Benedict, Guido Marnef, Henk van

Nierop and Marc Venard (eds), *Reformation, Revolt and Civil War in France and the Netherlands, 1555–1585* (Amsterdam, 1999), pp. 201–14.

Christin, Olivier, *Une révolution symbolique. L'iconoclasme huguenot et la reconstruction catholique* (Paris, 1991).

Cloulas, Ivan, *Catherine de Medicis* (Paris, 1979).

Cocula, Anne-Marie, *Étienne de la Boétie* (Bordeaux, 1995).

Collins, James B., *The Fiscal Limits of Absolutism* (Berkeley, CA, 1988).

Communay, A., *Le Parlement de Bordeaux, notes biographiques sur ses principaux officiers* (Bordeaux, 1898).

Communay, A., 'Les Gascons dans les armées françaises', *Revue de l'Agenais*, 21 (1894), pp. 379–91, 492–510; and 22 (1895), pp. 165–76, 229–39, 392–406.

Communay, A., 'Les Huguenots dans le Béarn et la Navarre. Documents inédits', *Archives historiques de la Gascogne*, 6 (Paris, Auch, 1885).

Connac, Emile, 'Troubles de mai 1562 à Toulouse', *Annales du Midi*, 3 (1891), pp. 310–39.

Conner, Philip, *Huguenot Heartland. Montauban and Southern French Calvinism during the Wars of Religion* (Aldershot, 2002).

Constant, Jean-Marie, *La Ligue* (Paris, 1996).

Constant, Jean-Marie, *Les Guise* (Paris, 1984).

Constant, Jean-Marie, 'The Protestant nobility in France during the Wars of Religion: A leaven of innovation in a traditional world', in Philip Benedict, Guido Marnef, Henk van Nierop and Marc Venard (eds), *Reformation, Revolt and Civil War in France and the Netherlands, 1555–1585* (Amsterdam, 1999), pp. 69–82.

Courteault, Paul, *Blaise de Monluc. Historien* (Geneva, 1970).

Courteault, Paul, *Douze lettres inédites de Blaise de Monluc, publiées et annotées* (Toulouse, 1898).

Courteault, Paul, *Histoire de Gascogne et de Béarn* (Paris, 1938).

Courteault, Paul, *L'invasion de l'armée des princes en Agenais (fin novembre 1569-janvier 1570)* (Agen, 1898).

Courteault, Paul, *Un cadet de Gascogne au XVIe siècle. Blaise de Monluc* (Paris, 1909).

Crouzet, Denis, *La genèse de la réforme française* (Paris, 1996).

Crouzet, Denis, *La nuit de la Saint-Barthélemy. Un rêve perdu de la renaissance* (Paris, 1994).

Crouzet, Denis, *Les guerriers de Dieu* (2 vols, Seyssel, 1990).

Dartigue-Peyrou, Charles, *Jeanne d'Albret et le Béarn* (Mont-de-Marsan, 1934).

Dartigue-Peyrou, Charles, *La vicomté de Béarn sous le règne d'Henri II d'Albret (1517–1555)* (Paris, 1934).

Dartigue-Peyrou, Charles, 'Une cabale politico-religieuse à Bordeaux en juillet 1562: le syndicat contre le parlement', *BSHPF*, 98 (1951), pp. 141–52.

Davies, Joan, 'Languedoc and its Governor, Henri de Montmorency-Damville, 1563–1589' (unpublished PhD thesis, University of London, 1974).

Davies, Joan, 'Persecution and Protestantism: Toulouse, 1562–1575', *HJ*, 22 (1979), pp. 31–51.

Davis, Nathalie Zemon, *Society and Culture in Early Modern France* (Stanford, CA, 1975).

Dawson, John Charles, *Toulouse in the Renaissance* (New York, 1966).

Delachenal, Roland, *Histoire des avocats au parlement de Paris, 1300–1600* (Paris, 1885).

Delattre, Pierre (ed.), *Les établissements des Jésuites en France depuis quatre siècles* (5 vols, Enghien, 1949–57).

Devic, Claude and Jean Joseph Vaissète, *Histoire générale de Languedoc* (10 vols, ed. Lacour, Toulouse, 1994).

Devienne, Dom, *Histoire de Bordeaux* (Bordeaux, 1771).

Devienne, Dom, *Histoire de l'église de Bordeaux* (Bordeaux, 1862).

Diefendorf, Barbara B., *Beneath the Cross. Catholics and Huguenots in Sixteenth-Century Paris* (Oxford, 1991).

Dognol, Paul, *Les institutions politiques et administratives du pays de Languedoc du XIIIe siècle au guerres de religion* (Toulouse, 1895).

Dubarat, Abbé, *Documents et bibliographie sur la réforme en Béarn et au pays basque* (Pau, 1905).

Dubarat, Abbé, *Le Protestantisme en Béarn et au pays basque* (Pau, 1895).

Dubédat, Jean-Baptiste, *Histoire du parlement de Toulouse* (2 vols, Paris, 1885).

Ducourneau, Alex, *La Guienne historique et monumentale* (2 vols, Bordeaux, 1844).

Dupré, A., 'Projet de ligue catholique à Bordeaux en 1562 et 1563', *Revue Catholique de Bordeaux*, 12 (1891), pp. 372–8.

Evans, A.W., *Blaise de Monluc* (London, 1909).

Evennett, Henry O., *The Cardinal of Lorraine and the Council of Trent. A Study in the Counter-Reformation* (Cambridge, 1930).

Farr, James R., *Hands of Honor. Artisans and Their World in Dijon, 1550–1650* (Ithaca, 1988).

Félice, Paul de, *Procès-verbaux de la prestation du serment de fidélité au Roi Charles IX par les huguenots d'Orléans en 1568* (Orleans, 1882).

Forneron, Henri, *Histoire de Philippe II* (4 vols, Paris, 1881–87).

Forneron, Henri, *Les ducs de Guise et leur époque: Étude historique sur le seizième siècle* (2 vols, Paris, 1893).

Fournel, Jean François, *Histoire des avocats au parlement de Paris depuis Saint Louis jusq'au 15 octobre 1790* (2 vols, Paris, 1813).

Freer, Marthe W., *The Life of Jeanne d'Albret* (London, 1862).

Frémy, Edouard, *Essai sur les diplomates du temps de la Ligue, d'après des documents nouveaux et inédits* (Paris, 1873).

Frémy, Edouard, *Un ambassadeur libéral sous Charles IX et Henry III: Ambassades à Venise d'Arnaud du Ferrier* (Paris, 1880).

Gachon, Paul, *Histoire de Languedoc* (Toulouse, 1921).

Galpern, A.N., *The Religions of the People in Sixteenth-Century Champagne* (Cambridge, MA, 1976).

Gardère, J., *Histoire de la seigneurie de Condom et de l'organisation de la justice dans cette ville* (Condom, 1902).

Garrisson-Estèbe, Janine, *Les Protestants au XVIe siècle* (Paris, 1988).

Garrisson-Estèbe, Janine, *Protestants du midi, 1559–1598* (Toulouse, 1980).

Gaullieur, Ernest, *Histoire de la réformation à Bordeaux et dans le ressort du parlement de Guyenne* (2 vols, Bordeaux, 1884).

Gaullieur, Ernest, *Histoire du collège de Guyenne* (Paris, 1874).

Geisendorf, Paul-F., *Théodore de Bèze* (Geneva, 1967).

Giesey, Ralph, 'State-building in early modern France: the role of royal officialdom', *JMH*, 55 (1983), pp. 191–207.

Gigon, S.C., *La révolte de la gabelle en Guyenne, 1548–1549* (Paris, 1906).

Glangeaud, René, *La basoche de Toulouse* (Toulouse, 1912).

Greengrass, Mark, 'Financing the cause: Protestant mobilization and accountability in France (1562–1598)', in Philip Benedict, Guido Marnef, Henk van Nierop and Marc Venard (eds), *Reformation, Revolt and Civil War in France and the Netherlands, 1555–1585* (Amsterdam, 1999), pp. 233–54.

Greengrass, Mark, 'Functions and limitations of political clientage in France before Richelieu', in Neithard Bulst, Robert Descimon and Alain Guerreau (eds), *L'état ou le roi. Les fondations de la modernité monarchique en France (XIVe–XVIIe siècles)* (Paris, 1996), pp. 69–82.

Greengrass, Mark, 'The anatomy of a religious riot in Toulouse in May 1562', *JEH*, 34 (1983), pp. 367–91.

Greengrass, Mark, 'The Calvinist experiment in Béarn', in A. Pettegree, A. Duke and G. Lewis (eds), *Calvinism in Europe, 1540–1620* (Cambridge, 1994), pp. 119–42.

Greengrass, Mark, 'The *Sainte Union* in the provinces: The case of Toulouse', *SCJ*, 14, 4 (1983), pp. 469–96.

Greengrass, Mark, 'War, Politics and Religion in Languedoc in the government of Henri de Montmorency-Damville, 1574–1610' (PhD thesis, University of Oxford, 1979).

Harding, Robert R., 'Revolution and reform in the Holy League: Angers, Rennes, Nantes', *JMH*, 53 (1981), pp. 379–416.

Harding, Robert R., 'The mobilisation of confraternities against the Reformation in France', *SCJ*, 11, 2 (1980), pp. 85–107.

Harding, Robert R., *Anatomy of a Power Elite. The Provincial Governors of Early Modern France* (New Haven, 1978).

Harvey, Howard Graham, *The Theatre of the Basoche. The Contributions of the Law Societies to French Medieval Comedy* (Cambridge, MA, 1941).

Hauchecorne, F., 'Le parlement de Bordeaux pendant la première guerre civile (décembre 1560–mars 1563)', *Annales du Midi*, 62 (1950), pp. 329–40.

Hauser, Henri, 'La préponderance espagnole (1559–1660), in L. Halphin and P. Sagnac (eds), *Peuples et Civilisations. Histoire générale*, IX (Paris, 1940).

Hauser, Henri, 'A Review of Courteault, Blaise de Monluc', *Revue Historique*, 97 (March–April, 1908).

Hauser, Henri, 'The French Reformation and the French people in France in the sixteenth century', *AHR*, 4 (January, 1899), pp. 217–27.

Heller, Henry, 'A Reply to Mack P. Holt', *FHS*, 19 (1996), pp. 853–61.

Heller, Henry, *Iron and Blood. Civil Wars in Sixteenth-Century France* (Montreal, 1991).

Heller, Henry, *The Calvinist Revolt in Sixteenth Century France* (Leiden, 1986).

Hipkin, Stephen, '"Sitting on his Penny Rent": Conflict and Right of Common in Faversham Blean, 1595–1610', *Rural History*, 11,1 (2000), pp. 1–35.

Holt, Mack P., 'Burgundians into Frenchmen: Catholic identity in sixteenth-century Burgundy', in Michael Wolfe (ed.), *Changing Identities in Early Modern France* (Durham, NC, 1997), pp. 345–70.

Holt, Mack P., 'Putting religion back into the Wars of Religion', *FHS*, 18 (1993), pp. 524–51.

Holt, Mack P. (ed.), *Society and Institutions in Early Modern France* (Athens, 1991).

Holt, Mack P., *The French Wars of Religion, 1562–1629* (Cambridge, 1995).

Holt, Mack P., 'Wine, community and Reformation in sixteenth-century Burgundy', *P&P*, 138 (1993), pp. 59–93.

Jaurgain, J. de, 'Les capitaines châtelains de Mauléon', *Revue de Béarn, Navarre et Lannes*, II (1884), pp. 241–341.

Jaurgain, J. de, 'Les capitaines châtelains de Mauléon. Appendice', *Revue de Béarn, Navarre et Lannes*, III (1885), pp. 13–81.

Jensen, De Lamar, *Diplomacy and Dogmatism. Bernadino de Mendoza and the French Catholic League* (Cambridge, MA, 1964).

Jouanna, Arlette, *Le devoir de la révolte. La noblesse française et la gestation de l'état moderne, 1559–1661* (Paris, 1989).

Jouanna, Arlette, Jacqueline Boucher, Dominique Biloghi and Guy le Thiec (eds), *Histoire et dictionnaire des guerres de religion* (Paris, 1998).

Julian, Camille, *L'histoire de Bordeaux depuis les origines jusqu'à 1895* (Bordeaux, 1895).

Kaiser, Wolfgang, *Marseille au temps des troubles. Morphologie sociale et luttes de factions, 1559–1595* (Paris, 1992).

Kamen, Henry, *The Spanish Inquisition. An Historical Revision* (London, 1997).

Kettering, Sharon, 'Clientage during the French Wars of Religion', *SCJ*, 20 (1989), pp. 221–39.

Kettering, Sharon, 'Patronage and kinship in Early Modern France', *FHS*, 16 (1989), pp. 408–35.

Kingdon, Robert M., *Geneva and the Coming of the Wars of Religion in France, 1555–1563* (Geneva, 1956).

Kingdon, Robert M., *Myths about the Saint Bartholomew's Day Massacre, 1572–1576* (London, 1988).

Knecht, Robert J., *Catherine de Medici* (London, 1998).

Knecht, Robert J., 'Military autobiographies in sixteenth-century France', in J.R. Mulryne and M. Shewring, (eds), *War, Literature and the Arts in Sixteenth-Century Europe* (Basingstoke, 1989), pp. 3–21.

Knecht, Robert J., *The French Civil Wars, 1562–1598* (London, 2000).

Knecht, Robert J., *The Rise and Fall of Renaissance France, 1483–1610* (2nd edn, Oxford, 2001).

Knecht, Robert J., 'The sword and the pen: Blaise de Monluc and his *Commentaires*', *Renaissance Studies*, 9 (1995), pp. 104–18.

Konnert, Mark W., *Civic Agendas and Religious Passion. Châlons-sur-Marne during the French Wars of Religion, 1560–1594* (Kirksville, MS, 1997).

Konnert, Mark W., 'Provincial governors and their regimes during the French Wars of Religion: the duc de Guise and the city council of Châlons-sur-Marne', *SCJ*, 25 (1994), pp. 823–40.

Labenazie, *Histoire de la ville d'Agen and pays d'Agenois*, I (Montauban, 1888).

Labitte, Charles, *De la démocratie chez les prédicateurs de la ligue* (Paris, 1865).

Labrunie, Abbé Joseph, 'Abrégé chronologique des antiquités d'Agen', *Revue de l'Agenais et des anciennes provinces du sud-ouest*, XV (Agen, 1888).

Lamouzèle, Edmond, *Essai sur l'organisation et les fonctions de la compagnie du guet et de la garde bourgeoise de Toulouse au XVIIe et au XVIIIe siècle* (Tulle, 1906).

Lavisse, Ernest, *Histoire de France depuis les origines jusqu'à la révolution* (9 vols, Paris, 1903–10).

Lecler, Joseph, 'Aux origines de la Ligue: premiers projets et premiers essais (1561–1570)', *Études*, 227 (1936), pp. 188–208.

Lecler, Joseph, *Toleration and the Reformation* (2 vols, London, 1960).

Le Palenc, 'La confrérie des avocats de Rieux au seizième siècle', *Bulletin de la société archéologique du midi de la France*, 25–8 (1899–1901), pp. 312–22.

Lestrade, Abbé Jean, *Les huguenots en Comminges. Documents inédits*, I (Paris, Auch, 1900).

Lestrade, Abbé Jean, 'Les Huguenots en Comminges. Documents inédits, II', *Archives historiques de la Gascogne*, 14 (Paris, Auch, 1910), pp. 1–160.

Lloyd, Howell A., *The State, France and the Sixteenth Century* (London, 1983).

Major, J. Russell, *From Renaissance Monarchy to Absolute Monarchy. French Kings, Nobles and Estates* (London, 1997).

Mège, Alexandre du, *Histoire des institutions religieuses, politiques, judiciaires et littéraires de la ville de Toulouse* (4 vols, Toulouse, 1864).

Mentzer, Raymond A., 'Calvinist propaganda and the Parlement of Toulouse', *ARG*, 68 (1977), pp. 268–83.

Michel, P., *Blaise de Monluc* (Paris, 1971).

Miquel, Pierre, *Les guerres de religion* (Paris, 1980).

Mirasson, P., *Histoire des troubles du Be[BL]ÿarn, au sujet de la religion, dans le XVIIe siècle* (Paris, 1768).

Mourin, E., *La réforme et la Ligue en Anjou* (Paris, 1888).

Mousnier, Roland, 'Les concepts d'ordres d'états, de fidélité et de monarchie absolue en France de la fin du xve siècle à la fin du xviiie', *Revue Historique*, 247 (1972), pp. 289–312.

Mousnier, Roland, *Les institutions de la France sous la monarchie absolue, 1598–1789* (2 vols, Paris, 1980).

Nakam, Géralde, *Au lendemain de la Saint-Barthélemy. Guerre civile et famine* (Paris, 1975).

Nakam, Géralde, *Montaigne et son temps. Les événements et les essais* (Paris, 1982).

Nicholas, David, *The Evolution of the Medieval World* (London, 1992).

Nicholls, David, 'Protestants, Catholics and magistrates in Tours, 1562–1572: The making of a Catholic city during the religious wars', *FH*, 8, 1 (1994), pp. 14–33.

O'Reilly, Abbé Patrice-John, *Histoire complète de Bordeaux* (6 vols, Bordeaux, 1863).

Orlea, Manfred, *La noblesse aux états généraux de 1576 et de 1588* (Paris, 1980).

Palm, Franklin Charles, *Politics and Religion in Sixteenth-Century France: A Study of the Career of Henry of Montmorency-Damville, Uncrowned King of the South* (Gloucester, MA, 1927).

Parker, David, *The Making of French Absolutism* (London, 1983).

Piaget, E, *Histoire de l'établissement des Jesuites en France (1540–1640)* (Leiden, 1893).

Picot, Émile, *Les Italiens en France au seizième siècle* (Rome, 1995).

Potter, David, 'The duc de Guise and the fall of Calais, 1557–58', *EHR*, 388 (1983), pp. 481–512.

Potter, David (ed.), *The French Wars of Religion. Selected Documents* (London, 1997).

Potter, Louis Joseph Antoine de, *Lettres de Saint Pie V, sur les religieuses de son temps en France, suivi d'un catéchisme catholique–romain* (Brussels, 1827).

Poumarède, Jacques and Jack Thomas (eds), *Les parlements de Province. Pouvoirs, justice et société du XVe au XVIIIe siècle* (Toulouse, 1996).

Powis, Jonathan, 'Gallican liberties and the politics of later sixteenth-century France', *SCJ*, 26 (1983), pp. 515–30.

Powis, Jonathan, 'Order, religion, and the magistrates of a provincial parlement in sixteenth-century France', *ARG*, 71 (1980), pp. 180–97.

Powis, Jonathan, 'The Magistrates of the Parlement of Bordeaux c.1500–1563' (PhD thesis, Oxford University, 1975).

Racaut, Luc, *Hatred in Print. Catholic Propaganda and Protestant Identity during the French Wars of Religion* (Aldershot, 2002).

Ramet, Henri, *Histoire de Toulouse* (Toulouse, 1935).

Ramet, Henri, *Le capitole et le parlement de Toulouse* (Toulouse, 1926).

Ramsey, Ann W., *Liturgy, Politics, and Salvation: The Catholic League in Paris and the Nature of Catholic Reform, 1540–1630* (Rochester, 1999).

Rey, R., 'Le cardinal Georges d'Armagnac, colégat à Avignon (1566–1585)', *Annales du Midi*, 10 (Toulouse, 1898), pp. 273–306.

Ricard, N., *Panégyrique de Saint-Yves, patron de MM. les avocats (prononcé dans l'église de Nazareth)* (Toulouse, 1764).

Ritter, Raymond, 'Jeanne d'Albret et les troubles de la religion en Béarn, Bigorre, Soule et Navarre, 1560–1572', *Revue de Béarn*, 3–6 (1928–33).

Roberts, Penny, *A City in Conflict. Troyes during the French Wars of religion* (Manchester, 1996).

Roberts, Penny, 'Religious pluralism in practice: The enforcement of the Edicts of Pacification', in Keith Cameron, Mark Greengrass and Penny Roberts (eds), *The Adventure of Religious Pluralism in Early Modern France* (Berne, 2000), pp. 31–44.

Roberts, Penny, 'The most crucial battle of the Wars of Religion? The conflict over sites for reformed worship in sixteenth-century France', *ARG*, 89 (1998), pp. 247–66.

Roelker, Nancy Lyman, *One King, One Faith. The Parlement of Paris and the religious reformations of the sixteenth century* (Berkeley, CA, 1996).

Roelker, Nancy Lyman, *Queen of Navarre. Jeanne d'Albret, 1528–1572* (Cambridge, MA, 1968).

Romier, Lucien, 'A dissident nobility under the cloak of religion', in J.H.M. Salmon (ed.), *The French Wars of Religion. How Important were Religious Factors?* (Boston, MA, 1967).

Romier, Lucien, *La conjuration d'Amboise* (Paris, 1923).

Ropartz, S, *Histoire de Saint Yves, patron des gens de justice* (Saint-Brieux, 1856).

Roschach, Ernest, 'Documents inédits concernant l'édit de pacification de 1568 et le régime des suspects à Toulouse', *Mémoires de l'académie des sciences, inscriptions et belles-lettres de Toulouse*, 10 (1878), pp. 318–57.

Roy, Ian, *Blaise de Monluc* (London, 1971).

Ruble, Alphonse de, *Antoine de Bourbon et Jeanne d'Albret* (4 vols, Paris, 1881–86).

Ruble, Alphonse de, *Jeanne d'Albret et la guerre civile* (Paris, 1897).

Salmon, J.H.M., *Society in Crisis. France in the Sixteenth Century* (London, 1975).

Salmon, J.H.M. (ed.), *The French Wars of Religion. How Important were Religious Factors?* (Boston, MA, 1967).

Samazeuilth, J-F., *Histoire de l'Agenais, du Condomois et du Bazadais* (2 vols, Auch, 1847).

Sarrasi de Capela, 'L'ancienne procession du 17 mai à Toulouse', *La semaine Catholique de Toulouse*, 20 (May 1874), pp. 474–6.

Sauzet, Robert, *Contre-réforme et réforme catholique en Bas-Languedoc. Le diocese de Nîmes au XVIIe siècle* (Louvain, 1981).

Schiffman, Zachary Sayre, 'An intellectual in politics: Montaigne in Bordeaux', in Michael Wolfe (ed.), *Changing Identities in Early Modern France* (Durham, NC, 1997).

Schneider, Robert A., *Public Life in Toulouse, 1463–1789. From Municipal Republic to Cosmopolitan City* (Ithaca, 1989).

Schneider, Robert A., 'Mortification on parade: Penitential processions in sixteenth- and seventeenth-century France', *Renaissance and Reformation*, 22 (1986), pp. 123–46.

Soman, Alfred (ed.), *The Massacre of Saint Bartholomew. Reappraisals and Documents* (The Hague, 1974).

Souriac, René, *Décentralisation administrative dans l'ancienne France. Autonomie Commingeoise et pouvoir d'état, 1540–1630* (2 vols, Toulouse, 1992).

Sournia, Jean-Charles, *Blaise de Monluc. Soldat et écrivain (1500–1577)* (Paris, 1981).

Stegmann, André, *Édits des guerres de religion* (Paris, 1979).

Sutherland, Nicola M., *Princes, Politics and Religion, 1547–1589* (London, 1984).

Sutherland, Nicola M., 'Review article: The foreign policy of Philip II and the French Catholic League', *History*, 51 (1966), pp. 323–31.

Sutherland, Nicola M., *The Huguenot Struggle for Recognition* (London, 1980).

Sutherland, Nicola M., *The Massacre of Saint Bartholomew and the European Conflict, 1559–1572* (London, 1973).

Tallon, Alain, 'Gallicanism and religious pluralism in France in the sixteenth century', in Keith Cameron, Mark Greengrass and Penny Roberts (eds), *The Adventure of Religious Pluralism in Early Modern France* (Berne, 2000), pp. 15–30.

Tamizey de Larroque, Philippe, *Lettres inédites de Janus Fregose, évêque d'Agen* (Bordeaux, 1873).

Tamizey de Larroque, Philippe, 'Lettres inédites du Cardinal d'Armagnac', *Collection Méridionale*, V (Paris, Bordeaux, 1874), pp. 1–134.

Tamizey de Larroque, Philippe, *Notes et documents inédits pour servir à la biographie de Christophe et de François de Foix-Candalle, évêques d'Aire* (Bordeaux, 1877).

Tamizey de Larroque, Philippe, *Antoine de Noailles à Bordeaux d'après des documents inédits* (Bordeaux, 1878).

Tamizey de Larroque, Philippe, 'Jean Lange, Conseiller au parlement de Bordeaux', *Revue Catholique de Bordeaux*, 1883 (Bordeaux), pp. 685–97.

Tamizey de Larroque, Philippe, 'Quelques pages inédites de Blaise de Monluc', *Receuil des travaux de la société d'agriculture, sciences et arts d'Agen* (Paris, 1863).

Tholin, Georges, 'La ville d'Agen pendant les guerres de religion du XVIe siècle', *Revue de l'Agenais et des anciennes provinces du sud-ouest*, XIV–XVI (Agen, 1887–89).

Thompson, James Westfall, *The Wars of Religion in France, 1559–1576* (New York, 1958).

Vaïsse-Cibiel, E., 'Notes rétrospectives sur la basoche Toulousaine', *Mémoires de l'académie impériale des sciences, inscriptions et belles-lettres de Toulouse*, 6 (1868), pp. 221–43.

Venard, Marc, 'Catholicism and resistance to the Reformation in France, 1555–1585', in Philip Benedict, Guido Marnef, Henk van Nierop and Marc Venard (eds), *Reformation, Revolt, and Civil War in France and the Netherlands, 1555–1585* (Amsterdam, 1999), pp. 133–48.

Venard, Marc, *Réforme Protestante, réforme catholique, dans la province d'Avignon au XVIe siècle* (Paris, 1993).

Viala, André, *Le parlement de Toulouse et l'administration royale laïque, 1420–1525 environ* (Albi, 1953).

Vigneron, François, *Éloge d'Armand Gontaut de Biron, maréchal de France sous Henry IV, suivi notes historiques sur les actes de valeur et de patriotisme de la noblesse de Guienne, et particulièrement de celle de Gascogne* (Paris, 1788).

Vindry, Fleury, *Les parlementaires français au XVIe siècle* (2 vols, Paris, 1910).

Weill, Georges, *Les théories sur le pouvoir royal en France pendant les guerres de religion* (Paris, 1891).

Weiss, Charles, *Papiers d'état du Cardinal de Granvelle (1516–1565)* (9 vols, Paris, 1841–52).

Wolfe, Michael (ed.), *Changing Identities in Early Modern France* (Durham, NC, 1997).

Wolff, Philippe, *Histoire de Toulouse* (Toulouse, 1974).

Wood, James B., 'The impact of the Wars of Religion: A view of France in 1581', *SCJ*, 15 (1984), pp. 131–68.

Wood, James B., *The King's Army. Warfare, soldiers and society during the Wars of Religion in France, 1562–1576* (Cambridge, 1996).

Wood, James B., 'The royal army during the early Wars of Religion, 1559–1576', in Mack P. Holt (ed.), *Society and Institutions in Early Modern France* (Athens, GA, 1991).

Yardeni, Myriam, *La conscience nationale en France pendant les guerres de religion (1559–98)* (Paris, 1971).

Zeller, Gaston, *Les institutions de la France au XVIe siècle* (Paris, 1948).

Index

accommodation, crown policy of 19,
  50, 91, 95, 97, 104, 119, 124,
  130–36, 163–4
Agen 83, 158–9
  archives 13–14
  Catholic nobility of 92, 95, 98, 100,
    102, 105, 107–8
  coalition government 5, 6, 87–8,
    91–9, 101–5, 108–9, 159
  correspondence with crown 84, 86,
    90, 105
  confessional violence 83–5, 91,
    93–4, 97, 100–101
  conseil militaire 87, 89, 94, 95,
    100–102, 107
  defence of 75, 83, 101, 103, 106–7
  fines (of Protestant community)
    102–3
  guard and militia 88, 95, 99–102,
    105–8, 164
  illegal assemblies 85, 86, 90, 94,
    101, 109
  Jurade 84–9, 91, 95, 100–101, 103,
    109
  League (March 1563) 96, 98, 108,
    127
  structure 98–9, 130
  moderate party 99
  penitential ethos 105
  profession of Catholic faith 95, 98,
    105, 107–8
  Protestant coup (1562) 93–5
  Protestant demography in 83, 87
  relations with Bordeaux Parlement
    83, 85–6, 96, 98
  sequestration of Protestant goods
    and property 95, 102, 106
Agenais, defence of by Catholic
  nobility 106–8
Albret, Louis d' 144, 151, 153
Alesme, Jean d' 62, 77
amnesty 77, 134

at Agen 89, 97, 163
at Bordeaux 163
at Toulouse 124, 163
Andrieu, Jules 52, 98
Anjou, Duke d' 151, 153
Armagnac 68, 152
Armagnac, George, Cardinal d' 116,
  124–7, 129, 132–3, 135, 158
  and Toulouse League (1563) 128,
    130–31
  as Inquisitor General 146
  opposition to Jeanne d'Albret 147–8
Arpajon, *vicomte d'* 140–41
Aspremont, Bernard d' 84, 87, 93, 148
Audaux, *seigneur d'* 150–51, 155, 157
Auger, Edmond 82, 126–7

Ban et arrière ban 102, 119–20
Bardaxi, Jean de 73
Basoche
  Bordeaux 25, 27, 29, 33–4, 82, 115,
    161
    performances 28–32, 161
    rivalry with *écoliers* 28, 31–2, 49,
      161
    roi de la basoche 28–30, 32
  Toulouse 113–15, 117, 121–2, 130,
    133, 161
    confrontations with *écoliers*
      114–15, 161
    performances 117, 130, 133, 161
    roi de la basoche 114
Baulon, François de 26, 33, 36, 57,
  79–81, 160
  and Jesuits 81–2
Béarn 90, 152
  Catholic rebellions 6, 143, 152, 165
  reform programme 143–5
Béarn, François de, *sieur de Bonasse*
  149, 153–4, 156
Béarn, Gabriel de, *sieur de Gerdrest*
  149–50, 154, 156

Beaullac-Tresbons, Pierre de, *grand-prieur de Fronton* 139–40
Belcier 65, 153
Bellegarde 120, 122, 126, 128, 135, 140, 156, 158, 160
Benedict, Philip 1, 8, 161
Beraud 26, 33, 41, 53
Bèze, Théodore de 21, 109
Biran, Guy de, *sieur de Gohas* 149, 153, 156
Boëtie, Etienne de la 23, 90
Boisnormand 19
Bordeaux 3, 158–9, 162
    administration 22, 24, 48
    archives 12, 14
    Registers of Parlement 12, 26–7, 39
    as frontier town 40–41
    confessional violence 27, 36–7
    confraternal militancy 25, 31, 33, 48, 82, 161–2
    Confraternity of Saint-Yves 25–7, 30, 34–5, 38, 44, 48, 82, 113, 115
        commissaires 25–6, 29, 41, 43, 48, 58
    guard and militia 34, 36, 44–6, 76, 79, 139, 164
    illegal assemblies 32, 38, 40, 42–3
    Jesuits 127
    Jurade 22, 27–8, 35, 42, 47, 78
    maison de ville 32, 81
    penitential ethos 139, 161
    profession of Catholic faith 43, 45, 76, 80
    Protestant demography in 18, 21, 29, 53
    surveillance of Protestant community 41, 80
    Syndicate 6, 33, 43, 47–9, 55, 82, 98–9, 101, 121
        as militia force 34, 44–6
        censure of 45–8
        formation 38
    tax on Protestant community 46, 76
    urban defences 22, 75, 78–9
    (see also Parlement of Bordeaux; *Écoliers*)
Bordelais
    Catholic nobles of 37, 49–53, 56–7, 62, 164
    confessional violence 19, 37–8, 45, 49, 51–5, 62, 64

Bordenave, Nicolas de 15
Bordenave, Jean de, *baron de Monein*, 144, 149, 155–6
Bosquet, Georges 120
Bossy, John 5, 160
Bourbon, Antoine de, King of Navarre 7, 10, 31, 34, 56, 63, 68, 71, 84–5, 143
Boyer, G. 114
Bryson, David 15
burial sites, contest over 119, 146

Cadillac, League of (March 1563) 59–62, 64, 98
Candalle, Frédéric de Foix, *comte de* 50, 56–60, 62, 65, 75, 78, 158, 160
    rivalry with moderates at Bordeaux 56–63
Carbajal, Don 72
Carcassonne 125
Carroll, Stuart 3, 8
Cassan, Michel 3
Casteljaloux 67, 80, 99, 102
Castres 124, 126
Catherine de Medici 10, 35, 61, 71, 82, 157, 164
Catholic League, The 1, 5–6, 82, 130, 139, 161
Catholic networks and associations 3–7, 11, 33, 60–61, 67, 153, 158, 160, 165
Caumont, *vicomte de* 92, 140, 153
ceremonials and processions 25, 81, 57, 105, 115, 133
Charles IX 139, 148, 153, 155, 157
Château Hâ 22, 31, 36
Château Trompette 22, 36, 38, 45, 58, 79
Châtillon 9–10, 68
Christin, Olivier 3
Clairac 91, 101
Clairac, Synod of 19–20, 30, 44, 89, 98–9
Catholic Clergy 5
    Agen 108
    attacks against 4, 19, 37, 41
    Béarn 143
    Bordeaux 41, 47, 76, 161
        indict Lagebaton 76, 79
        support of Catholic militants 61, 66, 76–7

Toulouse 113, 121–2, 131, 134, 161
  support of Crusade (1568) 138,
    140–41
Coligny, Admiral 8, 68, 75
Collège de Guyenne 27–8, 30–32, 44,
  49, 80–81, 112
Comminges 155
Commissioners, royal 62–5, 70, 93,
  132–3
Communay, A. 15
Condé, Louis, Prince de 74–7, 79, 85,
  93, 102, 105
Condom 94, 99
Confraternity of Saint-Yves (see
  Bordeaux; Toulouse)
Conner, Philip 3
conseil privé 11, 39, 44–5, 63, 79, 148
Couci, Charles de, sieur de Burie 32,
  38, 48, 57
  at Agen 90–92
  contention with Catholic militants
    at Bordeaux 35–6, 39, 44–9,
    55, 90
  troops and deployment 35–7, 46–7,
    54, 57
Courteault, Paul 10, 15–17, 54, 73
cross, wearing of white 121, 138–9
Crouzet, Denis 2, 4, 53, 118, 131, 141
Crusade 1568 (see Toulouse)
Crussol, comte de 117, 124

Dada, Charles 58
Daffis, Jean 125–6, 128, 132, 160
Damville, Henri de Montmorency- 41,
  68, 73, 129, 133–5, 139–40
  allegation of association with
    Catholic cartel 70–71
  rivalry with Monluc 154–7
dances and masks, ban on 135, 137
Dartigue-Peyrou, Charles 5, 14–15
Davies, Joan 3, 134
Delas, Gratien 90, 102
Diefendorf, Barbara 2
disarmament, crown policy on 40–41,
  80, 87, 90, 101, 115, 118
Domezain, Valentin de, baron de
  Moneins 150–51, 153–4, 156–7
Dominge, Captain 148
Dubarat, Abbé 14–15, 148
Dubédat, Jean-Baptiste 131
Dubois 35–6, 39

Ducourneau, Alex 12, 42
Dufaur, Michel 122
Dufranc 94
Dupré, A. 5, 38
Duras, vicomte de 45, 124–5

Écoliers
  Bordeaux 27, 30, 32, 44, 49, 80
    performances and rhetoric 28–31
  Toulouse 112–13, 115–16, 121
Edicts, royal 40, 163
  of Amboise (1563) 40, 50, 59–64, 67,
    73, 77, 95, 99–100, 129, 131–3
  of January (1562) 19, 44,
    118–19, 124
  of Longjumeau (1568) 77–9, 103–4
Elizabeth I, Queen of England 73, 75
Etats
  d'Agenais 92–3, 95, 97–100, 105,
    108
  de Béarn 144–5, 155
  de Guyenne 57, 61
  de Languedoc 112, 125, 130

Félice, Paul de 104
fines (see Agen; Bordeaux; Toulouse)
'first despoiler', Act of 147–8
Flavin, Melchior 137
Fleurdelis, Jean de, sieur de
  Lannevielle et de Gallos 154
Foix 68, 140, 151–2
Forneron, Henri 71, 73
Francescas 103
Francis II 10–11, 88
Freer, Marthe 148
Fronton 102
Fumel 93, 98
Fumel, François, baron de 38, 51–5

Gabelle riot (1548) 22, 50, 54
Galpern, A.N. 1
Garde, François de la 81, 124
Garrisson-Estèbe, Janine 52–4
Gaullieur, Ernest 30
Gontaut, Armand de, baron de Biron
  54, 83, 92, 164
graffiti on Catholic doors 139
Greengrass, Mark 3, 11, 15, 130, 139,
  164
Grenade, secret Catholic meetings
  (1563) 68, 71

Guard and militia (see Agen;
    Bordeaux; Toulouse)
Guise 8–12, 56, 71–2, 75, 79
Guyenne 3–4, 7, 11, 18
    as frontier province 7

Harding, Robert 7–8, 141, 164
Harvey, Howard 30
Hauser, Henri 54
Hélory, Yves 25
Histoire ecclésiastique 16, 44, 118,
    120
Holt, Mack P. 3, 52, 104

iconoclasm 3, 88, 94, 144
illegal assemblies (see Agen; Bordeaux;
    Toulouse)
Inquisition, Papal 12, 158
    jurisdiction in Béarn, Navarre, Foix
        and Armagnac 146
    monitoire 146–8
    opposition to Jeanne d'Albret 146,
        148
    visitations 146–7

Jeanne d'Albret, Queen of Navarre 7,
    67, 74, 85, 152–6
    accuses Catholic cartel of collusion
        with Spain 68–71
    accuses Catholics of plot to 'sell
        Guyenne' to Spain 150
    conversion to Protestantism 67–8
    reform programme 143–5, 147,
        149–50
    rivalry with Catholic militants in
        south-west 145, 149, 151,
        157–8, 165
    rivalry with Monluc 68–9, 151
    use of simultaneum 146
Jensen, De Lamar 130
Jesuits 2, 81–2, 126–7, 149
Joyeuse 125
Julian, Camille 36
Jurade (see Agen; Bordeaux)

Kaiser, Wolfgang 2
Kettering, Sharon 7

La Ferrière 42–3, 46–7, 77
La Mothe-Gondrin 106
La Rochelle 109, 152

Labenazie 15, 51
Lachassaigne 26, 139
Lafontaine, Jacques 86
Lagebâton, Jacques-Benoît de 31,
    39–40, 123, 163
    accusations of affiliation with
        reform movement 43–4, 57–8
    against the Bordeaux syndicate 39,
        44, 47
    controversy with Catholic militants
        39–44, 58–64, 76, 79, 101,
        108, 152
    moderating Catholic policy 44, 48–9,
        58–60, 65–6, 70, 101, 164
Lahet 47, 77
Lalande, Clément de 85–90, 92, 94–5,
    98–106, 160, 163–4
Lange, Jean de 26, 36, 40, 46, 50, 75,
    78, 81, 101, 121, 127, 160, 163
    and Catholic militia 37, 39, 41
    and Confraternity of Saint-Yves 27,
        37, 41, 44
    and Jesuits 81–2
    and Bordeaux Syndicate 43–4, 47,
        49
    attacks on moderate party at
        Bordeaux 35, 38, 43, 57–9,
        63–5, 70
Languedoc 3–4, 7, 11
Lanssac 65, 78, 157
Larroque, Philippe Tamizey de 36
Latomy, Nicolas 117, 120
Lauzan 62, 92, 153
Leagues, Catholic (see Agen,
    Bordeaux, Cadillac, Toulouse)
Lecler, Joseph 5
Lectoure 94, 102
Lescar 144
    Catholic rebellions 144, 149,
        156–7, 165
Limoges 138
Lomagne, Antoine de, sieur de Terride
    50, 68, 117, 120, 125, 127–8,
    133–5, 158, 160
    command of royal army in Béarn
        154–5
    defeat at Navarrenx (1569) 155–6
Lorraine, Cardinal of 10–12, 35, 56,
    67, 88, 146
Lur, Louis de, vicomte d'Uza 57, 60,
    62–3, 78

Luxe, Charles, *comte de* 145, 149–54,
      156–8
   appointed to administrate lands
      belonging to Jeanne d'Albret
      152–5
   defence of Basse Navarre 145,
      149–50, 154
   rivalry with Jeanne d'Albret 157–8

Mabrun, Jean de 58–9, 65, 153
Malvin, Charles de 26, 36–7, 42, 45,
      47, 57–8, 62, 77, 79–82, 160
Mansencal, Jean de 115, 120, 126
Melon 47–8, 50, 160
mi-partie chambers 88–93, 99–100, 108
Mirasson, P. 149
Moneins, Tristan de 22, 50
Monluc, Blaise de 9, 47, 67–8, 79, 83,
      158–9
   and Guise 10–11
   as Catholic leader in south-west 20,
      51, 53, 57, 75–8, 80, 153,
      160–65
   and his *Commentaires* 15–17, 94,
      102, 125, 129, 149
   as agent of Philip II 73–5
   at Agen 10, 85–8, 92–8, 101–3,
      106, 109, 129, 134, 151
   at Toulouse 120–23, 125–8, 130,
      133–5
   correspondence with crown 100, 126
   jurisdiction 9, 57, 71, 75, 144
   orders Catholics to wear white
      crosses 138
   relations with Spain 71, 73–4, 165
   rivalry with Damville 154–7
   rivalry with Jeanne d'Albret 68–9,
      81, 148, 151–3, 157
   secure Bordeaux 45, 75, 77–8, 98–9
Monluc, Jean de 9–10, 68
Montauban 3, 54, 70, 77, 102, 124,
      140
Montesquiou, Antoine de, *sieur de
      Sainte-Colomme* 144–5, 151–6
Montferrand, *baron de* 79–81,
      159–60, 164
Montgommery, *comte de* 102, 106,
      140, 156–7
Montmorency, Anne de 7, 10, 12, 67,
      125
Montségur 54, 85

Nakam, Géralde 52
Narbonne 127
Navailles, Henri de, *sieur de Peyre*
      149, 151, 155–6
Navarre 6, 67, 86, 143, 149, 152
   archives 14
Navarrenx, siege of (1569) 155–6
Nay, Synod of 149
Negrepelisse, *sieur de* 50, 55, 68, 92,
      120, 125–30, 154–5, 158, 160
Nérac 67, 87, 91, 94, 101
Nicholls, David 2
Noailles, Antoine de 36, 46
Nort, Antoine de 26, 87, 93, 102,
      109
Nort, Martial de 26, 85–7, 92, 107–8,
      160
Nort, Odet de 109
Nort, Pierre de 109

Oaths (see profession of Catholic
      faith)
Olhagaray, Pierre 14, 148, 152
Oloron 145
   Catholic League (1563/68) 149–51,
      153
   Catholic rebellion 145, 150–51,
      153, 156, 165
Orthez 154, 156

Palatier, Jean 137
Pamiers 124, 126
Papacy 67, 72, 123, 134
   opposition to reforms of Jeanne
      d'Albret 143
   sanction of Toulouse crusade (1568)
      137, 141
   support of Catholic militants in
      south-west France 158, 165
   support of Catholic rebels in Béarn
      and Navarre 146, 158
Pardaillan, *sieur de* 45, 61
Parker, David 163
Parlement
   Bordeaux 3, 9, 23–4, 50, 90, 102,
      164
      avocats 23, 25–6, 33, 38–9
      censorship of performances of
         basoche and *écoliers* 29–32,
         43
      conseillers 4, 23, 32, 37

grand'chambre 23, 28, 30, 32, 37, 39, 42, 59, 62–3, 65, 70
huissiers 23, 59, 63
Jesuits 82
moderate party at 11, 34, 43–7, 50, 66, 163–4
opposition to Jeanne d'Albret 68–9, 147, 151
  seizing lands of 152–3, 157
palais de l'ombrière 23, 26, 38
procureurs 23, 25–6, 33, 38
search of Protestant houses 32, 42
Toulouse 4, 102, 116–18, 122–3, 129, 135–6, 164
avocats 113
moderate party 119, 122, 164
opposition to Jeanne d'Albret 68–9, 147, 155
seizing lands of 152–3, 157
opposition to Protestant Capitouls 111, 116–21, 125–8, 132–4, 141
profession of faith 131–2, 135
sanctioning of Crusade (1568) 138–9
sanctioning of league (1563) 128, 130
structure of 110
support of Crusade (1568) 137, 141

Pau 10, 144
as capital and governmental seat of Jeanne d'Albret 73, 143–8, 151–7, 165
Paulin, *vicomte de* 140
Paulo, Antoine de 120, 125, 128
Pavie, Raymond de, *baron de Fourquevaux*, 123, 125–7
peasant uprisings 52–4
Penchéry, Helié de, *sieur de la Justinie* 95, 98
Penitential ethos (see Agen; Bordeaux; Toulouse)
Perrenot, Thomas, *sieur de Chantonnay* 19, 71–3, 143–4
Peyrusse, François de, *comte d'Escars* 34, 40, 50, 57, 63–4, 77, 81, 148, 160
Philip II, King of Spain 71–2, 143, 146–7

Piles, *vicomte de* 153
Pius IV 147–8
plot by Catholic powers to capture Jeanne d'Albret 148–9, 157, 165
Pontac family 58
Powis, Jonathan 3, 50, 63
preaching 86, 137
Présidiaux courts 23–4, 39, 86–9, 99, 101, 105, 108, 111
profession of Catholic faith (see Agen; Bordeaux; Toulouse)
Protestant
church structure in south-west 4, 8–9, 18–19, 32, 54–6
demography in south-west 4, 18
military infrastructure in south-west 19–21, 56, 64, 87, 140
psalms, singing of 32, 117

Quercy 99

Rabestans 157
Raemond, Florimond de 4, 16, 21
Raffin, François 88–92
Ram, Thomas de 35, 38–9
Ramet, Henri 121
Ramsey, Ann 2, 161
Rapin 69
Régin, Claude 150, 153, 155
Roberts, Penny 2
Roelker, Nancy 15
Roffignac, Christophe de 9, 26, 33–46, 57, 62, 65, 79–82, 127, 139, 159–60, 163
defence of Lange 35–6
opposition to Jeanne d'Albret 151, 153
Rouen 93, 161–2
Roussel, Gérard 145
Roussillon 146
Ruble, Alphonse, *baron de* 16–17, 60, 73, 130

Saint Bartholomew's Day massacre (24 August 1572) 1, 74, 138
Saint-Colomme, Jacques de, *seigneur d'Escoarrabaque*, 149, 151, 154–7
Saint-Foy, Synod of 20–21, 30, 98–9, 101
Saint-Sulpice 72, 148
Salefranque, Pierre de 14

Sanssac, Antoine Prévôt de 41, 64–5, 70, 76, 81–2, 139
Sauzet, Robert 1
Savignac de Thouars, *sieur de* 37, 153
Schneider, Robert 163
sequestration of Protestant goods and property (see Agen; Bordeaux; Toulouse)
Sevin, Herman de 90, 100–103, 108, 164
Souriac, René 3
Sournia, Jean-Charles 75
Spain 7, 41, 67 (see also Philip II)
 financial and military assistance to Catholic militants in south-west 72–3, 165
 foreign policy to France 73
 opposition to Jeanne d'Albret 143–4, 148, 151–2
 support of Catholic rebels in Béarn and Navarre 146–8, 152, 158
Strozzi, Lorenzo 125, 127–8, 130, 133
Supersantis, Jean de 149, 155, 157
surveillance of Protestant community (see Bordeaux; Toulouse)
Sutherland, Nicola 163
Syndicate (see Bordeaux; Toulouse)

Tarbes 126, 157
Tholin, George 87, 90, 94, 98, 100
Tholon, Antoine de 84, 87, 92–3, 100
Thompson, James Westfall 5, 74
Tilh, du 155–6
Cassagnet, François de, *sieur de Saint-Orens*, known as *Tilladet*, 50, 78–9, 160
Toneins 91, 94, 101
Toppiac, Captain 107
Toulouse 110, 123, 140, 158–9, 162
 archives 13
 capitouls 110–11, 116–17, 119–20, 135
 expelled from office 121–2, 132
 Catholic nobility of 120, 122–4, 128, 130, 133–5, 138, 141, 164
 Catholic response to Protestant coup (1562) 120, 123–4, 141, 159
 confessional violence 3, 116, 119, 136, 161

Confraternity of Saint-Yves 112–13, 115, 133, 162
Crusade (1568) 6, 123, 136–41, 161
guard and militia forces 116–21, 124, 127–8, 131, 133–5, 139, 141, 164
illegal Protestant assemblies 113, 118–19
imposition of fines on Protestant community 131, 136, 141, 159, 160
Jesuits 126–7
League (1563) 5, 6, 98, 123, 127–8, 130–31, 137
 dissolving of 129
 structure and statutes 128–30
penitential ethos 131, 135–9, 141–2, 161
processions of 17 May 122, 133
profession of Catholic faith 124, 128, 131, 135–6, 138, 141
Protestant coup (May 1562) 124, 141
Protestant demography in 110, 118, 160
Protestant insurrection 116, 119–20
search of Protestant houses 113, 135–6
sequestration of Protestant goods and property 122, 125–7, 131–2, 136, 141, 159–60
surveillance of Protestant community 127
Syndicate 117–18, 120–22, 130
united Catholic defence of 75, 120–22, 131–5, 142
university 112, 115
Trans, *marquis de* 62
Trent, The Council of (1545–63) 6, 73, 147, 161
Triumvirate, The Catholic 71–2, 84, 143

urban centres, strategic importance of 159, 162–3, 165

vagabonds expelled 79–80
Vaillac, Captain 36, 38, 45, 78, 81
Venard, Marc 2
Vignac 58–9
Villars, Marshal 83, 92

Villeneuve 86, 91, 94   Weill, Georges 52
Voisin, Jean 10, 86   Wood, James B. 3–4, 19

St Andrews Studies in Reformation History

Editorial Board: Bruce Gordon, Andrew Pettegree and John Guy,
St Andrews Reformation Studies Institute,
Amy Nelson Burnett, University of Nebraska at Lincoln,
Euan Cameron, University of Newcastle upon Tyne and
Kaspar von Greyerz, University of Basel

*The Shaping of a Community: The Rise and Reformation of the
English Parish c. 1400–1560*
Beat Kümin

*Seminary or University? The Genevan Academy and
Reformed Higher Education, 1560–1620*
Karin Maag

Marian Protestantism: Six Studies
Andrew Pettegree

Protestant History and Identity in Sixteenth-Century Europe
(2 volumes) edited by Bruce Gordon

*Antifraternalism and Anticlericalism in the German Reformation:
Johann Eberlin von Günzburg and the Campaign against the Friars*
Geoffrey Dipple

*Reformations Old and New: Essays on the Socio-Economic
Impact of Religious Change c. 1470–1630*
edited by Beat Kümin

Piety and the People: Religious Printing in French, 1511–1551
Francis M. Higman

The Reformation in Eastern and Central Europe
edited by Karin Maag

John Foxe and the English Reformation
edited by David Loades

The Reformation and the Book
Jean-François Gilmont, edited and translated by Karin Maag

The Magnificent Ride: The First Reformation in Hussite Bohemia
Thomas A. Fudge

Kepler's Tübingen: Stimulus to a Theological Mathematics
Charlotte Methuen

'Practical Divinity': The Works and Life of Revd Richard Greenham
Kenneth L. Parker and Eric J. Carlson

Belief and Practice in Reformation England: A Tribute to
Patrick Collinson by his Students
edited by Susan Wabuda and Caroline Litzenberger

Frontiers of the Reformation: Dissidence and Orthodoxy
in Sixteenth-Century Europe
Auke Jelsma

The Jacobean Kirk, 1567–1625:
Sovereignty, Polity and Liturgy
Alan R. MacDonald

John Knox and the British Reformations
edited by Roger A. Mason

The Education of a Christian Society:
Humanism and the Reformation in Britain and the Netherlands
edited by N. Scott Amos, Andrew Pettegree and Henk van Nierop

Tudor Histories of the English Reformations, 1530–83
Thomas Betteridge

Poor Relief and Protestantism:
The Evolution of Social Welfare in Sixteenth-Century Emden
Timothy G. Fehler

Radical Reformation Studies:
Essays presented to James M. Stayer
edited by Werner O. Packull and Geoffrey L. Dipple

Clerical Marriage and the English Reformation:
Precedent Policy and Practice
Helen L. Parish

Penitence in the Age of Reformations
edited by Katharine Jackson Lualdi and Anne T. Thayer

The Faith and Fortunes of France's Huguenots, 1600–85
Philip Benedict

Christianity and Community in the West:
Essays for John Bossy
edited by Simon Ditchfield

Reformation, Politics and Polemics:
The Growth of Protestantism in East Anglian Market Towns, 1500–1610
John Craig

The Sixteenth-Century French Religious Book
edited by Andrew Pettegree, Paul Nelles and Philip Conner

Music as Propaganda in the German Reformation
Rebecca Wagner Oettinger

John Foxe and his World
edited by Christopher Highley and John N. King

Confessional Identity in East-Central Europe
edited by Maria Crăciun, Ovidiu Ghitta and Graeme Murdock

The Bible in the Renaissance:
Essays on Biblical Commentary and Translation
in the Fifteenth and Sixteenth Centuries
edited by Richard Griffiths

Obedient Heretics: Mennonite Identities in Lutheran Hamburg
and Altona during the Confessional Age
Michael D. Driedger

The Construction of Martyrdom in the
English Catholic Community, 1535–1603
Anne Dillon

Baptism and Spiritual Kinship in Early Modern England
Will Coster

Usury, Interest and the Reformation
Eric Kerridge

The Correspondence of Reginald Pole:
1. A Calendar, 1518–1546: Beginnings to Legate of Viterbo
Thomas F. Mayer

Self-Defence and Religious Strife in Early Modern Europe:
England and Germany, 1530–1680
Robert von Friedeburg

Hatred in Print: Catholic Propaganda and Protestant Identity
during the French Wars of Religion
Luc Racaut

Penitence, Preaching and the Coming of the Reformation
Anne T. Thayer

Huguenot Heartland:
Montauban and Southern French Calvinism
during the French Wars of Religion
Philip Conner

Charity and Lay Piety in Reformation London, 1500–1620
Claire S. Schen

The British Union: A Critical Edition and Translation of
David Hume of Godscroft's De Unione Insulae Britannicae
edited by Paul J. McGinnis and Arthur H. Williamson

Reforming the Scottish Church:
John Winram (c. 1492–1582) and the Example of Fife
Linda J. Dunbar

Cultures of Communication from Reformation to Enlightenment:
Constructing Publics in the Early Modern German Lands
James Van Horn Melton

Sebastian Castellio, 1515–1563:
Humanist and Defender of Religious Toleration in a Confessional Age
Hans R. Guggisberg translated and edited by Bruce Gordon

The Front-Runner of the Catholic Reformation:
The Life and Works of Johann von Staupitz
Franz Posset

The Correspondence of Reginald Pole:
Volume 2. A Calendar, 1547–1554: A Power in Rome
Thomas F. Mayer

William of Orange and the Revolt of the Netherlands, 1572–1584
K.W. Swart, edited by R.P. Fagle, M.E.H.N. Mout and H.F.K. van Nierop,
translated J.C. Grayson

The Italian Reformers and the Zurich Church, c.1540–1620
Mark Taplin

A Dialogue on the Law of Kingship among the Scots
A Critical Edition and Translation of George Buchanan's
De Jure Regni Apud Scotos Dialogus
Roger A. Mason and Martin S. Smith

The Construction of Martyrdom in the English
Catholic Community, 1535–1603
Anne Dillon

Reforming the Scottish Church:
John Winram (c. 1492–1582) and the Example of Fife
Linda J. Dunbar

Huguenot Heartland:
Montauban and Southern French Calvinism During the Wars of Religion
Philip Conner

William Cecil and Episcopacy, 1559–1577
Brett Usher

Infant Baptism in Reformation Geneva
Karen E. Spierling

Moderate Voices in the European Reformation
Luc Racaut and Alec Ryrie

Music and Religious Identity in Counter-Reformation Augsburg, 1580–1630
Alexander J. Fisher

The Correspondence of Reginald Pole
Volume 3. A Calendar, 1555–1558: Restoring the English Church
Thomas F. Mayer

Women, Sex and Marriage in Early Modern Venice
Daniela Hacke

Piety and Family in Early Modern Europe
Essays in Honour of Steven Ozment
Marc R. Forster and Benjamin J. Kaplan

John Jewel and the English National Church:
the Dilemmas of an Erastian Reformer
Gary W. Jenkins

Religious Identities in Henry VIII's England
Peter Marshall